The Backdoor Hexologist

Hunter M. Yoder

OTHER BOOKS BY HUNTER M. YODER:

"HEIDEN HEXOLOGY, ESSAYS AND
INTERVIEWS" 20012

"NINE WORLDS" 2013

AVAILABLE FROM WWW.THEHEXFACTORY.COM

DEDICATION

I dedicate this book to to the entheogenic community and the plant
teachers who told me I needed to return to the Appalachian
Pennsylvanian German Schamanische of my youth.

Acknowledgements

Many thanks to the following contributors, living and dead, inadvertent and 'advertent':

Lee R. Gandee
Johnny Ott
Milton Hill
Bumbaugh/Mt. Bummy
Rabbi Joshua Saltzman
Jack Montgomery
Ivan E. Hoyt
Druid
Sachahambi
Burning Copal
Greg Farrell/Oracle
Dennis Boyer
Jesse Tobin
Susan Hess
Patricia Neidrich
Rob L. Schreiwer
Cody Dickerson
Yngona Desmond
Orva / Madame Lefeye
Rob Hewitt
Swanhilde
Valulfr Vaerulsson
Micalela
Brian Weis

Illustrations

Forward for 2nd Edition

Five years after the First Edition, It seemed appropriate to create a more streamlined version of what was a monstroue telephone book like document that comprised the first edition of this book.

The importance of this volume viewing it in perspective is not only my own personal spiritual evolution which was intiated by my growing and partaking of magical plants leading me to the warm bosom of mother Hexerei. But the evolution and growth of Germanic Heathenism in the Pennsylvania German community. A distinction between the Scandinavian model and the continental German versions of Heathenry had already been forming. What was new here was a distinctly Pennsylvania German version based on the already long established and documented Kultur of the Deitsch.

This book was created at the time of online forums, before Facebook, Twitter, etc. Much of the material here was extracted from the forums, Entheogen.com, Ayahuasca.com, and the Yahoo List, Hexenkunst as well as correspondence with many of the contributors noted in Acknowledgements. Many of the contributors were already published authors and many more would go on to distinguish themselves in different aspects of Pennsylvania German Magic. So it was a unique moment, a very idealistic time when Neotribalism based on prechristian European ancestry became more than just a dream.

Finally I would like to say that becoming a writer was never a personal motive of mine. The creation of this book and the two others that have followed is a result of two primary reasons. Firstly, as an already established and trained visual artist, I saw this vast amount of raw material, in the form of online converstions in the same way as wood, canvas and paint. Secondly, I see myself as not an author but as someone who simply has something to say.

Hunter Yoder, 09/13/2013

Foreward for First Edition

By PROFESSOR JOHNNY OTT, HEXOLOGIST.....

From HEXOLOGY, THE HISTORY AND THE MEANING OF HEX SYMBOLS, Jacob Zook

It's been gone on and on for centuries, that many tribes have believed in whattoday is called Hexerie, Hex, and today a lot of it is called faith, good fortune,breaks and good luck. The hex is of course Penna. Dutch, now called jinks.

While we all believe in it in some form or another, for instance cross fingers,nock on wood, under ladder, etc. Just about everybody, has good luck pieces,luckey pocket pieces, charmes, medals, luckey days. Religious people wearemedals, statuetts for faith, poker or card players change seats and decks, whenFriday falls on 13th the U. S. A. does fifty million dollars less business, thepeople just don't travel, spend or try new enterprizes ect that day. And whydon't Hotels have thirteen floors, be-cause people think they are hexed.

There is a reason for all this hexerie, and you cannot blame some people forhaving faith in it. They heard it at dinner table from grandparents, their mother and father and relations, they related many proven facts about the hex(witchcraft).
What these children seen and heard at home from parents they believe, and Idon't think they want to know different.

There are some clans who have their own hex signs, like a coat of arms, and ifanybody married in the relation they also use the insignia, then people passingwill know which clan they belong, the Millers, Snyders, Fishers etc.

And these hex signs realy pay off sometimes. A man came to me from Long Island N. Y. and said six month ago I bought a 2 ft. rain and sun and fertility now weare going to have a baby, now my next door neighbor wants a baby I have to haveanother sign.

A lady from Edystone, Pa. complained her husband slaped her around, I made her alove and romance, the next week she was back for two more for her relation.

A Mr. Davis in San Antonio, Tex. had no water for his cattle. I sent him a rainsign down, the next day it rained fancy. The San Antonio Light newspaper gave mea big write up.

I went fishing up to Sands Eddy along the Delaware river above Easton Pa to aJoseph James a retired cement worker. The fish weren't biting I ask Joe whatsthe reason he said we need rain. So I took Joe a rain sign up told him to put itout when he wants rain, when enough take it in, he went away and left it out,the rain come and washed away the shed where the Hex sign was on and did 5million dollar damage along the Delevare river 1955."

Introduction

The following is a diaristic account of my personal trek back to my own spiritual roots, the Pennsylvania German Culture. The account runs from July 2005 to February 2008 and includes correspondence with many of the contributors, magical and otherwise, who taught me more than I taught them as well as my own remembrances of growing up in Berks county in the 1960's and 1970's.

Frank Blank in Brooklyn

Saturday, July 02, 2005

Recent events have come to light which leads me to question my ability to anticipate "acceptable parameters" of normal human discourse. what does this mean? very little. so with that in mind i have decided to launch this book in an effort to connect the dots.

why do inanimate objects change? is it possible that they are alive? did they eat their wheaties? questions like this have lead me to wonder why food always comes in a box or a package. is it because we are in a symbiotic relation with the world of inanimate objects? do they have a union? can we hire

scab inanimate objects to do our bidding at a fraction of the price? could we consume food that is unpackaged? could we interact with the world as if it were a potential dinner, a forgive the cliché', "veritable feast" what if there isn't any money in it?

does it still have any value, probably not but maybe if it the marketing was handled carefully, differently then all the usual remakes, if was fresh and not out of a can who knows. perhaps we could make digital replicas of it and stick it on the web

maybe we should include a picture of the author as a young man.........

can we legitimately, (can't spell too good) include references from campy tv shows from the past? like the millennium files, how did Frank Black know that the girl was buried alive and able to locate her grave? I think not....generally i try not to think at all such a useless bungling habit why not just go straight to the point. Are there too many Frank Blacks? Pixies, millenium files, god knows who else. should we seek a state of blankness??? or blackness??? could we swim thru the river of gratuitous commercially exploitive references without getting wet?

we seek to find the answers to these and other interesting questions

Because, no one will ever read this and find out!

or because your subscription to the national Enquirer has run out

and you don't go to the supermarket anymore because you get your provisions (comes in boxes or packages remember) from fresh direct.com

Monday, August 08, 2005

Let's be clear, we, you and I can commune and it would be my preference that when it reaches the fork in the road that we take the way which has that good feeling about it, A groove about it, the obvious right decision for direction. But that is my preference however and the opposite of good may reach a higher potential. But it may just delay and fog the clarity needed to increase a mutual potential and get that sweat on your palms and the hair standing up on the top of your head and that buzz of connection in your ears and the racing of thoughts waiting to be touched via a random access association game we can play and you know what I'm talking about............

Every moment is a potential or has a potential that can continue and build till the potential is realized and the thing that needs to be known is revealed. Thus we exist in parallel continuums with whatever is affecting or I am effecting that dimension and thus increasing a potential crossover of the parallel continuums. These things are conducted as in electromagnetic attraction and repulsion, so that a third party creates a forum which not might otherwise exist. This is a classic third party hookup. The person conducting the forum for a potential crossover of parallel continuums may alternate between a positive and the opposite value to the potential but may remain only as the catalyst for the potential crossover. They may only remain as a random element in the opposite of positive switch and a booster rocket for knocking out the block on the positive switch. And this we know from experience.......

Saturday, September 10, 2005

Words and numbers are clouds, I seek clarity. Heaven is here on earth, Hell is here too. Where are you? Don't waste time or make excuses, If you do, you don't really know who you are dealing with here. If you are waiting to die in order to understand, then it's time for you to terminate

your lease, good luck getting your deposit back..........Don't indulge in
words to get your way....don't indulge in endless non repeating
numbers to mirror perfection.

I am convinced that esoterica, spirituality, wisdom, magic, etc. is just a
lack of focus from the actual real physical basic experience of life. Its a
quick buck as opposed to a real investment, a real commitment. One
has to use commonsense in dealing with supposed shamans, high
priests, witch doctors. Do you really need a 'spiritual broker'? Why not
spend a moment to listen to one's inner dialogue and then make the
right decision.

The same is true of Geometry. The esoterica surrounding certain
polygons and stars and the like is a cloud over their real beauty. Let
them reveal themselves for what they are, let the shapes and principles
associated be physical real shapes, not numbers, not letters squared.
Then true clarity is apparent, not just an unending sequence of numbers
after a decimal point. Perfection is unending, a desire to express it
numerically is imperfect.

What is unsaid is of more interest than what is said. What is written
merely provides a context for what

is unwritten.

When one mirror faces another mirror the reflection is an infinite
regression of the mirrors themselves, this is a matter of fact.......

The Man in the Maze

Figure 1 "Bretts Law" 2005 acrylic on scorched wood

Saturday, October 08, 2005

"The Man in the Maze" has several interpretations, my favorite is this:

It is a visual representation of the Tohono O'odham belief in life, death and life after death. The man at the top of the maze depicts birth, you get a sense of entry from the dominant wedge shape he inhabits. He is you and me. His life proceeds as a journey through the maze with its many turns and changes. As the journey continues, one acquires knowledge, strength, and understanding. Nearing the end of the maze, one retreats to a small corner of the pattern before reaching the dark center of death and eternal life. Here one repents, cleanses and reflects back on all the wisdom gained. Finally, pure and in harmony with the world, death and eternal life are accepted. From www.earthart.org

Figure 2 "TuBShvat" acrylic on shaped canvas panel, 2006

"The Man in the Maze" symbol has multiple interpretations naturally. However let me point out several characteristics that are always the same. It contains a seven circuit Labyrinth, seen as seven concentric circles. The Circle contains sixteen lines radiating from the center. It all most always has thicker radial lines than concentric lines or just the opposite, thicker concentric lines than the radial ones. This creates a three dimensional effect making the walls of the maze very real.

Lastly, "U'ki'ut'l"or "I'itoi", The Elder Brother, The Creator is always associated with this image. It is said that he is the man depicted entering the maze, it is said that, one meets him when reaching the center of the maze.

Friday, December 09, 2005

If and when you receive the sacrament of marijuana and it is after not partaking for a extended time. Do not take the time or circumstance lightly when you consume it. And most importantly, immediately after partaking take care to mark incidents that occur. they will make their presence known, this is not a recreational experience like shitting, pissing eating or drinking.....other things that have an intrinsic concern to your life experience, and it comes and goes very rapidly and the agent will induce forgetfulness. But if you see it, pure and true, don't forsake it's presence...........

Wednesday, January 25, 2006

possession of an object is more satisfactory than physical possession. Perception of a fixed object is a spontaneous event that is effected by weather, time of day, day of the year, age of the preceptor, and his personal weather conditions.....

Pleasure is the pathway to the divine.

Pain is the pathway to pleasure. The mind is a muscle that demands both equally. If there is pleasure in a thing, a thought, a decision, it is the right one. Pleasure is the engine that drives the mind. Physical acts that give pleasure are divine gifts not to be derided or regretted. The pleasure is heightened the glimpse the perception is deepened if the body and mind are disciplined. The body is a child and the mind has a dialog with the child and must know when to be strict and when to indulge this child. This is the key to achieving the impossible. That dimension that is impossible is unspoken.....

Figure 3 "Eyn-Sof," acrylic on shaped canvas panel, 2006

Figure 4 "Chichicastenango" acrylic on shaped canvas panel, 2006

Thursday, February 09, 2006

What is the meaning of "Go with God"?

The Universe moves in impulses, these impulses are not in units of time but in waves, like at the sea shore, the duration varies depending upon cosmic weather. The simplest way to synchronize yourself with these waves is by doing simple breathing exercises outside at some private place. Inhale slowly, hold the air in your lungs and exhale in time with ambient sounds such as trains or aircraft or traffic sounds seem to indicate. Repeat until you physically feel the wave motion of your environment crash against your body like waves breaking at the beach as you swim in the surf, So to "Go with God" or "God Speed" is to synchronize one's movements in everyday life to these impulses. If you do, all doors shall be open to you. All faces shall be known to you. And all things will be possible. Thus sayeth the

HUACHUMA!

The great Peruvian curandero don Eduardo Calderón - explained (Sharon, 1978:65) that the Four Winds correspond to the four cardinal directions of the compass. North - the place of Power, a positive direction, a place of strong magnetism, because of the position of the equator and the North Pole; South - the place of Action, because it's opposite to the forces of the North, and the strong winds come from the South; West - the place of Death, where the Sun dies into the sea; and East - a positive direction, the place of Rebirth, where the Sun emerge again, rising form darkness.

http://www.ayahuasca-shamanism.co.uk/Huachuma-SanPedro.htm

Saturday, March 18, 2006

"Being is not a thing but a space"

What are the properties of this "space"

Can it have form?

Does it expand and contract?

How does it interface with the physical?

Is it by definition alive?

Can it have children?

----- Original Message -----

From: hunteryoder@earthlink.net

To: joshua saltzman

Sent: 3/18/2006 7:18:36 PM

Subject:

" Being is not a thing, but a SPACE, AN Opening, which must remain
free. God is the freedom of human beings -take care of this liberty, do
not alienate it from anything or anyone - keep it alive and humble. Take
care of human being in that which escapes the human being, ".

posted by Frank Blank in Brooklyn at 6:20 PM 0 comments

My exploration into ancient Hebrew geometry and iconography is that of the complete novice.......the advantage is that the eyes are fresh. Early Hebrew geometry seems to favor the square and the equilateral triangle, or equilateral triangle in a square. It has a real primitive basic feel to it. No circles. We know they had contact with the Pythagoreans and picked up Tectraktys, an equilateral triangle and no doubt with it the mystical square, the Pythagoreans were the first to articulate "the golden ratio" later called Phi after the Greek sculptor /architect Phidias. But all of that was much later I think?

The Egyptians used "the ratio" in the pyramids and they were also influenced by the Pythagoreans so there is that connection.

My initial reaction to the phi analogy you made was How could this possibly be in the Tabernacle. Phi has a relation to the pentagram, thus the pentacle. It has a strong pull from the planet Venus, It seemed that this would be the very last geometric ratio there. Furthermore, such a architectural scheme would seem to be abit too sophisticated, in a western sense, a little too Greek to be precise.

Upon further reflection, the thought crossed my mind that maybe your construct was a better idea............than the original.

Of course I've always been a little bit bad. Har har har........

phi

you know-seriously yoder,i have been thinking not only about what i got right but what i got wrong - trying to see meaning where perhaps there is only history, in that case, I refer to the existential notion of the Divine expressed in the kabbalah (the historical is interesting as fact) -the Divine is existential as healing, the kabbalists interpret exodus 15:26 "and if you listen to the voice of YHVH" i.e. if you listen to the tetragrammaton and take care of it, Taking care of the tetragrammaton is taking care of being - Philo describes its thus" taking care of being and not my being or his being. Being is not a thing, but a SPACE, AN Opening, which must remain free. God is the freedom of human beings - take care of this liberty, do not alienate it from anything or anyone - keep it alive and humble. Take care of human being in that which escapes the human being, - I think all the techniques in kabbalah serve the purpose of keeping us open - idolatry is impatience, a frozen Image, rather than a dynamic process (as your own art so amazingly expresses) - so getting it wrong opened up more than i "thought" - it created the opening to allow that which is new to enter - i was called into question - ? and a new space opened - thanks for opening my mind -that is what I have been thinking about - take if for what it's worth, be well my friend

posted by Frank Blank in Brooklyn at 12:58 PM 0 comments

Thursday, March 16, 2006

i may need to go back to the factory - this is true - but there are various interpretations of the Hebrew - at least 5 different interpretations - so i need to continue to check this out - however, in terms of the sanctuary - i believe i was wrong - but let me get back to you on this - before i go back to the fact.josh"hunteryoder@earthlink.net" wrote:

The Tabernacle is a 1x1x3, 3 cubes, the sanctuary being one, the Sanctuary was a perfect cube!

Phi is a different religion see Baal, Ishtar, Beelzebub, Venus.

You may need to go back to the Factory...........

Figure 5"Salvia Divinorum Synagogue Mosaic" , acrylic on scorched

Ivan E. Hoyt, Pennsylvania German Folk Artist

Figure 6 "Budding Virginville Hex" acrylic on canvas, Hunter M. Yoder

Date: 2006/05/07 Sun AM 11:54:17 EDT

From: "hunteryoder@earthlink.net"

Subject: 8 pointed stars

Hello,

I like your work.

I recently purchased several of your screened hex signs while in Lancaster county, see attached pic.,I have a background in hex signs in Berks county, where the 8 pointed star is favored on barns. Johnny Claypoole's son's were friends of mine and I am familiar with Johnny Ott's work. I am not entirely happy with the commercialization of the genre, and prefer hand painted signs. The picture of your sign has elements that I refer to as the" east.

I noticed that you favor, several things of interest to me:

1.six pointed stars

2.odd numbered leaf arrangements, particularly the number nine.

3, nine doubled on your outermost border.

I would greatly appreciate any dialogue you may have regarding this and other aspects of Hexology, it seems that the language of hex signs is rarely spoken.

Hunter Yoder

Hello Mr. Yoder,

Thank you for purchasing several of the silk screened signs I designed. It may interest you to know the majority of my work is hand painted original designs. However, like some of my predecessors, including Johnny Ott, I design for a silkscreen manufacturer under a licensing and royalty arrangement.

I am also friends with Johnny Claypoole sons and have bartered work with Sean, Neil, and many times with Eric. Johnny and Helen were also my friends before their passing.

Don't be too unhappy with the "commercialization of the genre". In my opinion, the silk screen work of Jacob Zook, Don Greth, and others helped many people become educated or informed about this distinctively Pennsylvania Deutsch folk art. Without the volume of hex signs they sold around the world, I am afraid very few people would be aware of this genre. If you visit the Kutztown Pennsylvania German Festival this July, you will see myself, Bill Schuster, and Eric Claypoole working diligently to keep the hand painted art of hex signs alive, well, and flourishing.

You are very observant. The design basis for the sign you are holding in the photograph is called the Tree of Life and its inspiration was drawn from antique frakturs that portrayed family trees. Like all my work it is my original design done in the style and tradition of my Pennsylvania Deutsch ancestors.

The six pointed star, the basic single rosette, is the design that I believe started the folk art of hex signs and was modified or embellished as the folk art evolved.

The number 9 in the leaf arrangements means nothing other than spontaneous artisitc license as I attempt to vary my designs. I don't believe hex signs should be a stagnant dead art but rather an evolving art. I modestly think I will make my mark on the genre the same way the initial farmer folk artists did as well as Perry Ludwig, Milton Hill, Harry Adam, Johnny Ott, Johnny Claypoole, and other craftsmen have done.

The "nine doubled" border has no symbolic meaning. Eighteen scallops each 20 degrees make a 360 degree circle.

I am currently under contract to write a "How To" book for Stackpole Books. I hope to have it finished and ready for publication by next March.

I would appreciate it very much you would share information you have collected growing up in Berks County with the work of Johnny Ott and Johnny Claypoole or others involved with barn painting and barn decorating. This subject has fascinated me for over 30 years and my research and collecting is ongoing.

Sincerely,

Ivan E. Hoyt

Pennsylvania German Folk Artist

Sunday, May 07, 2006

Ivan E. Hoyt

KEY WORDS: Painted Decoration, Pennsylvania German, hex signs, Hoyt

Whether the hex sign barn paintings, which originated in southeastern Pennsylvania during the mid 19th century, were purely decorative or carried a more mystical meaning is a matter of debate; however, no one disputes their naive appeal. Ivan Hoyt expands the art of hex sign beyond traditional star and rosette designs to include motifs derived from other expressions of Pennyslvania Deutch folk art (frakturs, scherenschnitte, and springles) In his brochure he discribes the symbolism attributed to the flora, fauna, and folk of lore which find expression in his signs; but he admits a special fondness for the "distlefink" (goldfinch), because it allows for the most fanciful treatment and the broadest use of his wonderful, rich palette. An image of several signs can be seen in the Gallery; customization as to color, motif, and shape (dower chest panel, tavern sign, doorway arch), as well as personalization is available. All signs are suitable for indoor/outdoor display. Charming! (figuratively, and perhaps, literally?)

Ivan E. HoytRD2, Box 49D, Bell DriveWapwallopen, PA 18660717.379.3533e-mail: iehhex@epix.net

Monday, June 19, 2006

Three defines an activated space

Metaphysically speaking, three vertical axes side by side will define an activated space. This is a very real determination of a space, length, width and depth. I refrain from the use of "holy" or "sacred" and prefer "activated"

When a brand name is "franchised" the THREE also known as TREE means that this place is connected to the FACTORY. There are many different brand names however, THREE remains a constant.

Three will support and create a space for ONE. ONE central axis needs no explanation, it is supported left and right by secondary axes. Different Brands assign different names, symbolic roles, so forth and so on.....the point is the two secondary axes define and support ONE. They give ONE a home, a family.

Franchised locations are places to go to connect with the FACTORY. WHY? Because we all came off the assembly line and we will all go back for upgrades or junked for spare parts.

These spaces are volumes that are to be filled, after the space is filled via ritual, entheogenic plants, whatever it is thus activated. Once a space is activated it has a power, it can reveal things, it unifies individuals into groups. The truth is the individuals activate the space, they create the power, they tap into the ONE mind. One mind is power, neither right nor wrong but universal in the human sea where we all swim...........

Thursday, July 27, 2006

Datura stramonium, A thornapple grows in Red Hook

Red Hook, NYC's version of a Stalinist-Leninist State, or perhaps NYC's version of Mao's "Great Leap Forward" A grim reminder of what happens when Big Brother controls all aspects of its citizens lives. An example of what billions and billions of dollars achieves when flushed down the toilet, right you got it....a clogged sewage system. From the Projects to the Red Hook recreation area, to the razor wired pedestrian bridge over the BQE into the public school which sure looks like prison. You paid for it I paid for it, we all did......it might as well be a federal penitentiary, you get the unique view of the world through a high security fence. The occupants are....pretty vacant....all employed by the state...wards of the state, permanently damaged and in the business of self replication in a backdrop of a commercial warehouse zone with heavy trucks filled with hard toxic sewage, recycled paper and a pervasive odor of smoked fish/ a known carcinogen in the air. even in the new Brooklyn's spectacular real estate development miracle you can still get down to basics in a porto john in red Hook, where the homeless still can chill and shoot up in peace.....my kinda place. Be careful though, red Hook is the most police enforced zone in the 76th precincts' jurisdiction and those Gumba cops hate niggers and spics. They fund their personal retirements on the summons written here. Oh yeah this is where you go to take your drivers road test in Brooklyn. So amongst the garbage and deserted lots and places the park employees forgot to sanitize I found an old friend from my childhood......Datura Stramonium growing free and unknown to this mindless crowd. God bless the United State of my mind. Yeah I actually wrote this and took the pics, Frank Blank, July 27th 2006.

Tuesday, July 18, 2006

Figure 7 Datura Stramonium

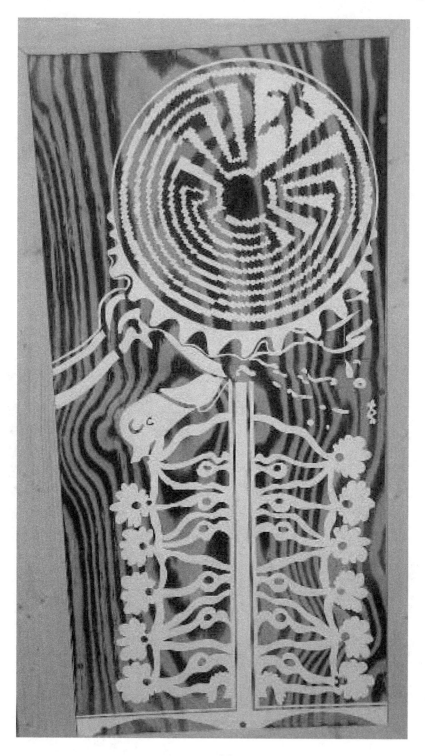

Figure 8 "It's the Real Thing"

Figure 9 Tohono O'odham Winged Disk

Figure 10 "Goddess as Tree" acrylic on canvas, 2006

Figure 11 Nicotina Rustica and Datura Stramonium, photo Hunter Yoder

Never mind the rabbit! Frank, perhaps we could have a small healing circle on the internet - for $150 registration payed through paypal, you have access to a tantric shaman, a kabbalistic rabbi, a hex/mosaic designer specializing in ancient symbols, a grower of herbs and bees for natural healing substance, a Buddhist monk from Thailand who specializes in healing meditation, a psychotherapeutic counselor trained in alternative therapies, a geometric designer and astronomer, dr. octogon, a specialist in spiracles, a philosopher of eastern and western esoterica and continental philosophy,

Dr. Mani Shushani

--- "frank_blank@earthlink.net"

wrote:

Update on my final nicotina rustica harvest, after receiving rave reviews on the stuff from my associate at the advanced herbal institute, i brought in the remaining stuff, the second generation stuff hanging outside underneath but still outdoor, been there a month, thank goodness the squirrels don't like it. and its i nice mild smoke blends well with other herbs, we used mugwort and amanita muscaria. the smell of a sweet philly cigar kinda stays with you afterward. still no frost here, nope not yet.

----

8 1 6

3 5 7

4 9 2

Thursday, January 18, 2007

Third Eye Sight Seeing

Frank Blank:

"Comet McNaught but I just looked , no luck, it peaked over the weekend but the weather was bad into Tuesday, oh well, sometimes the subjective and the objective weather don't coincide"

Reb Josh:

From: joshua saltzman

Date: 1/18/2007 12:16:09 AM

Subject: Re: Cosmograms Hexology/ a Shamanic Manifesto

true, but the objective is always a product of thesubjective, even if the objective exists independently of the subject, we can only know it in our minds,perhaps cosmology is refracted in the quantum level,>but i suspect that we have no choice but to writeabout our experience, zecher al majid, in the sufi, magician, alchemists, shamans and hexologists, among the many who may be privy to themysteris of mysteries" \

cosmic rabito bandito meshuganadito alchemetito

--- "frank_blank@earthlink.net"

wrote:

In Hexology we refer to this phenomena as "Third EyeSight Seeing" or "Seeing Eye Sight" it allows one to see through things or to see things somewhere else as though one was there. Its kinda the short cut between or as a resolution of, all that subjective objective mumbo jumbo and actually has many beneficial aspects for living........

From: joshua saltzman

Date: 1/18/2007 1:01:14 PM

Subject: Re: Cosmograms Hexology/ a Shamanic Manifesto

this might be what you call it, you may even fantazise and believe you are having such an experience, butwould say this third eye sight is more of a literary phenomena and less of an actual experience, however, i am currently investigating Jewish orientallist, a rather strange breed that existed prior to world war 1 - i will share more or my research progresses

sheik yehoshua al baktashi

--- frank_blank

wrote::

Very interesting, perhaps you are right, actually it may have been "second hand sight seeing" which contains residual imprints from previous second hand seeing eye sight, the second hand is usually the right one, and theseeing eye is usually in it.....

From: joshua saltzman

Iconic - got it, when we gonna try all your new shamanic concoctions?

"Third Eye Sight Seeing" 2007

In the Popol Vuh, a Quiche' Maya epic, the lords of the Quiche' underworld kill Hun Hunahpu and hung his head from the branch of a gourd tree or calabash tree. No tree of this kind had ever borne gourds until Hun Hunahpu's head was hung in it. While Hun Hunahpu's head hung in the tree, the daughter of a lord of the underworld stood before the tree. Blood Woman was her name. She stretched out her right Hand. Hun Hunahpu's head spat into its palm and the spittle disappeared. Soon she came to realize that there was life within her body and in time she gave birth to the set of twins whose names were Hunter and Jaguar Deer.

>http://www.darkfiber.com/eyeinhand/

Cosmograms Hexology/ a Shamanic Manifesto

Yes sachahamba, thank you for your cosmological model. Cosmological models are what I enjoy the most, I refer to them as "cosmograms" and being a visually oriented person, I speak much better in "images" But words are OK too and let's get right to the cart wheel, a classic iconographic symbol of the Universe, with a hub (Bindu), Circumference, and spokes (the number of which we will hold for another time)

Let me first say that the Sri Yantra best reconciles the Dualism/ Nondualism issue for me without the use of words and all the rhetorical nonsense that would follow.

"In this analogy, the outer rim is the manifest world, and the center axle is the unmoving, unchanging Oneness whose realization is the goal of Eastern religions such as Vedanta Hinduism. The region in between -- the region of the spokes of the wheel -- represent all the levels in between the manifest physical spacetime world of apparent individual objects and the level of totally undifferentiated Oneness. The levels of dreams and intuitions and visions, the levels where we are all connected and in constant telepathic interflow and negotiation. Usually, we enter those realms when our waking or "conscious" minds shut down, as when we are dreaming. Jung called that region the "collective unconscious," but did not seem to realize how dynamic that realm is, or that it is a world that can be visited and consciously navigated. But the conscious navigation of that ocean of collective consciousness is the art of the shaman. Essentially what shamanism is the ability to participate in this process consciously. "

What you have described here is a basis for my tradition, Pennsylvania German Hexology, and the wheel is a "Hex Sign" Obviously many traditions fit within this archetypical symbol, but first my own, which is the direction I come from and it's easier to start from the beginning. This also excludes myself from the set of American, westerners rejecting their tradition or lack of one in search of the truth.

Anyway, the Hex sign is divided into zones, "the outer most zone (circumference) represents the "outer world/ objective universe, the "spokes" or inner world represent the subjective universe of the hex master or the person for whom the sign is being fashioned, and the "hub" or core self of the hex master or the core intelligence within the universe" from NORTHERN MAGIC, Edred Thorsson, chapter "Operant Hexology" this parallels in many ways your "cart wheel"

The essence of the "Hex Meister's" skill is to make an intent (thought) into a material object (the hex sign) and by doing so project into the universe a telepathic blueprint image of what the hexerei wants to be materialized. The key is that sustained image must be sent out far enough to attract enough energy to make the materialization happen. This is dependent on the power of the Hex Meister. (see STRANGE EXPERIENCE, by Lee Gandee, the definitive work on hexology)

"Shamanism is, not a belief system, but it makes use of belief systems, belief structures as navigational maps to give structure to the space and as tools to be able to affect the way its energies flow.

For example, a traditional indigenous culture will have its own mythology, which is that people's evolving collective dream. Mythology gives a people a common language for their dreams and a way to dream collectively. The shaman will be able to navigate in that mythological world the way an explorer might navigate the physical world; the established mythology creates a pattern of blazed trails that can be used. The mythology of the group he comes from is a way of giving structure to that space; the mythology creates a kind of "map" so that the shaman isn't floundering in that space without any guidance. ..."

Your last statement confirms what I have felt and executed in my own "Hex Signs" That Cosmograms from various traditions, mythologies articulate symbols because as Lee R. Gandee says, "For thousands of generations, man's subconsciousness has used symbol as the language of instinct and emotion and the phallic symbols made by prehistoric man are so like those made yesterday by your neighbor's son in the public urinal that they could be interchanged without exciting professional comment"

The shaman/ hex meister is able to tap into the emotive power of these mythologies, consciously? I would articulate it in this manner, he is able to turn it on or off depending on the need, more need more emotive power, more sympathetic identification with the subject.

posted by Frank Blank in Brooklyn

Thursday, January 04, 2007

Towards Hexology as an Appalachian Shamanic Tradition

Figure 12"PA Deutsch Schamanische Spiral" acrylic on wood, 2007

Sunday, March 25, 2007

Black Hex Signs

Continuing on our little sojourn to the dark side, we have here a hex sign by LEE R> GANDEE from his 1971 book, "STRANGE EXPERIENCE" which is like the Castenada, "SEPARATE REALITY" for the Pennsylvania Deutsch, only Gandee himself is Don Juan. As I recently wrote to a former Berks County resident and childhood friend,

He was the real deal "using" Hexology and Pow-Wowing as one, which is our tradition which was distorted for commercial reason, I suppose, didn't want the tourists to know that these signs actually meant anything or could be used for anything except as decorations.........IE Kutztown Folk Festival or whatever it is now. Also Claypool, great craftsman Johnny's dead now, The boys are still in it, but no clue about certain aspects of these things. Johnny Ott, Claypooles predecessor, did and is referred to by Gandee.

Obviously the sign is for Rain, a reoccurring theme for the early PA farmer....

Rain: The basic sign. Do not leave exposed after rain begins-has been held responsible for disastrous floods when left outdoors during rainstorms. Also a black-hex sign for storm and flood

Again regarding hex signs in general and the ominous one above, Gandee continues in the chapter in the book titled "The Strangest Prayers are Painted"

If anyone wishes to prove the effect of a Hex sign, let him make one prayerfully and use it without explaining to anyone what it intends. Any in this book may be copied-I do not care-and all but the ominous looking rain sign that opens Chapter XVI are white hex signs. (I could not resist putting in one black-hex sign just to show the contrast)In it there is no earth-star to call for rain as a blessing to the earth, but only furious raindrops whirling in from all sides. It calls for storm and tempest, flood and destruction. Johnny Ott always liked to tell of a flood in the Delaware River that did $5,000,000 damage merely because one of his ordinary rain signs was left out after the rain started. I certainly would not want to leave the one I drew outside after the rain began-and because of the lightning drawn on it, I wouldn't want to go out and bring it in either!

He also describes his Great Grandfathers ability to control the weather:

My great-grandfather could command rain so well he could stop a shower at will. But finally, he grew angry when lightning struck his favorite shade tree. He shook his fist at the clouds and cried, "Burn a tree, will you! This is old Zach-let's see you flash one at me once!" A Hex should not say such things. The lightning obeyed him; he was killed instantly

And more about the weather from Frank Blank:

If the signal is good and the reward manifest, there is the
sacrifice............

Or if the signal is not good and the reward is not manifest there is
sacrifice...

It's like bouncing your voice off a wall. You seek to tweak the echo
and have it bounce back clearly and loudly. Of course interpretation of
echo in shamanic terms involves the reading of the ironic metaphorical
kennings, inter dimensional language/symbols, like a good tracker
reading the disturbed ground before him, yes this is the path of
enlightenment, friend.

Oh and one last thought, yes there is always humor in the
interpretation, always a good laugh to be had even if it is Death! Ha!

To elaborate just a bit more, One "uses" the ironic metaphorical
kennings to pierce and breakdown the physical world, the "everyday
routine" in order to diminish and minimize time/space. Distance is
eliminated, Time goes quickly and then very slowly. Perception of
environment/space is flattened. This allows "the User" to navigate
freely in a universe (in the familiar sense) solely of INTENT. The flatness
is like a continuously unraveling of spontaneous random events that are
woven together in whatever intent One wishes........this includes the
weather! Weathermen predict the weather, "Users" control it by
connecting the randomness and manipulating it through ironic
references to almost anything ....as long as it works! Sustaining the
energy level is the true measure of the "User's" ability. Flow is very

important here.

Tuesday, March 06, 2007

Shamanic Cosmology

Animism is the essential concept in a Shamanic Cosmological model.

Quote:

everything has a "soul", an "anima" in Latin, a "spirit"... including animals, plants, rocks, mountains, rivers, stars... each "anima" is powerful, spiritual, that can help or hurt them, including the souls of the dead, the "ancestors".

http://www.religion-cults.com/Ancien...sum/Animism.htm

Furthermore, God, is not a person, male or female instead

Quote:

god is the Energy, the Force, the Power, the Universal Mind, the Absolute, the Unknown, the Divine Being... is not a "he" but an "it"... it is not somebody but something... but something powerful able to get wonderful things for you using Magic... and worshiping it!... yes, worshiping the Force or the Energy...

And this energy, life force flows through the Universe, the living universe.

This is in stark contrast to science, astrophysics and empirical view of the universe, in which it is seen as vast dead empty space filled with dust with no life other than on the tiny planet earth.

Even God is hypothesized in ENTHEOGENIC circles as just a chemical in the brain.

Quote:

others have theorized that endogenous dmt is connected to being a visionary, ie jesus and buddha and such simply had higher amounts of dmt in their brain than those around them.

http://www.entheogen.com/forum/showthread.php?t=10958

To quote the Sex Pistols, we think this is "Pretty Vacant" WHAT DO YOU THINK?

Saturday, June 30, 2007

Hexerei's Disciplines And The True Meaning Of Braucherei

I did mention all 6 disciplines in earlier posts. Here's another list of them (now updated using more German correct terminology) and what they involve.

1. Spruchzauber, or "spoken magic", is a new term I've recently discovered. The Norse term for this would be "galdr". Anything spoken falls under this category, and all of the disciplines utilize some form of Spruchzauber.

2. Hexology. The "painted prayer", Always remember that merely painting one does not make one work. Both body and mind are required to activate one magically.

3. Runenzauber. The magic of the runes. Like the hex sign, these symbols must also be activated using both body and mind. Also used in divinatory activities.

4. Wahrsagezauber. New research materials have yielded a very German name for what the Norse call "seidhr". The term "wahrsage" means "soothsaying" in German according to the research of Professor Hasenfratz of Bochum University. Hasenfratz compares the terms "seidhr", and "shamanistic trance" to Wahrsagezauber.

5. The term "Augercraft", at least in West Virginia where a Thelemite friend of mine who grew up there in the same culture that yielded Lee Raus Gandee comes from, told me that is what the people in this area call operations of magic involving trees. The Germans were heavily involved in tree worship for those who didn't know.

6. Braucherei. Well I had planned to make this a topic all its own, but now is a good time as any to make sure our members understand what Braucherei is and what it isn't from the view of the traditional witch that practiced Hexerei. The term is more prevalent in the southern Appalachians and the practice is also commonly called "using". In Pennsylvania and the northern Appalachians, the term "PowWow" is better known. The term "PowWow" is a Native American one, and is a term totally unrelated in its terminology to the traditional German/Austrian/Swiss witchcraft that is Hexerei. Both the terms of PowWow and Braucherei eventually have come to be adopted and commonly used as terms to describe various other parts of the Hexerei practice after it was altered by Christians for their use. The Christian practitioners tried to divorce themselves further from the heathen roots of Hexerei and what they were really doing by relegating the term as a description of "black magic" and witches in general.

Now getting back to what Braucherei really describes, my own research and teachings I have received from my mentor, as well as from my advisor in Austria, have told me what it truly means. Alois comes from a old country family that kept their private heathen practices alongside of their Christian ones and he understands very well what Braucherei is and isn't. The correct use of the term Braucherei describes herbalism both magical and medicinal. The first "Brauc doctors" on these shores came from Germany, Austria, and Switzerland and were primarily herbalists and doctors, and did their healing work in a mostly medicinal sense. Some would use Spruchzauber here and there to magically charm and activate an herb or a plant, but very, very few actually did any spoken magic work for such things as removing diseases, breaking hexes, or other needs. The patient was usually given medicine by the Braucher if needed, and went off to someone else if any Spruchzauber was needed in addition towards curing the disease. The disease was not always viewed as being a natural affliction, other people and other unseen forces were also viewed as being possible causes, so again to everyone, the original Braucher was a primarily medical person who DID NOT DO spoken magic.

I see some devotees of Dennis Boyer have recently joined this club, so I "hope" this last section about Braucherei clears up the differences between the traditional Hexerei view in contrast to the Americanized Christian view of this particular discipline.

Blessings and frith to all,

Greg Farrell

Saturday, June 23, 2007

Helms Awe Hex Sign

As far as the runes and Hunter's Helm Of Awe sign, many different interpretations for the quarters are possible, it depends on the purpose. An elemental interpretation for example with a four pointed earth star in the center would be Jera for earth in the North, Ansuz for air in the East, Fehu for fire in the South, and Laguz for water in the West.

 Hunter, did you notice that the Helm uses 2 different runes? This is called a "bind rune", sort of like a compound word.

Blessings,

Greg

Yeah I think the "helm of Awe" is a combine of Gebo and Nauthiz?

In defense of "Northern Magic" I purchased it not for its European Germanic mysticism but rather for its lengthy PA German Hexology chapter and appendix, and it was there that the connection was really made between the two........I haven't seen that connection made anywhere else.

Hunter

Figure 13 "Berks County Helm of Awe", Spray paint on scorched wood, 2007

Sunday, July 15, 2007

Fecundity/ Venus/Netherland Dwarf rabbits/ Farming in Berks County

My apologies to all who do not possess a "green thumb" This is the time of year in which plant growth is so intense it becomes difficult for Frank Blank/ AKA Myself to contain the creative energies of the "Living Universe" that make him such a happy person. First of all he is the proud father of four beautiful children, 2 boys and two girls. Furthermore, Venus is very high in the Western sky until 10PM, and Jupiter is in the South probably longer. His ability to possess the "touch of life' is "macht gutt" His roots in Berks County allow him to extend that ability and he has these recommendations:

Have at least One rabbit in the garden, their innate irrationality isessential to fecundity.

Now is the time for the pepper plants, which is a sacred plant, more heat, the hotter the pepper, macht gutt

Thirdly , it is very important to have children, this is always in a sense a "mistake" a "chance" But sexual reproduction is always a chance we need to take.

The essence of Pennsylvania Deutsch magic is fecundity, as farmers we sought to increase our yield. Look to the west after dark and look for that Bright star, she is in a 8/5 relationship to us all and she has many names and She is painted on our barns..........

Did she unfurl her beauty to the welcoming arms of Venus?

I was selling my wares at our local farmer's market today (outdoors) and kept smelling whiffs and wafts of datura blossoms throughout the entire day. I went for a walk around the perimeter and found nothing... but that smell is unmistakable. Since I am home and indoors...I think it is still around me. Perhaps a strong southwest wind from Brooklyn?

Thanks for posting the pics on Hexenkunst...I considered doing so myself but shied away.

I only share with pals. Not convinced over there quite yet.

I will send you some garden pics soon.

But for now, feet up with a coconut popsicle on the 'hops' porch and a cat in my lap...

Venusian, eh? She rules.....

Sue

Last summer, it would definitely call to me at night through various senses. smell particularly. I use it's flower essence sometimes and would sleep with a bloom beside my head at night.

Honestly, I have to admit that I was totally enamored of it ... but also a lil shy about opening myself to it totally, as well. We did a flirtatious dance with each other all summer long.

Perhaps ,she hasn't given up on me yet.

"Well, did she unfurl her beauty to the welcoming arms of Venus?"

Nope.......not yet, probably waiting for the "horns" to appear, ha ha.

Although it's interesting that you put her in the same sentence as Venus.

Venus's rotation around the sun consists of 584 Earth days, earth's is 365 of course. Five of Venus's rotations equals eight of earth's or 2,920 days. Note the PHI relationship here. that's important because plant growth, growth spirals follow the "golden angle" or approx. 137.51 degrees. So it would only be natural that the planet Venus or Lamat in certain Mayan dialects be associated with, love, growth, fertility and so forth.......

The Datura is even more closely associated with Phi, its pentacle shaped flower is the very expression of the "golden angle"

+++

That coconut popsicle sounds good, up here brooklyn the thing is italian ices, coconut flavored but my favorite is pistachio, what a good Pa german I am, ha ha. I see you have a whole line of products very interesting, I might interest my wife in something, do you take paypal?

Well Ms Datura or what the Aztecs call, toloatizn more commonly called toloache by the indigenous, finally opened and I am abit surprised to find this one goes six instead of five like the ones you and photographed last year, kind of throws out my toloache-phi theory out the window, oh well...........ha! anyway heres the pic see what you think.............

Also is a pic of my Sinicuichi which is blooming profusely, this is another sacred plant of the Maya/Aztec very pretty bush, scientific name, Heimia salicifolia

Oh yeah,

Datura closes up during the day but this is definitely a "Hex" Looks like the last "hex sign" I painted, Intention is a subconscious process........

Anyway, I strongly recommend at least one rabbit in the garden, adds that irrational necessity essential for fecundity. They are not the best cartoon characters without a reason.

Actually I used to raise bees, had 50 hives at one time, I really miss that. I still use the boxes for plants.

The urban location, made this unrealistic so I went to the receiving end of their activities, flowering plants......

This time of year with the temps today here in the low nineties is ideal for pepper plants, especially the "hot ' varieties which actually become hotter in taste as the temp arises.

I have an ongoing relationship with the Tohono Od'ham tribe in SW Arizona who use the pepper as a sacred plant amongst others.

Here I went Gowanus which was so similar to Lenni Lenape.

We actually have some amazing gardens here in Brooklyn, the limitation of space is really an advantage.

The importance of participating in Hexenkunst is not so much to be their friends but to remind them that when they seek to represent PA German Magic they must deal with the reality of Berks County, we will not be obstructed from that dinner table.

I hope you took pictures..........

+++

Hey Ayla,

Can't take credit for those last pics but you are welcome all the same, A friend and were discussing this plant teacher elsewhere:

'"There is a lot of negative publicity out there in entheogen communities about these plants, they are potentially dangerous, as are many plants. But can be worked with, just hopefully one learns how

their plants live before it comes as a surprise. When it's said that the alkaloid content is variable, anywhere from 1-10x or potentially more the same plant can vary, in the same part of the plant, at different times. As I've never had testing equipment to get specifics as to how much this varies, I've had to base it on personal experience, but the 1x-10x variance is about the range I've noticed, within the same plant, of similar parts of the plants harvested at different times. Lunar cycle , and water availability are primary things to consider if one knows the nature of the plants they are cultivating. Datura tend to come true from seed, so most often a offspring will share a comparable chemistry to its mother plant, as these do not often cross pollinate."

"The smell of the leaves is considered by fetid to many people, now it just reminds me of peanuts, not even rancid anymore. Closest smell is that of rancid peanut butter however, foliage smells dreadful, however most of their flowers have a similar pleasant smell, that's IMHO beyond compare to any perfume.

"The smell is narcotic as well, Datura wrightii and Datura metel have very strong fragrances , Datura metelodies (inoxia) much milder scent, sometimes hardly noticable."

"And Frank, hopefully yours opens soon, have some Datura Wrightii blooming in yard, a few in containers (one overwintered from last winter open tonight) Datura metelodies will be blooming here soon too, birds spread seeds and now they've come up in gravel of patio, amazing what crappy soil conditions Datura can grow in , and still mature into beautiful plants, hard to tell the difference between a

Datura grown in gravel and one grown in potting soil in most cases."

Yeah the supposedly "fetid" smell is alotta bullshit, I likes that smell. And yes indeed BC it seems to grow wild in the worst soil possible, here usually in super compacted clayish stuff the color of yellow ochre in low lying areas that are poor draining, yeah abandoned lots and such, I think you have to have had contact with this one in childhood in order to lose the stigma attached to this one. That does not mean I recommend ingesting any part of this plant. the map shows distribution of Stramonium in the USA, it's probably in Wyoming too.....

http://plants.usda.gov/java/profile?symbol=DATUR

"I'm sure it's in Wyoming also. Those USDA maps are just where they have verified it to be growing, knowing datura, I'm sure stramonium has gotten loose from gardens a few places there, same with wrightii and metelodies.

And Frank, you may well be right about the issue with being introduced to these plants during childhood to avoid the stigma, the 'devils weed' view of the plants seems to be very prevelant. Stigma means little to those who trust and respect these plants, which if one had encountered them early on that may be more likely. These were consulted during rites of passage among other rituals. There is a good reason, the sharp transitions these plants can bring to the mind make it nearly ideal for that."

Yeah BC, for me my association with Stramonium was playing with it as a child, the supposedly "fetid" smell is my strongest recollection, I also remember the thorn apples in the early fall, this was way beforemy knowledge of its name and otherwise, for me its name is that smell, I think that's called synaesthesia...........

The true meaning of Braucherei

Hello All,

Well, although it has been a week since I received Greg's letter which clarified for all the many disciplines of Hexerei and the differences he saw between Hexerei and Braucherei. I would like to make some clarifications of my own. Although Greg seems to think that those of us teaching through the Three Sisters Center for the Healing Arts are devotees of Dennis Boyer, I must correct him and state that Dennis has been one of many teachers and mentors bringing us to the Braucherei Path, and since our initiation into the knowledge he passed to us he honors us as equals in the tradition. Secondly I must state our methods for research (including the methods of Dennis himself). We call a person a Braucher when he or she says they are a Braucher or a Powwower, when they say they practice Braucherei or Powwow, or when others in their community refer to them or their practices in this manner. This is the basis of our terminology, and in communities surrounding the Berks, Lehigh, and Lancaster counties of Pennsylvania we have never found anyone who said they practiced Hexerei. Third, as a group (those involved in the Three Sisters Center, and Dennis Boyer) our research includes information from over 80 Practitioners beginning in the 1960s and continuing to the present.

I must state that I am fully aware of the way in which the terminology surrounding Hexerei has been abused and demonized. I understand the ways in which the Church and secular authorities both in Europe and America demonized Spirits, beliefs and practices, and I am horrified by this history. However I choose to use the term Braucherei to describe my work and beliefs because that is the name I have been given by my elders to describe this living tradition. Also, I have been handed an amazing combination of Christianity (Gnostic, Medieval, Mystical, and

Protestant), Kabala, Greek arts and Sciences, and ancient Germanic, Celtic, Roman, and Lenni Lenâape tradition. In the practices I have been given I see no reason to regard either Christianity or Pagan practice with disdain. I have been taught that these are all teachers, beings of light, guides; that these beliefs and practices- many derived from pre-Christian tradition are in no way contradictory to Christian beliefs and practices. I have come to see all of the many cultural influences of the Braucherei Tradition as beautiful and complimentary.

Most importantly I must say that Greg has called Hexerei and only Hexerei- 1) Schpruchzauber, 2) Painted or visual prayers, 3) Runenzauber, 4) Wahrgezauber, 5) Magical acts involving trees and other plants, and 6) Medicinal use of Plants- Every single one of these practices and the belief systems that surround them have been taught to me by several teachers as Braucherei. Not only are these things Braucherei, but there much more. I choose to call my practices Braucherei to honor those many ancestors who had to carry on our sacred and necessary traditions regardless of what tyrant was in power at the time. I want to honor those who died as heretics and witches as much as I want to honor those who wept for those lost to the tyranny of the powerful. It was those who survived that passed on the heirloom that I have been given- those who maintained what was vital, added what was useful, and covered the entire tradition in a shroud of Christian, and later protestant terms to ensure their survival. I must also share some important words on the term Braucherei: En Brauch is a tradition (any tradition), or an heirloom. Brauche the verb can mean to need, to use, or to try. It is the understanding within the Braucherei tradition that these necessary cures are wrought not by the Braucher themselves, but by the use of the Braucher as a channel through which spirit flows, entering the body of the receiving person to bring them into harmony with the divine energy which is present in all the world.

I would love to have some open discussions about our common tradition, its many names and practices. And, this being a folk tradition, I would request some respect for that information that has come from the folk- from our elders- for their words, their beliefs, and their practices. After all, we would know very little about these practices if they hadn't borne them to us. Enough revisionist history has been written, I hope we can all just be open to what has come to each of us and share that information and vision with love of our common heritage. If I have learned anything in my study of Braucherei and Hexerei it is that there are many truths to be told, lets share them all and try to hold them all with the respect and love they deserve.

Thank you and Blessings to all,

Jesse Tobin

Three Sisters Center for the Healing Arts

Re: The true meaning of Braucherei

Hey Jesse,

Thanks for showing up here, Nice to have another Berks County persona in the house. I just love the dialog......... something you said that caught my attention was this: "It is the understanding within the Braucherei tradition that these necessary cures are wrought not by the Braucher themselves, but by the use of the Braucher as a channel through which spirit flows, entering the body of the receiving person to bring them into harmony with the divine energy which is present in all the world." This I think moves things into the realm of Shamanism, however the distinction between "witchcraft and shamanism" is very gray. From my own experience of growing up in Berks County in the sixties and seventies, it was local shamanism that shaped my identity of being Pennsylvania Deutsch. It was a not so distinct subculture relative to what was commonly associated with being "Dutch" and to this day I seek

to clarify my experience and extend it, not just preserve it....buts

that me. The shamanic aspect seems to be as you said, " by the use of the Braucher as a channel through which spirit flows, entering the body of the receiving person to bring them into harmony with the divine energy which is present in all the world." and this principle exists in many shamanic cultures throughout the world. Your quote specifically brought to mind the Shipibo shamanic tradition of the Peruvian Amazon, their textile design, pottery and "healing" principally includes complex geometrical patterns. The Shaman senses "holes" in the pattern which overlays the "patient" and through songs called "Icaros" seek to close the holes......... But back to Berks County, which is the heart of the matter here, possess what all Americans of Western European descent may lack, a direct connection back to their ancestral source of "power" Perhaps now is the time for these poor disassociated people to gain back their collective soul, and EXTEND IT!

+++

Hunter

Re: [hexenkunst] Re: The true meaning of Braucherei

Hi Hunter,

Actually this shamanic aspect of the tradition- the hands on healing doesn't even come close to showing the extent of shamanic techniques. We have a technique called Ziedschtrick (time cord) in which we follow the time cord of the client and tap into all sorts of things. Many techniques are very similar to what harner's institute describes as core shamanism- soul retrieval, extraction, psychopomp work. Alot of times we have to do healing work for anscestors before the client's own issues

can be adressed. We adress trauma's of the individual's past, and we
help to strenthen the future strands to facilitate a healthy future. This is
possibly my favorite technique, because it allows the individual to do
thier own work and come to true healing on their own terms, the
Braucher is just a facilitator. In addition to this there are many dreaming
techniques. One technique that I use with all of my herbal clients is one
we call Blanzeschwetze- speaking with plants. When creating herbal
protocols I spend time in ceremony with the appropriate plant spirits,
asking which will be most helpful in facilitating the individual's greatest
healing. Its amazing to see what can be done when Braucherei and
Herbal medicine are combined in this way. The shamanic end of the
tradition is my favorite aspect, as I think it connects people on a deeper
level. One thing I have been finding, though, is that people who are on
antidepressant drugs seem to have a really hard time doing timecord
work- it is interactive between practitioner and client, and they just
seem to have difficulty connecting, or maybe it is difficulty in believing
what they see. Again, these are some of my favorite techniques, but
they are just the tip of the iceberg when it comes to the richness of
techniqes we have been given.

Blessings

Jesse Tobin

Hey Jesse,

Nice Post!

I see we have much to discuss in the Plant world which is where you'll
find me.....The plants are very happy today and you can hear them
growing if you have an ear for that sort of thing. Yesterday I had to
catch my Black Netherland Dwarf Hare who had escaped into the
Datura patch that I didn't plant....Datura Stramonium has decided to

follow me around like an ex girlfriend or wife...oh well I like its pungent odor and then there are the "angels trumpets"

I grew up with it on the flood plane of the Saucony Creek, maybe you know where that is.........between The Old Dutch Mill and the Saucony Park on Crystal Cave Road......no one else on this forum will know where that is. I saw the piece in your website about Elderberry and I know that one! I don't have it here but I remember it well, Are the berries ripe now? You must get them before the birds do. It never occurred to me that the name "Elder berry" had significance....I recall they did better in a more acid soil than the lime soil of Berks County, my experience with them was actually Sullivan county. Anyway I used the woody branches as lacers on my authentic Blackfoot Tipi I built in Greenwich Township back in the day when i attended KU....cheap student housing-- I will be down in Berks this month to climb Hawk Mt (the road) on the bicycle, as I told you before I approach it from the Skuykill County side or as we used to say the "otherside" You must be right there near Eckville. Your garden must be extraordinary! Here are some coleus that grew up from the seedlings I got at Renningers Market outside from the Mennonites: It seems that they may have "usefulness" as well.....

Blessings and mahalo

+++

Hunter

Re: The true meaning of Braucherei

Hello Jesse, and I have a few clarifications of my own. Before I start, please be advised that none of it is intended as anything derogatory or to insult you or anyone associated with you. My approach is based on scholarly works as well as first hand information from European practitioners, as well as my own training and experiences as a Hexenmeister and an elder...

1. I believe I already explained that the terms "Pow-Wow" and "Braucherei" have been American Christianized, so in part your post is somewhat redundant. The views and terms I have presented are more traditional, and I might add much closer to the original, European views of the Hexerei practice. I am not trying to revise the Americanized view of the practice, if you want to call yourselves Brauchers, that's up to you. I was only pointing out that according to my most reliable source from Europe (Austria), whose mother still practices heathen arts mostly lost on these shores, Braucherei is the word she uses when describing the herbal practices of her ancestry...it doesn't make literal sense, but that's how it is. So while your definition is correct in meaning and in use for people on these shores who practice it, it is incorrect according to the Europeans from where it sprang. Also, the Germans, Austrians, and Swiss who landed on these shores were totally unfamiliar with the word "Pow-Wow"- just because it is accepted now doesn't mean it is an acceptable term- and most Native Americans I have spoken to consider the phrase as something borrowed from them.

2. The reason you will rarely if ever find anyone referring to the practice as "Hexerei" is because Hexerei means "witchcraft" in German and the term is antithetical to Christian views. It doesn't surprise me at all that they would prefer and choose to call themselves "Brauchers" or "PowWows" and describe the practice in those terms. As you pointed out, it was conducive and safer to not refer to oneself in those terms, and as these practitioners would never consider themselves to be anything but good Christians, it makes lots of sense. But yet, two published and renowned authors in the late Lee Raus Gandee (who trained the Hexenmeister that conferred the same title to myself and my wife, and who is still guiding us) and Karl Herr have referenced the

word. Lee was fond of calling what he did "Hex" in private, but outwardly and ostensibly he was a church

attending Christian. And Karl Herr noted that the tradition is called Hexerei while continually stating that he is a devout Christian who attends church and prays several times daily. Herr's view is an prime example of the confusion that has clouded and cloaked the true meaning of Hexerei.

3. There is nothing remotely "revisionist" about the extensive research I have done. Virtually none of the books, such as Valentino Kräutermann's 1725 guide to Zauber-Arzt ("magic doctoring" in English) that extensively describes the Braucherei herbal practices known to the first settlers in the same Southern German dialect (which thus far contain no Spruchzauber), have ever been translated. Several books I have translated or am currently working on were recommended as reading by my Austrian advisor and have validated much of what I have been sayingas to the original European views. I have seen many a clear reference to knowledge we have retained in America as well as discovered new things that may have been lost. So, while I understand that you are comfortable with what you have learned and what you like to call it, and I will state this with all due respect to those you have learned from, I will agree to disagree with all of you in both terminology as well as the mixing of heathen and Christian faiths that exists in your system. And that is what you practice, it is a revisionist system that has become very eclectic over the past several centuries and is not the religion I have come to know. Hexerei is a traditional witchcraft, as Stregheria is to the Italians, etc. We don't worship Christian figures or use Christian imagery. I would also recommend that you obtain a copy of "Anglo- Saxon Magic" written in 1947 by Dr. Godfrid Storms. The good doctor uses a very scholarly approach in explaining how Christian scholars added to and changed Germanic practices, as well as how one can differentiate a heathen charm from a Christian one in it's origin.

In closing, I have also noticed that you are in business and I wish

you success with that, truly I do. I am a PA German myself living in Bucks County, my ancestors settled just north of you in Schuykill County. I grew up just outside of Philadelphia yet I was raised with the same kind of family traditions and values. You may also wish to note that in this room, we openly discuss Hexerei and it's disciplines so contrary to tradition, oral transmissions are instead typewritten and must be free of monetary charge. Whether the view is heathen or Christian, I do believe it is important that it is shared so as a moderator, I hope you can reconcile this and be as open with your teachings as I have been with mine. It is the goal of Patricia and the other moderators for our membership to share information and have open discussions with one another.

Blessings and frith to all,

Greg

Re: The true meaning of Braucherei

Hey Greg

As you are fully aware, I think you are "the man" as we say here in Brooklyn where actually many Farrells are my neighbors, Your take on "Pow-Wow" is well taken, my view is that 200 hundred years ago, most of the Lenni Lenape's were gone from Berks County and all that really remained was the names, primarily of the rivers and streams, which you gotta love and respect. So that even 200 years ago, the European sttlers were seeking that esoteric extra from theindigenous "former" residents and used "Pow-Wow" to give that extra umf.

As far as Braucherei goes, you cannot dismiss the linguistic origins and meanings........can't do it or Bill O'Reilly will be in here in a flash You referred to Herr and Gandee, Herr repeatedly spoke of his nemesis the "Zauberer" according to the "magical practices of the Pennsylvania Deutsch" They scrape by making a living by making women infertile, putting the evil eye on innocents. They make work for the "Hexenmeister" The good guys.... What follows is a charm spoken by the Hexemeister to remove the evil eye and protect against it:

"I stand with Christ, who commanded evil spirits out of pigs, causing them to be dashed against the rocks below. As Christ commanded Satan, so do I, calling upon Jesus' name. In the name of Jesus Christ, who came to save us fro Eve's sin, Do I release thee of all foulness That has encompasses this child of God's glory. In the name of the four apostles, Do I surround you with angelswho shall protect you. Matthew, Mark, Luke and John stand by you. Go forthnow free of all evil, And be sure of your salvation through Jesus' blood

Amen. Amen. Amen.

from "Hex and Spellwork, KARL HERR

Your position on Hexerei vs Braucherei is not Pennsylvania Deutsch, however it actually maybe more interesting which is why I keep posting here.........

Raised Lutheran and UCC (my brother was a pastor in that denomination) and living side by side with the Mennonites and Amish, we're Christians baby, up and down, Usually I'm going up against the Hebrews who I love and respect and now i guess its the Hexes which i love and respect. But let me say it one more time, the Pennsylvania Deutsch are Christians, forgetta bout it.......dream on, har har har

Your "Restoration" is not revisionist its true religion, a real extension of mind and spirit for the "tradition" However its European roots may not be Pennsylvanian. Here we are tolerant of many many religious traditions and we love them all. We accepted influences that crossed "race" and "creed" and that has added to our importance worldwide. We are not about to return to the insanity and oppression that characterizes European history. My "people" burned no witches nor did they own any slaves and we are sick and tired of being held responsible for other peoples mistakes. My ancestors came here to escape all of that and farm a piece of land and enjoy life in all of its meanings.

Furthermore let us not forget how many Christian martyrs died for what they believed in and lets show some RESPECT! And lets not forget about the Christian miracles of healing and their founder Jesus Christ who was raised from the Dead to rule on the right side of the Lord! in parting I would like to repeat:

Our Father, who art in heaven, Hallowed be thy Name. Thy kingdom come. Thy will be done, On earth as it is in heaven. Give us this day our daily bread. And forgive us our trespasses, As we forgive those who trespass against us. And lead us not into temptation, But deliver us from evil. For thine is the kingdom, and the power, and the glory, for ever and ever.

Amen.

Re: The true meaning of Braucherei

**Sorry to interrupt. Well, (Har har har,) one of us is NOT. In fact more than a few of us on this list are NOT. Some of us follow the faith of our pre-christian Ancestors, and we are NOT bashing those who follow that faith, so I am wondering *where* one needs to bash those of us who ARE of a differing faith than you? Of course, we would agree that there are many who DO follow the various forms of christianity, but that's a given. What we are CHOOSING to do here is examine a people's Cunning and Healing ways that go beyond scratching the surface and go towards the radical formation of conscious healing that was found when their folksoul was formed.

Your "Restoration" is not revisionist its true religion, a real extension of mind and spirit for the "tradition" However its European roots may not be Pennsylvanian.

**that's the point exactly, is to examine what the Pennsylvanians DID and take it further back in the "way back machine" and see where the roots of this came about, in our Roots in European Seidhu traditions. The point is to see the evolution, and trace it's roots so there CAN be an authentic re-awkening. If you'd like to be a practising xtian Hexenmeister, be my guest. However, please don't think we are here to ONLY study the "Pennsylvanian period", but that which is encapsulated and has roots in the Germanic folksoul which was here thousands of years before Jeshua walked this earth.

Here we are tolerant of many many religious traditions and we love them all. We accepted influences that crossed "race" and "creed" and that has added to our importance worldwide. We are not about to return to the insanity and oppression that characterizes European history.

**Much of that insanity and opression is about CREED and religion and Politics and *who* could control things. This includes many churches, and various christian churches had a large part in the initial slaughter of many Pagans during the early conversion eras,starting with the fledgling Byzantine Orthodox churches from the 300's onwards up to the Northern Crusades where the Germanic Teutonic Knights killed off the original Prussian (Baltic) peoples, and forced conversions upon pain of death. Our ancestors went along because many did not want to see their children killed and everything lost. Much knowledge, much history has been lost to us by the burning of Sagas and tales, kept in dark monasteries,wanting to see the light of day. What WE did to many aboriginal peoples across the world in the post Columbus times on up were first perpetrated upon Europeans by Europeans.

I will weep no tears for those murderous wretches who commandeered a faith to use against simple folk, our ancestors, who wanted only to live in peace and harmony and know their ancestral ways, only to have to hide it under "folk tales", and other events like Harvest or Seasonal celebrations, etc.

Furthermore let us not forget how many Christian martyrs died for what they believed in and lets show some RESPECT!

**For what? For the last vestiges of a Roman Empire that wanted to lord it over Northern Europe and force us to accept a faith so they could control Princes, and land? I suggest you read some of the good books on the Conversion times, and you'd be suprised at how much Paganism is IN christianity!

And lets not forget about the Christian miracles of healing and their founder Jesus Christ who was raised from the Dead to rule on the right side of the Lord! in parting I would like to repeat:

Our Father, who art in heaven, Hallowed be thy Name....

**Spare me. I gave it up for Lent many years ago. He is NOT my God, please do NOT prosletize HERE. I don't quote Sagas or the Havamal at you.

Patricia

Re: The true meaning of Braucherei

Well it didn't happen in Pennsylvania which was founded on the principle of religious tolerance. And it certainly didn't happen amongst the Penna. Deutsch who are a model around the world for religious tolerance. Now if this page isn't about the Penna. Deutsch then its misrepresented. You insist you're tolerant but show little respect for any others but your own. Truth of the matter is that they're a few very few Pa Deutsch here. We have what you lack, a continuous tradition. The elements you possess are interesting very interesting but they played a very small part in the development of the Penna. Deutsch culture which was and is today inclusive not exclusive which is a more difficult path to walk........

+++

Hunter

Re: The true meaning of Braucherei

Well it didn't happen in Pennsylvania which was founded on the principle of religious tolerance.

**And as it seems, Christians very rarely show much tolerance towards others NOT (of one of) their persuasions. Seems they feel that they must "preach Salvation" towards us. We are not looking to be saved.

And it certainly didn't happen amongst the Penna. Deutsch who are a model around the world for religious tolerance. Now if this page isn't about the Penna. Deutsch then its misrepresented.

**It is about the people whom the PA Germans are descended from, our Ancestors, those from the various Germanic kingdoms and principalities that were "Germanic". It is also about the history of those people, we are NOT discounting that there WAS a Christian history, as I have written about in various posts. However, the AIM of this list is to explore what they did in the context of our Pre- Christian faith, and to see how that relates towards our reclamation of parts of our Native' Faiths'Cunning traditions, in a historical context. AND it has to do with the Pennsylvania Germans, as myself and many here have ancestors that are or were from those regions, or from the diaspora of those that migrated to other States.

You insist you're tolerant but show little respect for any others but your own.

**I think most of us have been very tolerant and polite towards the xtians, who are in the minority here. Many of us have parents or grandparents who/were Christians, so you are speaking about our relationship towards our nearest kin. I (and I am sure many others here do)work and live near Christians, and we realize that they are not going away soon. We can make the distinction between the individual who may be a very good decent person, and the Political Aspects of their Faith's Institution, which has shown clearly "other" sides of it's character over the centuries.

Truth of the matter is that they're a few very few Pa Deutsch here.

**I happen to be descended from one of them. He is my birth father. Does that make me any less because I was raised in Illinois? (There are also many Mennonites, Amish, etc. in this area as well..)Does that make THEM less "Deutsch"? It is a culture and heritage which we are looking at, as folk have left Pennsylvania for other areas due to what most do..move for jobs, better areas, location, etc. does that make them less.."Germanic"? We don't think so. The folksoul travels with the person, whether Xtian in belief or not.

We have what you lack, a continuous tradition.

**And where did the tradition come from BEFORE our ancestors ever settle in Pennsylvania, Mr. Yoder? We are interested also in examining THAT. You are looking at only PART of the equation. A folkway, is a living thing, and carries forth, it doesn't necessarily have to be "place-based", although I do realize that this was where the community developed and prospered. Mr. Yoder, you yourself now live in NYC do you not? Are you as a Hexenmeister lacking because you do not live there in that "continuous tradition"?

I don't think that there are many left there at all, and if those of

us that may be called to preserve it, are interested, we must all pull together to try. I think the modern world is interested in pulling many of the aspects of each culture's/people's Native healing traditions apart and modernizing them.

The elements you possess are interesting very interesting but they played a very small part in the development of the Penna. Deutsch culture which was and is today inclusive not exclusive which is a more difficult path to walk....

**I never wanted to be exclusive, we did welcome you, and you are still welcomed, but remember, the majority of us have aims here, and it may be that those aims may not be yours, because you seem to be called to "preach" to us. We are not interested in your converting us, we have our ways, and we do not seek to change YOUR attitude, and respect your faith (for you.) We are interested in the HISTORICAL use of Christianity because that IS history, and what some of our ancestors had to use due to the period they lived in. We look beyond that useage, and are wanting to reclaim our Heathen traditions. These may NOT be your aims, Sir, but please respect ours. You are also free to leave if these are not your aims either, you are NOT being asked to leave, however, this is a consideration youmay want to pursue as we will get nowhere at this point.

Patricia Niedrich

Re: [hexenkunst] Re: The true meaning of Braucherei

Braucherei is by its nature a path of many paths. It is a river of wisdom into which many tributaries have flown. When it reaches the sea of people by whom it must be carried it is a delta, wide and diffuse, rivulets of knowledge flowing in every direction but ultimately ending in the same purpose: wholeness, oneness, union with the larger spirit that encompasses us all.

I have heard over and over again from so many mouths about the "correct" way to practice, the "authentic" way to make a prayer, the "truth" of the tradition. These blanket statements have come from every angle: Christian, Pagan, academic, and folkloric. So many people seem to have interviewed one or two Braucherei practitioners and have decided that the truth they received is the only valid truth. If there is one thing I have learned from the stories and practices of the eighty something practitioners who have shared their tales with me, my teacher, Dennis, and my partners, Matthew and Susan, it is that there is a different path to healing for every single person in this wide and beautiful world. In our collective study of the Braucherei tradition there have been three well springs of knowledge upon which we have relied: 1) the direct oral tradition teachings of Elder Brauchers; 2) the written wisdom of mystics, historians, and scholars; and 3) the Spirit of wisdom that exists in our own hearts and connects us with the spirit present in every living thing.

Many wish to define Braucherei, pin it down, learn if and how it works, and discern it from other traditions. They want to document every cure, every prayer, every story. Ultimately however, this way of study will yield nothing but words on paper. It will not ensure the survival of the practice, and it will not bring the scholar to understanding of the practice itself. Understanding of the tradition itself defies definition. It refuses to be bridled. This is why we Brauchers cannot say whether or not a cure is possible: for there is no harness to spirit, it moves as it will, all we can do is hope and try to act as an open channel through which it can move.

To attempt understanding through a preservation of individual cures on paper is folly. It is akin to killing a beautiful bird, dissecting it, and placing its individual organs in jars of formaldehyde on the shelf to be studied. Perhaps the scholar can understand how certain organs interact, how a muscle contracts to drive a beating heart, lungs, wings; but there is no answer to why. Why does it breathe, hurt, heal, live, and die? These answers do not come in the form of words, words cannot hold them. They come only in the experience of spirit driving a heart to beat, a seed to sprout, the wind to blow.

Clear borders and boundaries are a human invention: the line between sand and sea is always shifting, and the border between field and forest requires constant vigilance. No matter how tirelessly we toil to maintain the lines and boundaries we create, they always return to the slow, blurred borders of the natural world. So too, that which can be defined as Braucherei is different in each pair of eyes, each mind, each heart.

The Braucherei tradition, as all culture, language, and tradition, and as every natural system on earth, has always been driven by that which is useful. Kabala was included because of the truth of its teachings; the knowledge of the Greeks leant its understanding of natural rhythms; the beliefs of the ancient Germanic tribes was the clear beating heart of a people; the wisdom of the Gnostics and later the German mystics gave an understanding of Christianity that did not condemn the inherent wisdom of a people, but simply built upon it.

It is not just Braucherei that refuses to be defined, it is culture itself. The living evolving being of language, art, religion, and healing that lives in our bones and our blood refuses to be static. How can it? That which becomes static and refuses to change or grow, as the natural world requires, quickly dies. It is the same with the spirit in every heart. The web of existence is continuously nebulous, bleeding across every line that can be drawn. In our commitment to the revival and remembrance of Braucherei wisdom we must also have knowledge of the culture from which it sprang. We must feed and care for this culture, recognizing that though this wisdom of healing and spirit may be the beating heart it cannot live without the being as a whole.

Most importantly, we cannot force our will upon this being, try to enslave it, or keep it to what it once was. Not only will its health and vitality decline, its beauty ebb; but we will have missed the point: to make the wisdom our own, to add what wisdom we can to this heirloom, to keep it vital and full, to pass it on in a state even stronger than when it found us. We have committed ourselves to openness in our mission of cultural revival. This means openness to every truth that can be spoken. After all, if Braucherei is a folk tradition, who better to teach it than the folk? Who better to learn it and carry it on than the folk? So we learn and keep alive the words of our elders, we enrich this knowledge with the wisdom of our hearts, and we rely on the hearts and hands of those yet to come to carry this heirloom as it has always been carried: with spoken word and open heart, from elder to apprentice, from person to person.

There are those who seem terrified that we will lose our path if we do not set it in stone. I hope to reassure them: the path that is lost was not meant to be had, the path set in stone cannot grow or change as a deer path in the woods, but is fixed in its purpose and function.

Already we have seen those bits of Braucherei that have been set to stone create an understanding of Braucherei that is dogmatic and empty. Dogma has a place on the healing path: it gives form and function. If, however, we rely on dogma alone to show us the path, wisdom is quickly replaced by ego, and spirit cannot flow where ego blocks the way. It is the light of spirit in the heart and soul of every being that serves to guide them on their path in life. This light makes a path in the wilderness where once there was none. It releases us from the bonds of pain in our bodies, hearts, and souls. It returns us to a state of wholeness and union with divine nature. We have spent too much time looking at our differences, dividing ourselves, and attempting to maintain purity. If there is one thing I am sure of in the future that stretches before us, it is that we must learn to see our commonalities, not only our differences. Diversity is beauty; it creates the same richness in human culture as it does in healthy ecosystems. In ecosystems, however, the many diverse aspects of the natural system have learned to work together to the greatest benefit of all. Perhaps it is time for us humans to sit back from our egoic and imagined control of our natural world, perhaps it is time to pay attention to what the natural world is telling us.

The light is present, my friends, the wisdom of Braucherei living in the flesh and blood of our elders, our descendants, and ourselves. The path shines out before us, and I pray that we have the courage and faith to follow, to bring our communities, our world, and ourselves to wholeness.

It is very confusing to me that this has turned into something that is about christian verses Heathen, as I count myself among both. My initial comment was only one of requesting inclusion and respect for the knowledge and research I have within this field, which is extensive. I think that an easy way to halt the arguement and put us all in the same playing field might be to simply say "according to ......" after stating a piece of information about our tradition. I say our meaning all of our tradition. My love and joy of Braucherei/hexerei/hexcraft/hexenkunst, ect (insert word here to describe Germanic Magical/religious/healing tradition) is that it holds all of our history as a people- all of our tradition. It does not see any part as conflicting with any other heathen and christian aspects of our history and tradition are well represented and loved. I never made a statement to prosteletize. Though I have found a dramatic measure of peace since being able to see all aspects of our historical development as relevent, and our current culture as beautiful, I am not asking anyone else to do so. What I am asking, I hope this clarifies it, is that we can act in a united goal to see a revival of this information that we all find inspiration and identity within. I love to hear specific information about heathen practices, and hope to continue to do so. What I also hope is that information I put out can be equally respected and included in discussion with out this type of blow up every time I mention anything Christian. From here on out I will tell you the location of the Braucher who gave me information that I recount, and I will also tell who interviewed them so as to keep everything clear.

If there is no interest in this type of information then I am quite willing to remove myself, I did not mean to stir the pot, just responded to what I took to be agression toward the work that I have done and the elders that I love. I joined this group because it seemed like something I would be able to learn from and contribute to, but I did not join to have more arguement about the heathens and the christians- that is a tape that has been overplayed. Lets have peace and learn together.

Blessings

Jesse

Re: The true meaning of Braucherei

Well that's been pretty interesting, I must congratulate myself and everyone for contributing to an interesting exchange of ideas.....cleared the air and I think we all know now where we stand. This certainly is far more interesting than anything that has happened here in the last 2 months anyway. If everybody agrees with everybody else .....its boring, I do tend to be a lightning rod. Nothing like a little galvanization, course they don't galvanize things like they used to.......

+++

Hunter Yoder

Re: The true meaning of Braucherei

Well it didn't happen in Pennsylvania which was founded on the principle of religious tolerance.

In word and history this is true. There have been no burnings here. But religious intolerance exists plenty and it rears it's head in many ways. Read on...

And it certainly didn't happen amongst the Penna. Deutsch who are a model around the world for religious tolerance

Oh, it didn't? Well, what do you call the infamous "Hex murder" in York County back in 1928? And Nelson Rehmeyer wasn't the only one. Wiccan author Silver RavenWolf researched quite a bit of PA Deutsch history and documented about 50 occult related killings in all from old reports. I grant that this pales in contrast to what happened in Europe. But it happens in other ways too. I know several people who were fired from their jobs after they were seen on TV about 10 years ago when LuAnn Cahn of NBC10 came to do a story about a Beltane festival we were in attendance at (thankfully a very sympathetic portrayal). I also remember Pagan Pride festivals in Lancaster and Free Spirit just south of York County in Maryland where radical Christians protested that we were, ahem, "devil worshippers" (hey Christians, he's YOUR bad guy not ours).

Back to the Rehmeyer killing, which was nationally reported- 12 years later in 1940, the Harrisburg Patriot printed an article that stated the following "State educators declared here yesterday that Hexerei, the terror of numerous farm communities for many years, is being banished from PA by the public schools. School authorities explained that instruction in the sciences, even in the lower grades, has proved the most effective weapon against the superstition. Court records show the "hex" is responsible for many crimes, including murder and arson, during the past 50 years". This attitude which also included bussing and the elimination of community "schoolhouses" was the beginning of the end for Pow-Wow and Braucherei. Now to your next point.

Now if this page isn't about the Penna. Deutsch then its misrepresented. You insist you're tolerant but show little respect for any others but your own.

We have said we want to talk about and have spoken about PA Deutsch customs, of which there are many that like the magic itself, were handed down by our Germanic ancestors. However, and this is a BIG however, we're simply not going to talk about the eclectic mix that is called Pow-Wow, Braucherei, whatever in a STRICTLY PA German context and ignore it's roots, history, and what it all meant to our ancestors. If you don't want to believe a little old Austrian lady with centuries of heathen practice in her family because of literal meanings, that's your call. I will say though that as a Hexenmeister and a teacher I must admit I'm a bit miffed with that and your latest response but I'll get over it. Back on subject, Braucherei according to Raven Wolf also meant 'witchcraft" to some of the settlers from where the term came. If this is to be believed then it explains why they were also generally avoided by the community (Lee Gandee fit this bill) unless there was a need. Lee sat in church with his wife on many a Sunday in South Carolina, but they still avoided him, you couldn't even get directions to his home unless you could convince the person you asked in his community that you weren't going there on "occult business". Lee's book was written 18 years before his death and Hunter since you persist, his views expressed in his book as well as his homosexual

87

admissions, led to the breakup of his marriage as well as his relationships in the community. He suffered mightily and not a single one of you knows anything about how he ended up in the years that followed. He knew and researched enough to know that many of the things a Pow-Wow or a Braucher does has firm, very firm, foundations in traditional witchcraft. My people, my wife's people, we're PA Germans as much as anyone here and our families knew this was true.

Truth of the matter is that they're a few very few Pa Deutsch here. Wehave what you lack, a continuous tradition.

Yes, a continuous eclectic tradition that has incorporated quite a few things alien to Germanic culture and is being rejected more and more as the growing fundamentalist and Bible literalist movement sweeps across America. The election of a fundamentalist and secular U.S president and his values shows this happening. These people don't even think that dinosaurs existed no matter the overwhelming proof, and my wife has a cousin like that, so I know this to be true. There is no room in their minds for Pow-Wow and Braucherei if it smells like witchcraft, and at least half of the system is exactly that. Nothing not in the Bible, no matter the intention, including Mr. Herr's prayer that you quoted, will change that.

The elements you possess are interesting very interesting but they played a very small part in the development of the Penna. Deutsch culture which was and is today inclusive not exclusive which is a more difficult path to walk.........

I would not assume that about the first waves of settlers. How else do you think we got this culture? Many of them left the old country on

William Penn's promise that there would be no religious persecution. Quite a few among them were witches and Hexenmeisters and I would not discount that at least a few knew about and worshipped the German gods and goddesses, after all it was part of the culture through their sagas and "marchen". Remember the lady interviewed in North Carolina who was using "Thor" in a healing incantation- and where it came from. They knew the truth and it is plain to see for anyone with an open mind about it. Much of it has disappeared among the Germans of today, this is true. But the true traditional nature of Hexerei that was known to them and lost still exists according to several people I have spoken with directly, people who have first hand knowledge of it.

This said, I hope we all can come to some sort of compromise here. Arguing other than in a scholarly and factual manner is nothing but counterproductive. I believe anyone can learn something from someone else.

"Cooling down" lol blessings and frith,

Greg

Re: The true meaning of Braucherei

Well I have to admit it, you guys seem to have your fingers on the "buttons" which is probably why I am hanging around. As I was telling a friend of mine, "there is nothing more stubborn than a PA Dutchman" I know of a case where some old Dutch guy was so stubborn and dumb (worked hard all his life) that he was too stubborn and dumb to realize he was dead. Now this went on for some time now and the neighbors were complaining about the stink, but Paul, his name was Paul Getz just refused to accept the fact and kept getting up in the morning anyway.

Finally his wife told him, "Paul, you stubborn, dumb dutchman" you're

dead as doornail and you stink time to put you underground" "Oh yeah?" He said, "That might explain why my schnicke doesn't work anymore and I'm attracting flies"

So anyway, we weren't all those different National christians you were talking about we were Lutheran, United Church of Christ (practically the same thing as Lutheran), Mennonite and Amish. Lived on a farm. I still get calls from runaway Mennonites who find my name in the phone book. My choir instructor at Lutheran Evangelical Church we attended was Richard Wagner and the minister was Rev Heckman. When we went to school the townies complained that we smelled, well like the farm, but the smell wouldn't come off no matter how much we washed.

The neighbors were Amish and they had twelve kids. People would drop off shoes and clothes for them because the limited income from the farm wasn't quite enough. On Sundays, the Amish would observe the Sabbath and sometimes a bunch of them would bicycle 100 mile roundtrip to the Philly Zoo.

I would get my saw blades sharpened by one Mennonite family, they had no electricity but had a telephone. He ran the shop equipment off of the wind using a series of belts and pulleys. The Amish and Mennonites always had the best land on the plain in Berks County. My grandfather, Maurice Yoder and his kin came out of the Oley Valley in southern Berks County, Oley was originally called Friedrichsberg. it must be some of the most haunted country in the State. It was the "backway to Philly from Reading. Dennis Boyer was from the "south mountain" and describes the area well. Yeah 10 cent beers at the Grand Central tavern in Fleetwood with sausage and hot mustard.

And if you have Don Yoder's "coffee table" book "Hex Signs" and look at page 19 which shows the frequency of hex signs in the SE part of PA, right where the dots all converge and it gets all black......yeahthat's where I'm from...........

Re: [hexenkunst] Re: The true meaning of Braucherei

Of course Braucherei is also considered witchcraft, as was my point in
my very first response: What you are calling hexerei others call
braucherei. Braucherei is simply another name for the magical/ healing/
spiritual system of the PA Dutch. Here in Berks county it is the
predominant name. Yes, you are right that many of the old gods are still
present in our system, some renamed, some not, that is my very point.
There is actually very little evidence for much of an influence from
native american people except in western PA Traditions, some of which
contain a Willow Lodge or other sweat lodge tradition which was
created on purpose in the hopes of creating a place where healers of
many cultures could come together and exchange information. The
tradition I have been handed from over 80 practitioners across the state
is one that is at its core Pre-christian (as Christianity is at its core Pre-
christian). Like most European wisdom traditions there is a thin icing of
Christianity on top of a big fat pagan cake. If we want to talk about
original, how far back do we go? Is it necessary to discount the people
who simply added to the traditions? Truly, not much was lost, mostly
things have been added, which, from a healers perspective is natural- if
something works it will be used again, simply put. My point was not to
heat up this whole arguement over christian and heathen practices, but
simply bring to the table the fact that there are many different terms,
many different names that have been given to these practices, as many
as there were dialects in germany before the advent of high german.
And I am glad to respect, believe, and appreciate your little old austrian
lady, I am positive she has much to offer. I actually have contacts of my
own in germany, contacts who called this practice all sorts of things-

greidehex, Brauche, Braucherei. My original response was not written to disregard your research or your teachers, it was simply to broaden it with information from my little old rhineland lady, my little old Oley valley lady, my little old piketown lady, snyder county, bucks, lehigh, etc. I thought that was the point here. Though many americans have a big problem with the idea of "witchcraft", I do not- I understand the history that brought us here. I do choose not to use that word or the term of hexerei because of its current day connotations, though I wish these connotations did not exist, there is no rewriting history, and I have more important battles to fight. I just do not want our practices and traditions to be discounted because there is also christianity- I do not operate on a basis of either or- but instead:both and. I think you would be surprised, if you let me get past this arguement, the aspects of our tradition that have remained intact since ancient times. Also- most of the "eclectic" aspects of the tradition have been around as major influences in germanic culture since nearly 1000 years ago, perhaps more. The Greek arts and sciences entered Germany in many ways, but by the time of Hildegard von Bingen were very well known; Kabala has possibly been an influence since before christian times as there seems to have been a Jewish presence in the Rhine River valley very early on; The gnostics were possibly some of the first christians to reach germany- and shared their wisdom in a peaceful way (our tradition tells us it was Mary Magdelene who first brought the teachings of Jesus, coming up the Rhine River valley). These influences are movements that shaped and changed our culture irrivocably. I most certainly don't like every change that has been made. I don't like much of the violent and terrible history. But what of those who were not violent, who were not prosteletizing, but were simply living humble quiet lives filled with the wonder and magic of the world-of creation, regardless of whose it is.

Also- the Hex trials is what happened when a paranoid and sick man made an unfortunate act of violence. It is what happened when PA German Culture came out of the closet to the Englishmen that surrounded them. It is the sensationalization of the media, and overreaction of the state to an isolated subculture and its oddities. It is a sad point in PA history, and one that nearly destroyed our culture, language, spirituality, and healing practices. The peasantry of Germany, Austria, and Switzerland have endured much of the same, it just came later in PA. This lateness is what has allowed Braucherei to still be a vital cultural force in this region. There are vehement religious wackos everywhere, which is exactly why I take the stance I do- one of inclusion, one that respects all the many ancestors in our history and seeks to include their wisdom- that of their teachings which is life affirming, whose goal is to grow the spirit. My hope is for a flexibility about terminology and beliefs, seeing as these things changed with each valley along with the dialect of language, the costume, the food. It is the practices themselves I am here to discuss. I will call them braucherei, as that is what I have been taught, you may call them hexerei or what ever you want. What I want is not to be informed of the "correct" dogma, when I know the dogma perfectly well, it just might be different than yours. When one wishes to collect a coherent understanding of culture, it is often important to exist in a place of plurality. Trying to correct Braucherei practitioners with correct terminology, beliefs, or ideas would only end in not learning anything from them. I like to learn.

Blessings

Jesse

Hi again Jesse. My responses to follow. Please remember that this is a healthy and friendly debate and that I am only presenting a different point of view :)

Of course Braucherei is also considered witchcraft, as was my point in my very first response: What you are calling hexerei others call braucherei. Braucherei is simply another name for the magical/

healing/spiritual system of the PA Dutch.

My research indicates that Hexerei and Braucherei are similar yet different animals. In the literal meaning of the latter in the German tongue, which you previously gave, there is no reference nor association whatsoever between Braucherei and witchcraft, whereas Hexerei literally means "witchcraft". Other than my Austrian source, I have never heard nor read the word Braucherei used in any context to describe witchcraft except in works describing American practices. The European books continually refer to witchcraft practices as "Hexerei". I once asked my mentor (a non-Christian) for an explanation about this very thing, because when you read the various books on the subject you are presented with names such as Hexerei, Braucherei, and Pow-Wow. Even Lee Gandee himself used the terms Braucherei and Pow-Wow to describe U.S practices, yet he (and this caused him a mess of problems) called himself a "Hex", which upon publication of his book led his wife and community to believe he had been "turned away" from God and Jesus by Satan, the devil, etc. Before I digress any further, my mentor's response to me regarding what Lee said to him about this echoes what I stated previously. Hexerei is it's original and root name. Hexerei describes the practice when using the names, imagery, and power of the pre- Christian gods and goddesses of the Germanic people. Braucherei and Pow-Wow are the name Christians gave to it as they practiced it. It's that simple and I don't see the need to debate it any further than that.

Here in Berks county it is the predominant name. Yes, you are right that many of the old gods are still present in our system, some renamed, some not, that is my very point.

My question to you, in the spirit of learning, is how many of the old gods and goddesses do you actually see as still present in your

system? In the Braucherei/Pow-Wow system, I have learned and read virtually nil about this. It's certainly not present in the spoken magic, the Spruchzauber. The instance I described in North Carolina is far from the norm. The second Merseburg charm is another exception to this. Very few if any have been otherwise uncovered. And naturally, in the cloaking used by practitioners who were Christian in ideology, there are several versions from Scandinavia and the British Isles.

There is actually very little evidence for much of an influence from Native American people except in western PA Traditions, some of which contain a Willow Lodge or other sweat lodge tradition which was created on purpose in the hopes of creating a place where healers of many cultures could come together and exchange information. The tradition I have been handed from over 80 practitioners across the state is one that is at its core Pre-christian (as Christianity is at its core Pre-christian). Like most European wisdom traditions there is a thin icing of Christianity on top of a big fat pagan cake. If we want to talk about original, how far back do we go? Is it necessary to discount the people who simply added to the traditions? Truly, not much was lost, mostly things have been added, which, from a healers perspective is natural- if something works it will be used again, simply put. My point was not to heat up this whole argument over christian and heathen practices, but simply bring to the table the fact that there are many different terms, many different names that have been given to these practices, as many as there were dialects in Germany before the advent of High German.

How far? Well, we don't have to do this for Braucherei, it is what it is. Hexerei is a different matter. My ideal approach would be as I mentioned previously, to discuss it with a European hereditary who has the knowledge of it in a heathen sense. That is the very best way it can be fully comprehended. In absence of that, what has to be done is what Dr. Storms noted in his book, which is where I was at anyway, and therefore most gratifying. I'll avoid a full dissertation and simply say that it has to be uncloaked. This isn't about all the different names or disrespecting persons who have contributed, not at all. To me, the only versus is simply that one is an elder, heathen version and one is eclectic with elements of the former incorporated into it. My practice is the former, that's all.

I could address every point that went further, but I don't have the time to spend on it right now. Bottom line, we can talk about all of it. I come from a family who had Pow-Wows and Brauchers, and most likely witches or cunning folk, terminology whatever you prefer, even farther back. I respect what you do and look forward to exchanging ideas and hopefully information. For example, here's what really interests me- Lee Gandee spoke about a magic grave lamp and a "dead man's mirror", but couldn't find a person who knew the Spruchzauber and/or prayer to activate one. The remainder of the procedure is otherwise known to me. Would you know anything about the words?

Blessings and frith,

Greg

Hi Greg,

About the presence of the old ones in our current tradition: There are several who are mentioned as a side note or a spirit here or there, but there are also several who are still important and vital forces within the traditon. One is Hollerbeierfraa (Fraa Holle, aka Hella, Holle, Hulda, etc)- goddess of the underword from ancient lore, she continues to be our guide in the realm of the dead, and a translator on the otherside. Another is none other than Woden himself. It is interesting to see on the Northvegr website that there is an article about the association between Odin and the ancient grain god traditions. We actually have information about Woden by his own name, and we also have a grain god tradition- we call him the Butzeman and there is very specific protocol surrounding his creation, his purpose, and his funeral pire. These traditions are very similare to english traditions surrounding John Barleycorn. Another is the White Haired woman- and here we have an enigma- honestly she could be associated with so many different Goddesses, one part Baba Yaga one part Walpurgis- her face and being shifts- now young and beautiful, now ancient and wise. She is said to be the spirit of the tradition of Braucherei itself. Also there are the three sisters- these are the wyrd sisters of old- they have the same description and function, but in braucherei they are called either "die Drei Schwestere" or collectively "Sophia". There are others, but I will have to expand another day.

As to the many less well known aspects of the tradition. There is a reason they are not found in written form. When PA Germans experienced the whole hex trial spectacle, they went through quite a bit culturally. Brauchers who continued to practice went very far underground, many stopped practicing- especially after two world wars made topics about Germanic Magical traditions rather unpopular. For a long time my husband, Matthew and I were very frustrated about the fact that these old timers just didn't seem to want to trust anyone with this tradition. At the time we were researching with an eye toward publication, not practice. Now that we have shifted our focus to one of wanting to learn what they have to offer, and our willingness to learn it accordiing to their context and beliefs, and honor their wishes about the information, we now we have people asking us to interview them! That has been a very exciting shift. However, many of the prayers and less well known practices are kept exclusively in oral tradition- the prayers, the willow lodge, timecord work, and the information about pre-christian dieties and spirits. Some practitioners regard these prayers and practices as living beings, and say that they die when you write them down. Some simply want to honor the tradition of passing down one person to the next. Some believe that if you can't memorize the prayers instantly and spit them back perfectly, you are not meant to have them.

There are all sorts of different reasons for the oral tradition. I have made vows to these elders, in respect of their wishes not to bring these specifics into written form, and I have to honor that.

I have not heard any specifics on the particular charm you are talking about, although we do have some information about death ceremony both for the deceased and for the survivors.

Blessings

Jesse

Re: The true meaning of Braucherei

Hey quote me some sagas sock it to me give me some of that if you have the power don't hide it don't be shy my rabbits bite but I don'tI'm country

+++

Hunter

Tuesday, July 10, 2007

Statement for understanding

This is a statement from the Native American Church about their sacramental use of Peyote and following the Peyote Road. in the context of our work, I thought this was interesting.

Statement for understanding

The use of 'sacrament' is contained within the community. Any other use of this would not be a correct use of 'medicine'. While it could be said that the whole world is a community, which is true, it also can be seen that at the spiritual level this is not always true. By being part of community there are conditions of coherent belonging. There must be impeccability or a serious personal aim in that direction toward one's personal community (Kiva). Responsibility to your personal spirit/soul is a sacred relationship. This relationship must be growing and alive in your everyday environment.

And as you know an understanding between the participants of a community is one of trust. This trust is founded upon time spent together and the shared effort of being one with the Creator as much as possible. As you see, the community is one of constant evolvement, adjustment and renewing...

Ancient Spiritual tenets are to heal the body and spirit. Further, to teach impeccability, correct 'seeing', and power of Beingness. Peyote is not used to obtain 'visions' but to open portals to Reality. Always seeking centeredness within this existence. Peyote is the road back to the true Self. This should suffice in order to allow personal compreshension of this Sacrament

There is much more to the 'Church' - 'Kiva' than just the Sacrament but, all things flow from the existential awareness of Being Here. This "Diazine" leads to the second, and a most powerful teaching perception. Which is to maintain the integrity of this Existential Beingness in the environment in which one finds their self manifested (Weltanschauung). There is energy to affectively change, from searching to understanding.

Let me give you an example of a couple of self-realizations that can allow you to become mere harmonically in tune with the Relativity surrounding you. For each of us gravitate to the freedom knowledge brings with it.

Truth is like the Air we breathe; We cannot live without It. Many things present themselves to fragment each one of us away from Truth

Within the 'Church-Kiva' we are ourselves. Feeling and emotion of each other make the relative space harmonic or, off centered (fragmented). Outside the 'Church-Kiva' we have learned that in order to exist in that environment, we have to strategically hide behind our 'Images'.

While this can be said to be universal behavior, the difference is in the "psychological defenses" of our objective self. When a person is ego-centered in the image, the psychological strategies come into play automatically. This movement is Conserve the projected image at all costs! Loss of this Image could be dangerous to the well-being of the person. These complex psychic interactions cause problems-cause problems-cause problems.

These situations, when encountered on the outside, are only IMAGE conflicts and it means that there has to be a Reality check on our INTENT and DIRECTION.

If you heal the Spirit, you heal the body, and to Be yourself is a step in the right direction. Furthermore, there is a discipline and a structure to everything that surrounds us. To vibrate harmoniously with these things is definitely healing. (feels good too)

The learning of 'Human things' and the knowing of relationships opens portals of existence which are the Spiritual Legacy of each one of us. This is the rightful place of man-kind as we step into the future second by second.

http://www.nativeamericanchurch.com/peyote.html

Figure 14"Datura Star" paper collage, 2007

Dennis Boyer

Hey Dennis

Got a hold of a copy of "Once Upon a Hex" Really liked the Berks County stuff. I've been hanging out with a bunch PA German Witches, yeah alittle Hexerei, Jesse's over there too, very bright lady..... Anyway I wrote this, just off the top of my head from my own experience growing up in Berks......I know all them places, Bowers, Lyons, Fleetwood, all those "hotels" brought tears to my eyes....

So anyway, we weren't all those different National christians you were talking about we were Lutheran, United Church of Christ (practically the same thing as Lutheran), Mennonite and Amish. Lived on a farm. I still get calls from runaway Mennonites who find my name in the phone book. My choir instructor at Lutheran Evangelical Church we attended was Richard Wagner and the minister was Rev Heckman. When we went to school the townies complained that we smelled, well like the farm, but the smell wouldn't come off no matter how much we washed.

The neighbors were Amish and they had twelve kids. People would drop off shoes and clothes for them because the limited income from the farm wasn't quite enough. On Sundays, the Amish would observe the Sabbath and sometimes a bunch of them would bicycle 100 mile roundtrip to the Philly Zoo.

I would get my saw blades sharpened by one Mennonite family, they had no electricity but had a telephone. He ran the shop equipment off of the wind using a series of belts and pulleys. The Amish and Mennonites always had the best land on the plain in Berks County. My grandfather, Maurice Yoder and his kin came out of the Oley Valley in southern Berks County, Oley was originally called Friedrichsberg. it must be some of the most haunted country in the State. It was the "backway " to Philly from Reading. Dennis Boyer was from the "south mountain" and describes the area well. Yeah 10 cent beers at the GrandCentral Tavern in Fleetwood with sausage and hot mustard.

And if you have Don Yoder's "coffee table" book "Hex Signs" and look at page 19 which shows the frequency of hex signs in the SE part of PA, right where the dots all converge and it gets all black......yeah that's where I'm from..........

The only thing is your hex sign on the cover, the hearts are going the wrong way...............

Other than that, I loved it

Blessings

+++

Hunter Yoder

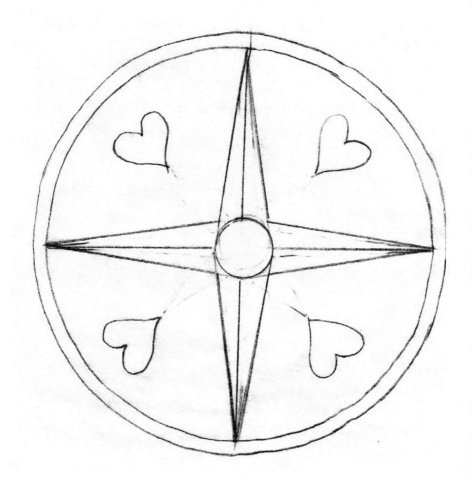

Figure 15 "Corrected Once Upon a Hex Book Cover"

Hunter: Enjoyed this communication! My family denominational background was diverse: mostly Fraconia Mennonites in Mom's side(with some Brethren and German Methodists), paternal grandfather Reformed

(but with Moravian and pietist ancestors), and paternal grandmother Lutheran (with some Bally Catholic ancestors). On my father's side there were many Oley valley roots in what I call ground zero for pow wow. And a number of family practitioners.I attended a slew of different churches as a boy, but was confirmed Reformed at Huffs Church, was rebaptised by a Brethren pastor in the peace movement after my return from Vietnam and am now the only VFW life member I know who is a Mennonite.

Regarding the hex sign on the cover: I handpainted it on my barn in SW WI after a shamanic journey in the colors and configuration you see. If you think that one is nontraditional I'll have to send you a jpeg file of my medicine wheel hex (star of david, with points of white, balck, red, yellow, blue and green on copper field with gold triangle in the center). This also came out of a shamanic journey.

machs goot!

Dennis

Hey Dennis,

Wow that's pretty diverse!

We were just straight up Lutherans, Trinity Lutheran Church on west Main street, Kutztown. Big ole organ, lotta Martin Luther hymns, "A mighty fortress is our God, a bulwark never failing; "

Yeah but my memories of the area are inevitably about all the factories that abounded that I worked in such as Caloric Stove in Topton where I worked on the assembly line in the summer, and Red Cheek apple Juice in Fleetwood, The Tannery in Fleetwood, and all of the shoe factories in Kutztown, Saucony Shoe which is still an International trademak name, the creek is still there but the factories are long gone.....

But up your way there, Huff's Church, "Five Point Road" The Dryville Hotel and then that short cut down the hill to Bowers to the UCC Church my brother was ordained as a minister in....yeah the Bowers Hotel the really old cemetery . Or Up the hill from Dryville to New Jerusalem where I used to get my '52 Dodge Pickup worked on at "Rhodes Garage" yeah its the same truck that was in the 52 production of "White Christmas" with Bing Crosby singing.....

Working and living side by side with the Mennonites, yeah it rubs off, used to use them all the time in the trades, either in their wood shops or for welding and fabrication, the bike shops, "Weavers Hardware comes to mind on the Lyons Fleetwood Rd. Always the best produce and seedlings at a great price, tractors with steel rimmed treads.

Finally regarding the hex sign on your book cover,

Who am I to be correcting a published author but, what you have painted there on your barn is an "earth star" (a circle with 4 directions) sometimes associated with the planet Venus (fertility, love abundance good luck) This symbol goes straight back through thousands and thousands of years to the "fertile crescent"

Of course what would be more approriate for the PA Dutchman to paint on his bank barn to decorate it and promote fertility and abundance. On yours, I think the intent was to radiate the love outwards by pointing the hearts in the way that you did. However the central part of a hex sign refers to the "subjective universe" the artist's personal identity and source of inspiration . The outer area of a hex sign is the "objective universe" the outside world so to speak. By pointing the hearts inward you actually will produce your desired intent, it will strengthen the subjective "core" allowing it to reach outward into the objective universe "invisibly"

I am interested in you viewes on Pa Deutsch Shamanism and have formulated some ideas of my own. To my limited knowledge the two are seldom seen together in the writing that has occurred on the subject of "Braucherie" other than your own.

How this Shamanic viewpoint differs from the Hexerei perspective is something I am trying to wrap my mind around. I think there is a difference, shamanism has more of a direct conection to the land the plants and animals, the weather. the rivers and streams and perhaps less emphasis on "blood' and verbal charms. I think that PA Deutsch shamanism may be connected to the Appalachian MTs. I think that it may also be a more recent revival or discovery of connecting directly to the "living universe" It may be more visceral or experiencial than hexerei.

I think it uses different plants. Plant teachers in my personal experience are invaluable , not only consuming them but then growing, coexisting with them as they passively effect life around them. Some plants speak very clearly and loudly, others come in dreams.

But anyway I'm still working on that.....

Blessings

+++

Hunter Yoder

Hunter: I appreciate your thoughts. And the trip down a fond memory lane. The information about my barn sign is interesting. It kind of flows from my experiential framework of Braucherei, remaining open to what Spirit sends my way (like the encounter with the particular symbol in the journey state).

As for my view of Braucherei as PA German shamanism, it is still evolving. I've interviewed over 70 pow wow practitioners and found their accounts so varied and eclectic, that i became convinced that what I was seeing were fragments of a once integrated system that was a little worse for the wear from church/government suppression.

I use journeying to "track" my lineage and have encountered dozens of teachers in the recent and distant past. I have encountered the following rough "stages" in that lineage:

Paleolithic shamanism of nomadic proto-Europeans

Neolithic Celtic and Germanic shamanism

cross-cultural dissemination (Egypt, Greeks, Romans, middle east)

Dark Ages (alchemy, Kabbala,Gnostics)

Inquisition

Reformation and Pietists

New World (native American contact)

multi-cultural contact (Scotch-Irish, African, Roma,)

I don't rely a lot on word definitions. I describe my view of Braucherei as the sum total of the above periods and experiences (which I find "accessible" through shamanic work). For me it is more than healing practices, it is a world view, dare I say cosmology, that flows from affinity for a view of Creation and one's place in it. I approach this with the attitude that one can be part of the world of Braucherei without being a Braucher. As for Hexerei, my teachers usually portrayed as a use of power to the detriment of others, but that too is a definition and may be too narrow to describe what was going on.

I'd like to hear more of your thinking on this. DB

Hey Dennis,

Thanks for replying to my email, it means a lot to me.

My point of origin in all of this has always been the hex sign. Painted them on my father's barn in Richmond Township near Virginville when about 16 years old. He grumbled at the extra cost and expense since the "job" was to just paint the whole barn, ha! But there they were actually inscribed into the wood, the usual three on the front "bay" and one on either end, none on the back bank side. Eight pointed stars, with a radiating outer border. Made a big impression. I also grew up and went to school with the Claypoole family whose Dad you might know, Johnny who took up hex sign painting from Johnny Ott of Lenhartsville not too far down stream.

I loved Ott's work it still was pretty visible then, he was basically a commercial painter with alittle something extra. The interior of the Lenhartsville hotel, the main dining room is the "Sistine Chapel" of PA Hexology. He free form decorated all the walls, I think he owned the place at one time. Ott is referred to by Gandee in "Strange Experience" A "rain" hex sign Ott painted evidently was left outside too long causing so much rain that the Delaware River flooded causing 4 million dollars damage, a large sum back in the fifties.

So I'm pretty familiar with this tradition, I practice it. Don't have to remember all those prayers and charms although I have incorporated some of them in my work. recently I wrote:

"Even the mere layman can enjoy and benefit in many ways from the practice of painting "earthstars" Certain geometric and numerical configurations have always been held "sacred" since the stoneage. Painting, or pecking symbols in the rock cliffs has been so easy that even a "caveman" could do it. I like to make the analogy between "hex sign painting" and growing plants. Perhaps more precisely planting seeds,. They both are creative acts, when planting a seed, all of the components of the mature plant are there in a very compact form, The results of the "planting" are not always known and the conscious intent of "planting" can be misleading. "Growth" occurs sometimes in such away that is not always anticipated, The subconscious mind needs only to be exposed to a conscious experience inorder for it to manifest that experience's essence into a creative result........all the stylized intent in the world cannot be a substitute for the irrational power of the paradox. Making a connection with the "Living Universe" is inevitably paradoxical and the results frequently a surprise!"

My interest and focus is what I believe to be the primary focus of the Berks County farmer, fertility and weather control:" The essence of Pennsylvania Deutsch magic is fecundity, as farmers we sought to increase our yield. Look to the west after dark and look for that Bright star, she is in a 8/5 relationship to us all and she has many names and She is painted on our barns.........."

You are right, all the rest may be just different names for similar things, the simplicity of my concerns and their basic primitive nature may meet the criteria of being called "shamanism"

Thanks again Dennis

+++

Hunter

Hunter:

My primary pow wow teacher "prescribed" hex signs, but did not paint them herself. She often referred to them as "picture prayers" . Her method and concept were also present in a number of other Berks and Lehigh brauchers, mainly in a belt from Oley to Macungie, though I heard of a few others up in the Mahoning Valley.

Other terms that popped up were visual prayers, dream signs, wish symbols, and magic marks. I've been told of brauchers of long ago that drew such symbols on the body of others and of one who had india ink tatoos in the palm of her hands. I had a dream of having such a tatoo on my left upper arm. Haven't moved on that yet. DB

Hey Dennis,

From the Brauchers perspective prescribing a "painted prayer" makes perfect sense. Lee Gandee was the king in this regard. I however, seem to be coming from the shamanic direction and see these things as "tribal symbols" expressions of identity. I assure you that the quickest most recognized "Pa Dutch" icon in the media universe is that rossette, problem is everybody think the Amish paint them.......ha ha

These things are "cosmograms" or abbreviated cosmologies. Many cultures have them, ours are directly related to Icelandic "Galdor Staves , my favorite is the "helm of awe" These actually articulate the flow outward and and the retention inward in a more sophisticated manner then ours........oh well, I just appropriated from theirs what I wanted and I'm back in the game. I used this:

and incorporated it with something I picked up from a virginsville hex sign painter, Milton Hill and now its ours again:

added some Runes, The German Hexs freaked out because they were from the Younger Futhark, but hey I liked that version of Hagall (sure looks like that rossette configuration) better..........

So it is a fluid living cultural entity that I am determined to EXTEND.

+++

Hunter

about the ancient ones

Hielsa,

I am very much enjoying this discussion and I'm learning a lot from it. On the Goddess portion, Hella and Holda(Hulda, Holle) are not the same Goddesses as per lore, histories, traditions, etc.:

Hella(Hel)- the keeper of the dead until: rebirth, guardian spirit, Hall of God or Goddess, Niflhem (really bad people).

Holda(Hulda, Holle)- in northern Germany she is also known by Perahta and Frau Berchte - she is a generous Goddess of home, family and women's crafts(spinning, weaving, etc), flax

Three sisters, wyrd sisters - Urda, Werdanda, Sculd

Hi Jesse and Judy,

Judy is right for the most part, as far as I can see. Where I would disagree is that Holda is better known by Holle/Perchta/Berchte in Southern Germany, where a good deal of the original settlers came from. All these names get confusing, again, this is a tribal thing in my estimation.

Jesse, what the European lore says about Holda (whose energy I am very familiar with) is that she can appear young and beautiful, or she can appear old and ugly, a kind but stern taskmaster. She has attributes similar to Frikka, wife of Wuotan/Odin (Wuotan also is known as a triple god, and his attributes are much more vast than what you've mentioned), in that she is a spinning goddess, and spinning has sometimes been linked with weaving the threads of Wyrd. She has also been called a goddess of the underworld and of witches, and according to witch trial transcripts from the 1500-1600's (if those can be believed) she sometimes shows a visitor what will happen and who will die, in the example I have read it was a year's time. The latter attributes, the theme involving witchery and living inside a mountain, have also been attributed to Frouwa Walpurga, a.k.a Freyja, mistress of seidhr (the Norse term) and the "similar in meaning" German term of Wahrsagezauber. I believe your white haired lady is more than likely Holda/Perchta. Hella seems to be more of a Scandinavian rather than a continental entity, at least in what I've read and researched, I believe the Germans associated Holda/Holle with Hel. The names I've read that are commonly used for the "drei Schwestere" are Urd, Verdandi, and Skuld, they're also known as the "Norns". Sophia, as you may know already, is associated with Gnostic Christianity.

I am disappointed that you cannot write anything down here, but I respect your vow. Of course, that doesn't mean we cannot speak about it orally, does it not? I propose payment should, in this case, be an exchange of information, of which as a Hexenmeister I have plenty to offer. I hope we can work something out and I will give you a call :)I did have to chuckle at the one thing you said about a prayer losing it's power if you write it down. I recently had to have my niece (one of my students) write down my burn charm so that she could help someone with 2nd degree burns. Normally I would have done this over the telephone for the patient but that wasn't possible. My niece did what I instructed to the letter and the patient experienced immediate relief from the pain. So I feel that this is more of a superstition than anything else, because many of the charms have been written down at this point in history and they are working just fine for myself and others, and that includes those using different god and goddess archetypes.

Faith is the driving force of any magic. This is why what I do works for me. I have experimented with Psalms and other Christianized charms by simply changing the words and imagery (uncloaking if you will lol) and they work as intended with sometimes spectacular results. I can honestly say that I have never failed to heal someone in my 19 years of being a witch (and I never take credit, that goes to the Divine and ancient ones for sending me the energy and faith to do so), and have rarely missed in casting a spell. The few times that happened, someone involved didn't do what they were supposed to.

Blessings, frith, and also enjoying this very much!

Greg

Hi Greg,

Yes, everything you are saying about the old ones is reflected in my own research and what I have gained through the brauchers I have talked with: the nature of Holle, woden, and the different names for the three sisters. I have a different feeling about White Haired woman, however. According to what I've been told she is the spirit of the tradition itself, and she was once alive on the earth. There is a story about her called the first woman who dreamed- sort of an origin story of our shamanic practices. The story says that she has returned to the earth several times to revive and renew the tradition when it has needed it. It also says that her last incarnation was mountain mary.

The transmission of the prayers is something that I never charge for, something I am not allowed to charge for. I like to get to know someone pretty well to give them the prayers, though, to give myself a chance to feel them out energetically, to be sure of intentions and future use of the information. I would be open to talking about meeting to talk about all of this since you are in the bucks county area.

Blessings, Jesse

Figure 16 Datura Stramonium thornapple

Datura Stramonium, the new moon and friday the 13th July 2007

I did some work for myself and my man today. I hope that's all going to help! Thanks for the picture! It was lovely...

Ayla

Why not mark the moment?

And Venus is very high in the Western sky

Enjoy!

Hey Ayla,

Your man is very lucky indeed!

here are some more pics from another member who has fallen under this

one's spell........

Figure 17 Datura Stramonium, six pointed flower

Blessings

+++

Hunter

,

Oh, they are so beautiful! They are one of my favorite flowers! Thanks so much for sending them...........

Ayla

Datura Hexology

Because of the interest this plant has created from the feedback I've received, I've decided to "do" a little hexological sojourn into the subject. According to the Hexenmeisters, this is supposed to take place in secret in the closet so to speak. the old timers didn't have access to the internet as we know it. Since I am interested in just doing this for pure pleasure, which is pretty much my guiding light, I thought I might open the process up to this group. The subject is a "no brainer" really Datura or what I like to call "Tolache" pronounced Toe Lock is such a weirdo, that merely its presence has an enormous effect. liken it to having a wife. You really don't get much satisfaction out of her but she certainly has alot to say and won't shut up, or go away, ha ha

My dilemma is should it be a five or six pointed star or both, also what other iconography should I attach, I will try to refrain from any Christian references but I only have so much control over these matters. I'm seeing leaf arrangements probably four, two pairs. Anyway any reaction to this would be nice and this plant is such a Dr Strangelove, that the "sign" will probably work. If not keep the receipt and you get various confusing warranties depending upon your port of call or state of mind which ever you can recall............

+++

Hunter

My dilemma is should it be a five or six pointed star or both, alsowhat other iconography should

This is a dilemma...The six points would easily give you an appealing, balanced design for your placement of the four leaves. And according to Gandee, 6 representing the feminine aspect. Just curious if you've considered just 3 leaves? You also have the inspiration of the six petaled Tolache growing in your yard. Hard to resist the call of that.

Having only ever experienced the five petaled blossoms, I am attracted to this one personally and would possibly incorporate the glyph for Venus (the crosses emanating from a small circle in the center of the star?) hearts or the rose shaped pentagram ...all historically symbolic of the feminine principle, love, fertility, the eight year path cycle of Venus...etc. I would definitely have to balance the linear angles with some kind of feminine flowing or circular element. The design possibilities are slightly less appealing (and limited) than the balance of the six.

Really curious to see what you have come up with so far.

Susan

Hey Susan ,

Thanks for the input, yeah six pointed stars such as the rossette arereal basic hexology. I'm not quite sure what Gandee was saying in regard to six being feminine, the usual interpretation of six pointed stars is that they are the union of the male and female , the descending equilateral triangle is female and the one pointing up is male together they form a fusion of polarities, a very powerful sign. But I think you are right, 5 is better for this one. The glyph you speak of is Lamat and the cross works well for that but Toloche maynot tolerate that. Besides Venus being an influence, the moon may even play a larger role here, Frequently the rabbit is associated with Venus and the image visible on a full moon has been associated with the rabbit as well

The pentagram will be a refreshing change from the usual six and eight I'm much more familiar with. And it has a spooky aspect that suits this spooky plant. I'll work out a basic star design and then an "intent" can be slipped in there ......

+++

Hunter-

True North / Magnetic North /Local North

The importance of "True North" seems relevant to this forum. My preference is a more "local" approach. Once again , in Berks County, "North" was never a abstract concept, North was always a daily part of our lives, it was more than a direction it was a Mountain, the highest point in Berks county, a place called the Pinnacle. We gazed on it every day unless the weather would not allow. Sometimes there would be snow on the mountain. It is visible everywhere in Berks County which also has a "South Pole" or South MT, which is lesser than the North but defines the fertile valley between. These Appalachian Mts are just large enough for the farmer psyche to feel comfortable, safe and in synch with.

I am sure all of us have a similar "True North" that we can visualize in our minds. This is all intuitive, there are those here who know more the basis for this Northern way.

:

Figure 18 Niger Bilsenkraut, Black Henbane

Niger Bilsenkraut

Schwarze Bilse was used in the 20th century (with excellent results) as a truth serum in political interrogations .Quite possibly, still is. How magical. Made most potent by being harvested by a young virgin, standing only on her right foot, using the little finger of her right hand to pull the plant out of the ground.

A more inviting Solanaceae would be ground cherries

Least you can make pie out of it.

Sue

Excellent Sue and Hunter,

 especially the harvesting techniques. I love this stuff. The harvesting instructions sound almost like a game of Twister lol, my 9 year old daughter will probably be laughing if we ever have her do this.

I'm not surprised at all it would be used in truth serum, it is known to be a hallucinogen. My few notes mentioning Bilsenkraut say that it was believed to be used in the infamous "flying ointments" of witches. It was mixed with other hallucinogenic substances in a lard base and rubbed into varied parts of the body.

Blessings and frith,

Greg

.....It was mixed with other hallucinogenic substances in a lard

base and rubbed into varied parts of the body.

yeah, very hidden parts of the body...1) for quick absorption and 2) so as not to be detected by the outside world.Being caught with flying ointment meant absolute death by fire. yup.

Sue

LMAO at "Naked Twister", Patty and I are no strangers to this one! My daughter...guaranteed Mom and Dad will have blankets circling her if anyone could possibly see her!

Middle Ages author Karl Kiesewetter writes about his experiments with the flying ointment in his book "The Secret Sciences". He mentions rubbing Hyoscyamin extracts into his heart area and, well, basically he was tripping and experiencing flying-type sensations. It doesn't take much imagination to do some "rubbing", sit on a broom, and think you really are flying. There is also an incantation given to reinforce this type of "flight" that mentions the Blocksberg. From a 2001 German book- "According to newer presumptions the mixture consists of extracts of jimson weed (thorn apple), nightshade plants, hemlock, sunflower, poppy or henbane".Of course as I have mentioned and others here know, this type of travel can also be accomplished without use of drugs. The term "Entrücken" in this case describes the "driving out" of the soul, hence astral/shamanic type travel. Other terms we have mentioned for this are "Wahrsagezauber" and the Norse "seidhr".

Blessings and frith,

Greg

Romanusbüchlein

Guten Tag Alles!

I just posted in the links section a link to the legendary "Romanusbüchlein". According to noted scholar and professor Don Yoder (no relation to Hunter unfortunately), this small but valuable book was (and I agree) the primary source from which John Georg Hohman culled his "Long Lost Friend". It attributes the Roma Gypsies as the authors.

Those familiar with Hohman's book, of which I assume most of us have a copy or two of, should immediately recognize the majority of the charms. There are also a few others contained within that Hohman did not use that could be considered useful. For those here of a heathen mind, you can adapt these to that view and if you are familiar enough with the writings of Dr. Godfrid Storms, you should be able to determine which are heathen in origin.

My thanks in advance to Joseph Peterson of the Esoteric Archives website for his kind permission for this link, and also full acknowledgement and credit for the work he did in translating the material. He has an excellent website that has many English translations of material from some of the pioneering German mystics such as Agrippa and Paracelsus, particular medieval grimoires such as the 6th/7th Books Of Moses, Roten Dragon, Grand etc, and much more. He is also the owner/moderator of a Yahoo club dedicated to Moses book study that some may find fascinating. Hopefully, someday, someone will do a study and scholarly translation of the Hebrew letters and writings and see if the actual origin of any of these correlate to our pre-Christian heathenism in some way, or if they are simply a case of Kabbalism finding it's way into and being adopted into our magical culture.

Blessings and frith and enjoy!

Greg

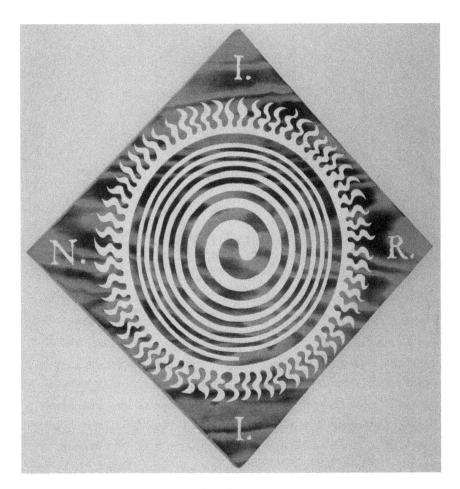

Figure 19"Long Lost Friend Hex" 2007

Pilgrimage to Berks County

Frank Blank has just returned from a wonderful trip back to his native soil. He enjoyed meeting so many like minded friends. He climbed his favorite Mountain via his favorite trail (Appalachian) He rekindled his relationship with the rattlesnake, the copperhead, the fruit fly bat, he met many wonderful plants and seeks to remember their names lest they fail to remember his, he found abundant water supply which he rejoiced over. He also passed through Schuylkill County for which he has a special place in his heart, in a way its industrial past and resultant decay appeals to Frank, He also finds a cleansing in the poverty and ancient industrial grunge of the mines. He frequents places like South Tamaqua Coal Pockets, he enjoys the company of the working man, he always will......just as he prefers the company of those who grow plants and are knowledgeable in them. He spoke with Susan's husband who was able to articulate in a better way the manner in which the plants speak to us. Clearly the husband and wife work in the garden. My friends at "3 Sisters" and their family and friends and our discussions and hospitality, much of which would only be comprehensible to Berks County "locals" took place at their location at the base of Frank Blank's favorite Mountain. And Jesse I will pay more attention to the rotational direction my "Hex Signs" spin. I would like to thank everyone for their gifts, especially Susan for her gifts to my wife and daughters and for the "Elder"

Blessing and Frith

+++

Hunter

Figure 20Susan Hess, Hunter Yoder and Jesse Tobin, 2007

Susan Hess, Hunter Yoder, Jesse Tobin at Sustainable Living Festival, 2007, Kempton, PA

Heimia salicifolia "tea"

Oh, wow Druid, I've been hoping to find good first-hand information about this plant for years!

A friend is growing a small shrub from which I could probably pick some leaves.

Can you describe your fermentation process in a little more detail? And you could you give us any details about the effects?

It's not hard. Just take your fresh plant material and put it in a cookie tin. Spray with a little water, or wash the sprigs first and put them wet into a cookie tin (preferably plastic so it doesn't rust, or else line it with wax paper or plastic wrap). Leave in the sun until it wilts. This is called "fermentation". The heat causes the natural sugars of the plant to come out and ferment. I let it sit in the sun for 2 days and then the leaves start to give off a nice scent that is moving away from "planty" and towards "aromatic".

I then put the 5g of wilted leaves, flowers and even branches into a yogurt maker with 1 cup of water (the yogurt maker keeps them at 110 and no more than 120F for three days. Not much water evaporates, but I do add more if it does). It is ready after the third day. I only need 1/4 cup, and then I replenish the water and let it referment for the next session. You can do this for 3 or 4 times, and it doesn't lose potency because you keep reculturing the populations of microorganisms (I guess -- no one has ever proven this, but it seems to be absolutely correct, since the potency doesn't drop once I consume and then dilute the brew).

The aches and pains do not come if you don't exceed 5g of leaf. I have had very powerful experiences with Sinicuichi, very intense, very fully immersive, but only with a properly fermented brew from my own plant (fermented leaves followed by keeping warm in my yogurt-maker for 3 days, replenishing the water as it evaporates). Regular tea doesn't work and smoking the leaves is mild at best. The full effects come from brewing for many days at no higher than 120F (best if no more than the sun can heat 100-110F). Some people just put it out in the sun and make sun-tea. That has worked as well. 5g of fresh leaf lasted for four sessions, but I kept refermenting from day to day, since the current theory (which seems to be true) is that the microorganism that is cultured through leaf-fermenation and low-heat cooking is responsible for the entheogenic effects, much like an ergot mold. Fermented sinicuichi, I assure you, is *extremely potent*.

I have recently been asked to try commercial leaf to see if I can get it to work from dried leaf.

Also, one can potentiate the Sinicuichi so that you can get the high-dose effects without the penalty. Kava and kratom, or even a combination of both can do this very effectively. Salvia taken with Sinicuichi blends the two plant spirits, making the Salvia much more colorful and vivid, and adds auditory effects that Salvia does not have on its own.

Hope this helps clarify some stuff about a very difficult-to-use entheogen that really has a very deep trance if you can get fresh leaf.

http://forums.ayahuasca.com/phpbb/viewtopic.php?t=11295&postdays=0&postorder=asc&start=0

Pennsilfaanisch Gebeden Fia Rehhen?

How would a Pennsylvanian do for rain? Did they learn something fromthe Native Americans? or from Judaism?

One thing that was done at the summer solstice to ensure rain through the season is that they would pour water over the Butzeman (corn doll, scarecrow). He is the father of the corn, and giving him rain would mean that his children would get enough. This would only work until the grain harvest, however. It comes out of the ancient germanic tradition of the corn god. I am sure that both native american and judaic practice contain similar traditions... if you look in the right places.

Blessings

Jesse

I read that he's also called "Der Strohmann". Thanks. I will remember der Butzemann. Of course! it makes sense to grow a home garden if you're into Braucherei. Then the Butzemann would be purposeful.Bis Schpaeda! (Bis Später- Later!)

It is amazing to see not only echos of our own culture and stories, but to see the archetypes essential to human nature- always the same characters, different names and details. To me it shows how we are all so fully connected through spirit.

Blessings

Jesse

Rain is a basic motif of the PA Deutsch Hexologist. These things being in many ways not only talismans, warding away harmful elements but also sympathetically effecting sufficient rain and sunshine. Raindrops or what I have always called "Yods" usually are found dancing between the rays of an eight pointed "Earth Star" They are similar to a "Ying and Yang" sign. Here is one by Lee Gandee :

Rain is also a metaphor for spiritual purification, and on this level of meaning the sympathetic effect is obviously more profound and not "praying" for physical things but for spiritual change, evolution. I Judaic mystical thought, which I think was introduced early on in this discussion, There is a seeking to "gather the scattered sparks" The spiritual is seen as flames, embers emanating down from "Ein Sof" Usually as the words of God or YHWH. In PA Deutsch iconography this is usually shown as "raindrops" which rotate either clockwise or counterclockwise as in this hex sign of mine in which the rotation alternates in the successive orbits around the sun.

Figure 21 "Virginville Helm" Spray paint on scorched wood, 2007

They also "emanate" down from Heaven and are blessings from God. This use of "holy water" obviously has very strong ties to christianity as in the rite of baptism and the purification by sprinkling "holy water" This tradition has even earlier ties to the ancient Assyrians who have images of an emanation from "god" possibly Shamash and his earthly counter part, the King, whose responsibility was to assure this continual emanation from above and fertilization of the Female Date Palm trees, assisted by Genii or angels. Part human, part animal, part god.

Figure 22 "Datura Hex for Susan" 2008, spraypaint on scorched wood

Susan Hess

Hi Hunter,

Just thought I should finally introduce myself since Ive been reading the posts at the Hexenkunst group for a few weeks without jumping in....wowzer...been an interesting few days, to say the least. I think I shall continue to lurk for the time being!

I am a friend of Jesse's and part of the Three Sisters Center. It is our hope that we can all get together when you are in the area and talk about plants, as that is my strong interest, as well.

We are currently putting together our next newsletter, Hollerbeier Haven and I wondered if you might like to add a small piece about hex signs, symbolism or something else? Let me know if you are interested...I know its short notice.We will be going to print in about a week. If not there is always next time.

Sincerely,

Susan Hess

Hey Sue,

Yeah that's straight up and down shamanism, don't have to be born from certain kin neither, just have a green thumb. And I'll talk with you.

All my tomatoe and pepper plant seedlings I got from the Mennonites at Renningers market in the beginning of May, oh yeah I got som Coleus as well, are very productive.

By the way, Venus is very high in the sky in the West now.

This is as about as good as it gets! My Brown Turkish Fig tree has the first ripe figs, the dwarf meyers lemon trees always produce and my first datura stramonium which i didn't plant is about to bloom probably according to a phase of the moon......ha ha ha and eggplants are on the way. Cone Flowers and Heliopsis are kicking, Black Eyed Susans are coming and the meadow flox, 3 different varieties...

Yeah i have netherland dwarf rabbits and I'm hooked.

Any experience rooting out fig trees?

Blessings

+++

Hunter

and my first datura stramonium which i didn't plant

I also had one of those also 'volunteer' last year. t grew at the very epicenter of my garden. So glad I waited out weeding it when it was small....even at that small size I knew it was something important. It grew to an enormous size.

This is my fave......I often use this visual for journey work.....cool, eh?? It looks like a painting.

You're right about the fragrance. Its totally intoxicating. There is a seedling from last years plant but its growing at a much slower pace than the big mamma from last year.

Sorry, I have no experience with figs at all.

Sue

 Hey Sue,

I actually have some in pots and will bring it close to the house, this one speaks very loudly and clearly and will have an effect on your life. Sometimes it comes in dreams also. Just keep it away from children and animals. Its related to Eggplant and tomatoes and the leaves are very similar to eggplant. I like the odor of the leaf and stem, that real pungent unique odor, I use that for ID as well.

Actually this year the loudest plant to speak to me was a Valerian plant who demanded that I pick her up buy her and take her home now! So what could I do?

Hunter

sorry, Hunter,

let's try that again....attaching three datura pics. Last summer, it would definitely call to me at night through various senses. smell particularly.

I use it's flower essence sometimes and would sleep with a bloom beside my head at night.

Honestly, I have to admit that I was totally enamored of it ...

but also a lil shy about opening myself to it totally, as well. We did a flirtatious dance with each other all summer long.

Perhaps,she hasnt given up on me yet.

Sue

Real Nice pics Sue,

I have actually quite abit about Datura stramonium, probably more than any other plant and know other people like yourself who have to one degree or another fallen under her spell. heres a pic from mine last year, this year is just about to open, probably tonite.

Hunter

Datura stramonium, A thornapple grows in Red Hook

wow. Very interesting piece. I am such a country girl that I cannot even begin to relate to a world such as this. I am intrigued to read more Frank Blank material. However, looks like I need an official invite to read the blog.....howz about it?

Well, did she unfurl her beauty to the welcoming arms of Venus?

Sue

Good morning Sue,

"Well, did she unfurl her beauty to the welcoming arms of Venus?"

Nope.......not yet, probably waiting for the "horns" to appear, ha ha.

Although its interest ing that you put her in the same sentence as Venus.

Venus's rotation around the sun consists of 584 Earth days, earth's is 365 of course. Five of Venus's rotations equals eight of earth's or 2,920 days. Note the PHI relationship here. that's important because plant growth, growth spirals follow the "golden angle" or approx. 137.51 degrees. So it would only be natural that the planet Venus or Lamat in certain Mayan dialects be associated with, love, growth, fertility ands so forth.......

The Datura is even more closely associated with Phi, its pentacle shaped flower is the very expression of the "golden angle"

Your website is wonderful, tell me more about the plants you grow.

+++

Hunter

I was selling my wares at our local farmer's market today (outdoors) and kept smelling whiffs and wafts of datura blossoms throughout the entire day. I went for a walk around the perimeter and found nothing... but that smell is unmistakable. Since I am home and indoors...I think it is still around me. Perhaps a strong southwest wind from Brooklyn?

Thanks for posting the pics on hexenkunst...I considered doing so myself but shied away. I only share with pals. Not convinced over there quite yet. I will send you some garden pics soon.

But for now, feet up with a coconut popsicle on the 'hops' porch and a cat in my lap...

Venusian, eh? She rules.....

Sue

Hey Sue,

That coconut popsicle sounds good, up here Brooklyn the thing is italian ices, coconut flavored but my favorite is pistachio, what a good Pa german I am, ha ha. I see you have a whole line of products very interesting, I might interest my wife in something, do you take paypal?

Well Ms Datura or what the aztecs call, toloatizn more commonly called toloache by the indigenous, finally opened and I am abit surprised to find this one goes six instead of five like the ones you and photographed last year, kind of throws out my toloache-phi theory out the window, oh well...........ha! anyway heres the pic see what you think..............

Also is a pic of my Sinicuichi which is blooming profusely, this is another sacred plant of the Maya/Aztec very pretty bush, scientific name, Heimia salicifolia

Hunter

Six instead of five like the ones you and photographed last year, kind of throws out my toloache-phi theory out the window, oh well

... a trickster, too? Maybe go back and count again later! That's the only glitch with geometry. One errant number throws off the entire universe. I found a few more datura pix...attached one that took my breath away when I found it. Back outside....before the morning gets away. The light is perfect for garden photos.

Sue

Oh yeah,

Datura closes up during the day but this is definitely a "Hex" Looks like the last "hex sign" I painted, Intention is a subconscious process........

Anyway, i strongly recommend at least one rabbit in the garden, adds that irrational necessity essential for fecundity. They are not the best cartoon characters without a reason.

Actually I used to raise bees, had 50 hives at one time, I really miss that. I still use the boxes for plants.

The urban location, made this unrealistic so I went to the receiving end of their activities, flowering plants......

This time of year with the temps today here in the low ninties is ideal for pepper plants, especially the "hot ' varieties which actually become hotter in taste as the temp arises.

I have an ongoing relationship withe the tohono od'ham tribe in SW Arizona who use the pepper as a sacred plant amongst others.

Here I I went Gowanus which was so similar to Lenni Lenape.

We actually have some amazing gardens here in Brooklyn, the limitation of space is really an advantage.

The importance of participating in Hexenkunst is not so much to be their friends but to remind them that when they seek to represent PA German Magic they must deal with the reality of Berks County, we will not be obstructed from that dinner table.

I hope you took pictures..........

+++

Hunter

Tolache

TOO-LOCH-AY?? Is this correct?

All of those photos I sent are from the one and only D.stramonium momma bush/tree. She was here with me last summer. I never let a seed drop from her for fear of the chickens who are always at my feet in the garden.I collected the thorn apples at the moment they ripened and started to split open.Regardless of my collection measures, a few of her babies sprouted this year, the largest being only a foot tall at this point in the summer.The seeds I collected last year are in a jar, very clearly marked here on my desk...perhaps I should release them. What are your thoughts?

I don't believe Brugmansia was here at all.no. It was just a very large stramonium. The flowers were not even remotely pendulous and the stalk was herbaceous, not woody. However,even though I am still in awe of her, I am very happy to keep my close and gentle associations with mugwort and hops among a few others.

Have you a S. Divinorum?

Last night was the third evening ingesting 3 drops of datura flower essence as I drifted off to sleep.

Not sure if it was the power of suggestion, since I also ingested your email about tolache before I went to bed, but I awoke a few hours later, in a dark fog, not being able to remember anything about my dream (rare)but certainly feeling the dread, dark tone surrounding it or me. I think I will cease from this activity now.....also worth noting:I purchased this essence and did not make it myself. As you know, the intentions and methods by which these plants are approached and harvested can make all of the difference in the world.

Susan

Hey Susan,

Tatula seems to be distinct from stramonium, very interesting, save all the seeds, they are viable forever. I don't ingest Tolache, its presence is enough and I would not have it in my garden without the presence of other entheogens that I already mentioned. But its variation and tenacity and strength as a plant and all its multiple variations really remind me of Trichosereus, of which I have maybe three distinct "species" Pachanoi, Peruvianus, Bridgesii but its so unpredictable if sexually propogated that cuttings are the safest way to get a sibling that is the same as the parent. It has so many subspecies that it just boggles the imagination as does Tolache. Check this guy out who is a genius in the field: http://flickr.com/photos/msscacti/

But back to the Tolache both Stramonium and Tatula, there is definitely a "hex sign" here, but a five or six, I'll have to sleep on that.

+++

Hunter

Hey Hunter,

Thanks for the links to the cacti guy and the Huichol piece of Tolache. I will study them carefully after I emerge from the creation of the newsletter and big class here Saturday.

I'd like to be certain that I have your permission to include this quote of yours for our 'harvest' issue. I think the creation of a hex sign is indeed a harvest of sorts and I'm sure your beautiful words about their creation will help readers to conceptualize hex paintings as a living presence, instead of a schlocky tourist momento.

"Even the mere layman can enjoy and benefit in many ways from the practice of painting "earthstars" Certain geometric and numerical configurations have always been held "sacred" since the stoneage. Painting, or pecking symbols in the rock cliffs has been so easy that even a "caveman" could do it. I like to make the analogy between "hex sign painting" and growing plants. Perhaps more precisely planting seeds,. They both are creative acts, when planting a seed, all of the components of the mature plant are there in a very compact form, The results of the "planting" are not always known and the conscious intent of "planting" can be misleading. "Growth" occurs sometimes in such away that is not always anticipated, The subconscious mind needs only to be exposed to a conscious experience inorder for it to manifest that experience's essence into a creative result........all the stylized intent in the world cannot be a substitute for the irrational power of the paradox. Making a connection with the "Living Universe" is inevitably paradoxical and the results frequently a surprise!"

If you wish to, add a lil bio and which name you prefer to use. also, I'd like to put a picture to the quote.....which one? I can't find the link right now but it was definitely floral looking like the center of a zinnia in color.... or have you the daturahex or another you'd like to see with it? maybe the one you have of you holding a sign in front of grafitti...that's cool too....

Coriann der Sveetbirch

Hey Hunter,

Thanks again, so much for responding so quickly to my frantic request for your pics and bio for the newsletter.The page looks great. Always the best stuff comes in at the final hour! Makes fitting it all together such a great pleasure. Also got a last minute surprise addition from Dennis Boyer so you are in great company as a "guest".

I'll be sure to keep a few copies set aside for you. along with those seeds.

Sue, Susan

Jesse calls me SuebeeKy

Hey Susan

Great!

I liked the additional slide shows, and its forced me to document my "other" plants that will blow your mind........There may be no end to that. Gotta an email from Greg regarding the August meeting, he's really a nice guy with a good heart. They just sort of ran into a brickwall called Berks County, but I'm sure he and Jesse have much to share.

I actually have been in contact with Dennis and that bio I sent you was from an email to him.

The seed exchange is good, I have also something for you that I'm sure you will find very beneficial. I am also interested in some Elderberry plants, any suggestions on variety?

The chickens could probably eat all the datura seeds and have no ill effects...........the rabbits have developed a taste for cactus, har har har

Mulching with straw eh? I'm using crushed stone...............

Hunter

Dear Hunter,

Thanks for all the hexerpics......so many to choose from...they are all so beautiful and intriguing.

I keep going back to this hexenkunst post you made (pre-braucherei battles). I have saved it to read again and was what was inspired me to ask if you would submit something to the newsletter: (Even use of this thought stream would be thrilling, as is or expanded....what say you?) I paired a trillium along side a six pointed rosette earlier today which I had dreamt about months ago...finally brought it to this reality for the newsletter......

anyway, you said.......

Even the mere layman can enjoy and benefit in many ways from the practice of painting "earthstars" Certain geometric and numerical configurations have always been held "sacred" since the stoneage. Painting, or pecking symbols in the rock cliffs has been so easy that even a "caveman" could do it.

like to make the analogy between "hex sign painting" and growing plants. Perhaps more precisely planting seeds,. They both are creative acts, when planting a seed, all of the components of the mature plant are there in a very compact form, The results of the "planting" are not always known and the conscious intent of "planting" can be misleading. "Growth" occurs sometimes in such away that is not always anticipated, The subconscious mind needs only to be exposed to a conscious experience inorder for it to manifest that experience's essence into a creative result........all the stylized intent in the world cannot be a substitute for the irrational power of the paradox. Making a connection with the "Living Universe" is inevitably paradoxical and the results frequently a surprise!

I read your re: post about sock-it-to-me-sagas and rabbits at about 5 am this morning and nearly choked on my tea when I laughed out loud. Such an unexpected and great way to start the day...

Your mugwort looks great! Much further ahead than mine. I am anxious to harvest, too. Running low on supplies. When Jesse, Matt and I do work, we burn it as you would sage. I have to say, this plant has been the most profound "speaker" to me. I love it very much...

That bunnie of yours is too much.Makes me wanna go to Green Dragon and pick up a few. gGot a tip on an old farm in Oley (Powwow central) that needs care takers-rent free.

It is an old farmhouse with barn and several outbuildings, 10 acres and has never had, no will ever have electricity.The owners are looking for the "right people" to live there in the "old way and keep up the property.

I HAVE to check on this.Could be the lifestyle change that Ive been dreaming about. Gotta hear more about years in a tipi. wow.

Susan

My grandfather had a farm in Oley, most of those ole farmhouses are haunted, ha ha.

I have tons of mugwart picked by virgins on a new moon.......my daughters, also Mopacho (tobacco) I grew last year. Here is a pic of my Datura Hex.

+++

Hunter

oh yeah!!.....I LOVE IT!!!! Plan on any other additions? It is certainly complete on it's own. I was also envisioning the spinning or rotation movement of the 5 nearly opened petals. Sketched it out a little myself. On a new moon, huh?I always pick mine by the light of the full moon. Also the old standby that makes the herbal circles, is to harvest bare breasted. Not sure the young virgins would appreciate that but out here in the country anything is possible.

Unfortunately, there are no vestal virgins in sight. The mugwort is cool with it, though. I have heard the Oley farm ghost stories, also. We have already dicussed powwowing the whole house, just like we did here-- 36 total windows and doors--took all freakin' day!!

Susan

Thats just the bare bones star, gotta put it into a circle with a border and add things to it especially between the outer rays.......maybe a more detailed center, like a crescent moon, yeah

Ghosts can be cool, lived in two houses with them, experienced the white fog visitation in the middle of the nite. The house here in Brooklyn from the 1880's has none, I was somewhat surprised.

+++

Hunter

like a crescent moon, yeah sounds great. and /or crescent moon scalloped border. maybe you can squeeze out 28....

Squeeze? Pi (3.14159 into infinity) times diameter divided by 28, (lunar cycle) scallop as in smooth sailing thru life?Hah, fat chance with this weirdo plant, if there was a picture of a garden with all the plants, and the question was "Whats the matter with this picture?"

What do you think the answer would be?

I would go with 26 the gematric number of the Tetragrammaton. This was just a toss off, working on a piece "Rampid Caprids being fed by the Tree of Life as Goddess" Who was the Jesus's wife? Who was YHWH's wife? silly monotheism

+++

Hunter

Hey Hunter,

Have a tenative plan for the weekend yet? Saw Jesse in K-town this morning and she said that Sunday is best for her in the Kempton area, Monday's out for her altogether. Me, I'm Miss Flexibilty...just need a little notice to plan around.Too late to make red beet eggs though (my eggs are too fresh!), but I make a mean pie. and Yeungling...nope. Nothing but a fine variety of home brews in this house. I found that old farm in Oley today...and then scouted it out on the internet.The Keim Homestead. Do you know it? no water (justa spring) no power, no heat.... It is much better than I could have ever imagined....Jesse says that many of the Keims were Indian Dietsch meaning they mixed it up with the local Leni Lenape.

http://freepages.genealogy.rootsweb.com/~bierhaus/Keim/index.htm
http://www.historicpreservationtrust.org/hist_sites/jkfarmstead.html

How goes the tolachehex?

Susan

Thanks Susan,

Yes I'm definitely going to be in PA Sunday, probably get into Berks in the mid to later afternoon and will stay over into Monday maybe stay over Monday Nite and return Tues first thing. Just cleaning off some graffitti from the van windows so hopely the cops won't pull me over. Are you looking to buy the place? that's the way to go all the work and everything.

The Tolachehex has revealed itself to me, just have to execute, all 28 phases of the moon on the circumference, rabbits running one between every outer ray, the center needs alittle defining but that one made itself, by the way where's your drawing?

I do look forward to meeting you Susan.

+++

Hunter

Hey Hunter,

 They live on Pine Creek Road, but Im unsure of the exact number on the mailbox. Not sure if you are still planning to visit here at any point as I live a good 45 minutes south. Just give me a head's up if you would like me to transport elderberry bushes to Kempton Sunday. Very much looking forward to meeting you also.

Have a cool powwow dream to tell you about.

 Susan

Hey Susan

Great I don't plan everything down to the second, weather and such
This is what I had thoughts of doing

1. Visit 3 Sisters

2. Visit your place

3. Get up on the Pinnacle and chew on some cactus spend a night on the rocks

4. Cycle , climb Hawk Mt. from Skuykill County side

5. Yes I want elderberry plants, will trade for cactus or other sacred plants (sinicuichi, etc.)

Thanks

+++

Hunter

Hey Hunter,

Great to meet and hang out with you this weekend!! Much more enjoyable than typing!

Thanks again for all the gifts.

You probably have a list of solanaceae going but I stumbled upon this today and thought you might like to see.......

Click here: Solanum - Wikipedia, the free encyclopedia

Susan

Hey Sue,

Susan might be better, after seeing all your pics and slide show, I have to say that you are a true Pennsylvania Deutch Fertility Goddess and you remind me of Glinda, Good Witch of the North from the Wizard of Oz, if either of my daughters grow up to be as beautiful , knowledgeable, and "productive" I would be very pleased....and they are aware of you and I have spoken to them about you. My one daughter, Brigitte is especially a farm girl, she knows all of the plants that I have by name, she does most of the transplanting and she handles the rabbits. Not bad for eleven years old. She constantly asks me about the farm I grew up on.

On a completely different note, the entheogen you have in your garden, I prefer to call Tolache, which you have in Stramonium form and the tree looks like a Brugsmania. Please be careful, this one is like a jealous lover. I am pleased that you have her, but there are others that are kinder and sweeter that would suit your good nature. And yes they are legal to grow. Also be especially careful with the "thorn apples" and seeds especially keep them away from the beautiful chickens that look very pampered.

Blessings

+++

Hunter

Hunter,

You have no idea....'Pennsylvania Deutch Fertility Goddess?' It is a compliment of the highest form, you putting those words together to describe me.I have been trying to put this puzzle together forever.

Until recently, I had not been able to rectify these life long "conflicting" illustrations of myself:

100% Pure Grade A PA Deitsch, by blood and Berks, yet always searching, so as not to "be" that, feeling like I belonged to some 'other' clan.I swear the wolves must have carried me gently, and laid me at my parents barn door.My mother lovingly tells me still that she doesnt know where I came from.

It didnt help that my parents were of the generation that was intentionally trying to lose their Dutchness, the dialect and the ways. I was separated by one generation and an hour's drive from my Brethern Grandmother who spoke the dialect, made soap, gardened, canned, quilted, raised sheep and chickens, etc. (interestingly, I came to learn all of these things on my own much later, as a new wife with a new home....her influence on my life was not recognized until she was nearly gone)

I have spun the wheel of 36 flavors of culture and religion,tried some different tastes, yet came up less than satisfied.The Holy Roman Patriarchy and ultra feminist Goddess "Womyn" worship both made me angry....but, as always, I found some beauty in both.Just was not able to fit into any one box .

In Methodist Bible School as a young kid, I was removed from a class for " asking too many questions" one of which (the straw breaker)' Who was Jesus' wife?' Another time I saw a vision of Christ on the wall during an Easter church service. I was ten and no one really believed me. A few more mystical Christian experiences before the age of 15, with no one to hear me or explain. I pretty much just shut it down after that and moved on to more readily available experiences of the 70's. It filled a hole.sort of....

When my Emily was born (she is 23 now and a recent grad of KU) something cracked open in me....and I began to find Indian arrowheads and feathers in my garden and surrounding farm fields (dropped in the very place by a dream animal or bird the night before) I had amazing dreams and meditations that were rich with information and symbology.Often geometric symbols that would reinforce themselves in waking reality...and I kept it all a secret.Just journaled about it all. I knew no one in my Deitsch clan that I could share this with.

Fast forward through 20 years of the big stuff: another child (Riley is 18) and ending of a marriage,and eventually the beginning of another.I have lived on this farm since 1995 honing my craft(s) and growing more comfortable in my various skins. yeah, I think I got it now, right?

About a year and a half ago, I went to Kempton for a day of Permaculture workshops.

One being about Powwow medicine. Me thinks Native American?? Sure,as an herbalist, I love native medicine. Go to the Swiss hills of PA...no problem. It feels like home to me there.

Jesse Tobin spoke for an hour to a small breakout group of 6, perhaps. For 55 minutes of that talk, I wept uncontrollably, like a baby.You could have knocked me over with a feather afterwards. I was moved beyond belief.

Jesse loves to tell this story when people ask how we met.It was her very first speech on powwow...also the very first day she met Dennis Boyer face to face (as did I) ...and the day she made a sensitive Libran woman cry with her words about Braucherei. hahaha

I like to think of it as the day I was reborn a PA Deitsch girl and embraced it...finally all of my "conflicting" parts were not conflicting at all. It was always a beautiful, complete and moving mosaic of which I didn't have the eyes to see. I didnt sleep for two days after, the joy was so great. Jesse and I havent been apart for more than a few days ever since that moment in time.My already wonderful life has become even richer and more meaningful since then.

It is wonderful that your daughter enjoys her farming responsibilities. Mine embraced it as children also and then gradually moved away from it as they grew older and outside of my bubble into the wider world.I hold onto the hope that as they move into their own nests, the influence will move with them there.

Whew...more later. My chickens need to run.....

Thanks again for the enourmous compliment.

I will keep it as a recognition and confirmation of my path.

Susan

Figure 23 "Long Lost Friend Hex", Hunter M. Yoder

"Long Lost Friend Hex", Hunter M. Yoder

"Within the shamanic context of Braucherei and Hexology, Christianity

is a useful tradition/structure. The question has quickly arisen here and elsewhere and having already been through the war I am well seasoned in this respect. My defense of Christianity comes not (unfortunately) from being a devout Christian, rather I see it as an inevitable tradition that is "useful" for which I have been also criticized. I am a pragmatist and a practical person, and frequently use the materials at hand".

I understand this point completely. Many of us here were raised as Christians. Why I turned to the faiths of my ancestors was simply that I always felt disconnected, despite the best efforts of my family, and yes myself, to try to connect. Within Pow-Wow (notice I don't say Hexerei in this instance) practitioners of the Christian faith are called to service and they consider the calling to be from their version of faith, and all that entails. It works for them because that is what they believe, and when belief is strong, anything can be accomplished. My experience as a traditional witch following the ancestral root faith of these same practitioners is exactly the same. No matter how practical it may be, use of Christian imagery and names of power would not work for me because I don't accept nor believe. However, when I work within my faith and use the imagery I am comfortable with, I get immediate results. I will give you 2 comparative examples using a charm to alleviate and reduce bruises and explain as such.

Pow-Wow version- "Bruise shalt not beat, bruise shalt not swaet, bruise shalt not run. No more than the Virgin Mary shall bring forth another son".

Hexerei version- Bruise shalt not beat, bruise shalt not sweat, bruise shalt not run. No more than Mother Frikka shall bring forth another son.

In the ancestral Germanic faith, Dame Frikka is considered to be our mother figure, as Mary is to the Christians. Frikka's only son is Lord Palter. Palter has many similarities to Jesus, he "died" and will also be "resurrected", he is a god of the light and represents all good things.

Now, when you speak about substitution and/or elimination of religion and imagery- the fact is that the 2nd Merseburg charm has been uncovered in both Heathen and Christian forms. Thorsson/Flowers has identified the Heathen version as the elder, no surprise there, polytheistic beliefs are generally older that monotheistic models. The point I am arriving at, is that it is clear that Christians obviously revised the charm with substitutions that fit their imagery and their beliefs. I can understand this and I don't have a problem with it- the Divine is the Divine and faith is what an individual perceives the Divine to be. I respect all Hexenmeisters whether they are Christian or not as my equals, I can learn from them as they can learn from me. My feelings aside in regard to all the atrocities committed by Christians over the centuries for reasons that are completely contrary to what they preach, what I am advocating here is that Hexerei was originally part and parcel of the Germanic faith before it was adapted for Christian use. And that it should be returned to it's roots and be recognized for what it is.

Blessings and frith, Greg/Oracle

What follows is an exchange from the Ayahuasca forum recently:

Quote:

it took me years to warm up to the San Pedro Mesa tradition because ofthe catholic stuff... but after a while of really doing the research... i could see that it was a syncretic tradition that's core was still more then likely the same as it has been for a very long time... possibly since the chavin culutre.

I think its pretty hilarious the idea of separating the Catholicism from the work of the Curanderos in Northern Peru. It certainly isn't something that would occur to them to do. Clearly such an idea shows how out of touch this community is from the realities of Shamanicpractices in South America, Central America, and North America. I guess if you hate yourself enough you'll believe that you can turn back the clock to a time when Western man didn't exist. It seems to me such thinking indicates the use of plants to alter ones state and to indulge in inner dialogue enough to fantasize that its the PlantTeachers doing the other side of the conversation. Seems to me that the Catholic tradition may have added to the power of the Curanderos. Certainly the Mesa evolved as a direct result of the Catholic tradition. And by the way, I'm not a Catholic, just calling it as I see it. Good call, Frank! Self hate, and hate of one's own culture in many cases leads some into a kind of escapism that seeks out a romanticized deal of purity. Just witness some of the subtle attitudes pervading the American/European/Australian ayahuasca community. The tribes are the most pure because obviously natives communicate with Gaia herself on a regular basis. Second best are mestizos, but these guys partake of that icky Western culture; and it's even worse that their Catholic. Third, Goddess forbid, are the syncretic churches out of Brazil. The Christian ritual and symbology here almost certainly make their ayahuasca use blasphemy to the point of cultism. It's all imagery, and different ways of expressing the unknowable into some sort of cohesion. It really doesn't matter what metaphysical system someone uses to perform the work; as the Spirit simply uses concepts and images that one has been raised with to communicate itself. In other words, the Catholic san pedro shamans are just as powerful and effective as the indigenous ones (if there are any left?).

Andesvirgo

Very well stated Andesvirgo,

I wasn't expecting that positive or ironic a reaction. Edred Thorsen said:Quote: We in the "West"have often made idealized models out of othe exotic cultural traditions: the American Indians, the Indians of Asia and even the Afro-Carribean just to name a few.What we have idealized is their sense of continuous tradition and their deep level of spiritual authenticity. If we want this for ourselves-collectively or individually-we must find it within ourselves. It cannot be gained from sources outside our tradition of body-mind-spirit unity. We can learn a great deal from other traditions-but from a holistic viewpoint they remain something outside ourselves. from "Northern Magic" Further, he states

:Quote: If you are interested in living a Whole-istic life in which the integration or unity of body-mind-spirit is gained and understood, it should be obvious that a key to knowledge concerning your spiritual heritage is to be found in the "heritage" of your body-in the genetic code which you have inherited from your distant ancestors. Thus your own most natural, most intuitive path is an ancestral path.

So, Christianity functions in the "Pennsylvania Deutsch" Braucherei the same way it does for the Curanderos of Northern Peru. There is another level behind it, an older one and nothing makes the metaphorical kennings more powerful than even more multiple levels of meaning..........

Eduardo Caldereon said:Quote:

Actually, what we curanderos are doing is giving guidelines to the patient in regards to his problems. Always in accord with his beliefs, particularly his religion, whatever it may be, because all religions lead to a point which is God. Many think of God the way the Christians depict him: as a bearded man with the world in his hand. Others in other forms. But God is the cosmic energy within ourselves. Yes, we are a part of God because we have that energy, and this energy ia an elemental force that allows us to converge at an important point, which is curing.

from "Eduardo El Curandero The Words of a Peruvian Healer"

The PA German Lutheran "Braucherei" and the Peruvian Catholic Mestizo Curandero are as different as apples and oranges on the surface, but underneath we all swim in the same ocean. And there are many more than just these two fish in the Sea.

Frank Blank finds it of interest that Satanism and Judaism have been associated with one another.

Just for the record Frank Blank has been asked repeatedly to renounce Jesus Christ as his Savior, and has been unwilling to do so. His parents would be so proud.

Frank Blank has a tribe and a tradition and has identified it clearly. What is your tribe and tradition???? Is it continuous and linked by blood?

Hekura knows where Frank Blank stands and Frank has asked Hekura for additional information because we seem to share a Mountain Range in common. Mountain ranges are "geological religions"

Strength and knowledge will protect us.

+++

Blessings

Frank Blank

http://www.entheogen.com/forum/showthread.php?t=12699&page=1 0

My tradition has been complicated by the emerging revelation that behind much of the "good" Christian Braucherei is an older heathen Hexerei, which were considered to be , not good. Hexerei in PA Deutsch is witchcraft. Maybe it is not widely known but "witches" were murdered en mass by Catholic Christians in Europe and in New England. So it would not be surprising that they, the Hexs hate Christianity. Much in the same way those of Jewish descent are very wary of Catholic Christianity for very similar reasons. Good and Bad Hexerei are a manifestation of Dualism, a simplistic solution to far more intriguing issues............

It isn't viewed as good or bad Hexerei in my Pennsylvania Deutsch tradition, rather the Christian Braucherei and the Heathen Hexerei, the latter was viewed by a Christian culture as "evil" Pennsylvania was founded on the principal of "freedom to worship in whatever manner one see fit" This is not a strictly Catholic community, quite the opposite. The various communities were kicked out of Europe because of their different religious views. The first Synagogue was built in Philadelphia , the first Buddhist temple, and so on and so forth.

The Amish and Mennonite communities have always been internationally respected for their unwillingness to compromise their religious practices.

Braucherei or Pow Wow was largely a Lutheran or Germanic protestant phenomena, but behind this Christian veil were other influences including Heathen , Qabalah and others, so what else is new ....

Subject: The Pentateuch

Hey Jesse,

Thanks so much for your recent hospitality, means much to me............

I sense that you are a Christian and I want to clarify my position regarding the 6th and 7th book of Moises which you brought up in our conversations. To put them in perspective.............

Pentateuch, is the first five books of what Christians call the "Old Testament" Genesis, Exodus, Leviticus, Numbers, Deuteronomy. and they were written my Moses, in my opinion, well that's worth very little, anyway he is a very big heavy weight, probably the biggest Magician who ever shook a staff.

I actually have a rabbi, who has been very useful in helping me be a better Christian (he doesn't know that) if that makes any sense, his name is Rabbi Joshua Saltzman. I strongly believe that it may be impossible to separate aspects of Christianity from Judaism.

Not raised "Catholic" and well versed in Jakob Boehme's "Aurora" I find my fundamental belief in Jesus Christ to be a line I will not cross, but I am willing always to listen............always.

Hunter

So I am confused about what you mean to say about the 6th and 7th books of Moses. Do you think they are completely fabricated? If so, from what? How about the 8th, 9th, and 10th? I certainly consider myself a Christian, though not exclusively. As you have seen with my perspective in Braucherei, I see no reason not to include other belief systems and tradition. I very much embrace Prechristian Germanic and Greek beliefs and practices as well as Kabballic judaism. I take my inspiration in Christianity from Meister Eckart, the friends of God, and Jacob Boehme, as well as Mary Magdelene herself. I see the man, Jesus of Nazereth, as a teacher sent here to show us the path and an example of salvation. I do not believe he died for our sins, but instead he died to show us how to escape from the world of sin. I very strongly believe in what Meister Eckart described as the divine spark in the soul- the tiny spark that we are all born with, the inherent presence of the holy spirit in each and every living thing. I believe what Jesus taught us was how to attain Christhood by growing this spark until it overwhelms our being. In truth, these teachings of Meister Eckhart were nearly Buddist, though they seem to have sprung forth from Gnostic teachings. Faith is such a nebulous world,

Jesse

Hey Jesse

What I mean is that these "books" are of dubious quality when
compared to the Kabbalistic work of the same time which they seem to
be mimicking. My associate, Rabbi Saltzman is a kabbalist and he says
an alchemist........he is currently translating the "Hebrew Book of the
Dead" which is difficult he says , because written Hebrew operates on at
least 3 different levels and it is numerical in nature, every letter has
numerical value, Greek is similar, its called gematria.

What went on in Southern Germany during this period was however
extraordinary, I wish I knew more about how this German/Hebrew
transfer occurred.

 Meister Eckhart was definitely very cool, I think the Catholic Church
sentenced him to death but he died from natural causes before they
could do the deed. His Yogi Berra isms are terrific:

" All things are created from nothing; therefore their true origin is
nothing. "

" Go completely out of yourself for God's love, and God comes
completely out of himself for love of you. And when these two have
gone out, what remains is a simplified One. "

"for that now in which God made the first man, and the now in which
the last man will have his end, and the now in which I am talking, they
are all the same in God and there is not more than the one now. "

I wish I was facile as you and able to believe in so many religious ways,
my experience with belief is that its very singular, but I'm such a sinner
maybe that's all I can come up with, ha ha ha.

By the Greeks I assume you mean the Pythagoreans? They also had a
great influence on the Hebrews with Tetraktys and the
Tetragrammaton.

the Gnostics I have not yet delved into.

Mary Magdalene was the wife of Jesus and the first to utter the words, "He is risen" I love the "Last Temptation of Christ" the book.

The Catholic church and even Nicea made some alterations to fit their agenda

In Judaism, Archaic Hebrew artifacts state that YHWH had a wife and her name is Asherah, her name is always associated with a tree or grove of trees. The Hebrew temples included asherahs at the alter up until Deuteronomy, which was when Judaism became monotheistic.

Canaanite Pantheon which is distinct from the Hebrew also had asherah, she is shown many times as a "tree of life" feeding "rampant caprids" later this "tree" changes into a goddess and she is shown feeding the "rampant caprids"

I have been working on asherah imagery and have included it into the Hexology.......

+++

Hunter

Hi Hunter,

The Greek influence I am talking about includes astrology, four humors medical theory, and alchemy. The Greek Scholars fled west when the Turks took over istanbul in the late 1300's. There was an influence that came earlier than that-Hildegard von Bingen used the four humors theory in her classifications of herbs. This earlier influence came via the Arabic and Jewish communities in Spain and france. Apparently Greek, Arabic, and traditional Jewish medical theories operate in the same basic system. All of this system is naturally mixed in with the four element theory, alchemy, astrology, etc. I expect that much as you described to me earlier the basis of this system evolved in ancient Babylon.

As to the Hebrew/German exchange: Our oral tradition tells us that Mary Magdelene traveled up the Rhine, bringing the Gospel with her (as well as the child of Christ), and she supposedly settled in communities of Jews in Rhineland France. This Historical presence of Jews in this area is documented outside of this Oral history, so I think that the Presence of Jews in that area of the world and their influence on surrounding cultures goes back as far as the crucifition, if not before. Interestingly there is no evidence of Germanic Tribes until this time either- before the ad/bc switchover the folks to the east of the Rhine were still considered Celts, the Teutonic tribes came south after the Romans had set up the Rhine River as a Barrier between the civilized world and the heathens. Anyway, I would love to learn more about Kabala, as I know shamefully little, maybe you have some books or websites you could recommend?

Blessings

Jesse

Frank,

your history is a bit off but not bad. the early German Jewish influence was know at the Pietists, or Hasidim, which means holy or piety, they were later compared to the early Jewish mysticism of the fifth century BCE as we find in the Book of Creation – Genesis Book of Palaces and Chariots - Ezekiel, we are talking fifth century b.c.e. - about very early Jewish mystical tractates and oral traditions handed down from generations dating back prior to Babylonia, some from Egypt, and what was know as Mesopotamia, (later known as Babylon)

Convergence of mystical traditions in the Axial age, Vedic and Early Buddhist from India, Mesopotamia. Dualism with Zoastrian and earlier roots, Gnosticism was a relative late phenomena - during the time of

Rabbi Yehoshua which those of the Christian faith like to refer to in the Greek as Jesus Christ, the arisen one, though the Prophet Elijah rose way before Rabbi Yehoshua, Reb Elijah was a mystic of the Chariots, through which he ascended to HaShem (literally, the Name)

Now, how many wings do the angels have and where are they positioned?-

Michael, Gabriel, Uriel, Raphael,

ADAM Kadmon

so, anyway, from here the study of the deeper levels of Jewish mysticism requires direct contact with a teacher, a text, and a tradition (kabbalah lit. means to receive the tradition - passed down from teacher to disciple, we will have to look into those early texts and read them in the original which performing certain spiritual practices of meditation, visualization, (gemetria it is true is greek, but the science of tzeruf, or of mixing and adding and using mathematical formulas applied to these traditions comes much earlier than the Greeks, Sefer Yetsirah, including the infinite dimensions of HaShem will blow your mind,yes, from here we must read and talk together, there are 4 levels of reading

Peshat or the literal level

Remez, or the metaphorical level

Drash, the Homelitical level

and Sod, the mystical, secret level,

and then a fifth, i.e. a return to Peshat.

like the Zen monk says

" Before i was enlightened the trees were trees and the mountains were mountains, now the trees are trees and the mountains are mountains."

Rabbi Saltzman

by the way, i apologize for claiming that i am either a Kabbalist or an alchemist, i am neither, just a simple Reb,

Reb Josh

you must be asleep, because 12 am and after is the time of the jewish mystics, perhaps after we meet, you will be persuaded to temporarily switch your diurinal cycle -

Henbane: Breaking Hexes, Weather spells,Clairvoyance and Love charms.

Gathered by a naked man, standing on one foot, alone, in the morning to gain love of a woman.

Sometimes thrown into water to make it rain.

Hunter,

. Last evening a possible rabid raccoon stumbled through the garden (maybe was distemper....) Cats, chickens and daughter were freaked. Husband was warrior.

Today I found a large grey-white toad on top of my patio table (alive and blinking at me) How on earth did it get up there??oh yeah, and a dead rat on my porch.

All very strange occurrences.

Holy henbane.

Just means your "country" girlfriend, ha ha ha that's what shotguns are fer.........

Well if there were more than three toads fornicating, like altogether I might have had something to do with it, but one by itself, no babies ....I can't take responsibility..............and that's the truth +++

Frank

Magic rainmaking, one of my fields of endeavor............. Maybe also of interest if things get stormy while you hone your skills: Mullein will ward off lightning strikes. Best keep that in your back pocket or growing at your house if you are calling in the rain.

Susan

Sent: 9/10/2007 9:45:44 AM

Subject: Re: Blanzeschwetze

Hey Brother,

Heck Yes,

I actually did have another great market day on Saturday!! Next big retail event will be the Sustainability Festival in Kempton in a few weeks so I have a little bit of a production break..

You drying all that mugwort in yer van? Ahhh, the smell must be incredible! I made a dozen Sweet Annie (Artemisia annua) wreaths for the market (and made some while I was there, too) It was funny to see people walk by, take a whiff of the Artemisia, and turn right on their heels and come back looking for the source of "that incredible smell". Sold 'em all!! Need to make one for me before its all gone.

Thanks so much for the sinuichi tip...I was going to ask you about harvesting cuz it has grown so huge and I need to think about bringing it in at some point. Not sure I will get into the infusion/fermenting process this year but I am happy to know I can dry it and enjoy that way.Im' curious what will you do with the valerian and stramonium leaves. Have a plan?

Can't wait to tell Jesse about you at the Annex chasing the farmgirls....She'll get a big kick outa that and we'll definitely consider you there with us while we dig up our 4 square garden.Keep your fingers crossed.

hey, guess what?

One of my late blooming tatula plants has come out with 6 petal blooms! I must say I never heard of this until you mentioned yours.on Friday, I found a yellowed old paperback copy of Carlos Castaneda-Teachings of Don Juan at a yard sale. (never read any of these before) so I am immersed, of course, but happy to keep my 'relationship' with her at arms length.Ever finish your daturahex?

Not working too hard this week. nope.

Sister SuebeeKy

Hey Sis SueBee,

Nicotiana rustica is different than regular tobacco, When grown the Rustica has a yellow flower and the regular tobacco is white.

It might even be in that Castenada book your reading. In South America, rustica is considered the most powerful plant of all. It has much higher nicotine levels than the regular stuff. Its kinda harsh though, unlikely to get hooked on it. Goes well in a mix as previously stated.

I'd try your ornamental out anyway, a bird in hand is worth two in the bush...........just cut the leaves and hang outside somewhere underneath, turn nice and brown just like tobacco.

Heck I don't hardly smoke anymore anyway, just dry and make these mixtures outa habit. When the Rabbi comes over he always has the best 420 and we add it in there, the way 420 is these days you have to have it in a mixture. Heck I really miss growing it, really beautiful plant, I used to get'em up 12 feet. Male and female plants, very curious creature, oh well.............Yeah that book you got there, I think 1970?, yeah that really got the ball rolling as far as shamanism is concerned.

I'm talking to the krauts over at Aya and they tell me that the black henbane goes in good with a pilsner beer, I guess the seed? [and I just luv beer)

Speaking of Castenada, how did you make out with those cactus chips? any luck.........

I hate to say it Frank, but corporate America has made sacred cactus accessible to the masses. Is this such a wrong thing? I don't think would ever have been given the knowledge I have been given if I hadn't taken that misguided trip to Home Depot and found my unique Bridgesii specimen.

Figure 24 Bridgsii Cactus, collection of Frank Blank

Tobacco

Tobacco is the number one power plant of the world. Tobacco is the Plant of Power. The name he has told me is Power Food. Tobacco is food for the spirits. That is why we offer pinches of Tobacco to herbs when we gather them. Tobacco is nourishment that feeds the spirits and strengthens them. You can use it for protection against negative energies, because if you dedicate it to Protection it will feed the energies of Protection. Like feeding your watchdogs to make them strong. In the same way, it makes prayer-energies more Powerful. If you place prayer intentions and songs in Tobacco when it is growing, it absorbs that energy and acts like a kind of spiritual megaphone for your prayers when you release them. You can enlist the help of elemental-type spirits that don't care about you normally by offering them Tobacco as a kind of payment. The same thing is said among peoples here in Turtle Island and in the Amazon, that the reason humans were placed on Earth was to cultivate Tobacco for the spirits, because they cannot do it themselves.

Tobacco feeds our own spirits when we consume it. We can become addicted to his food, more so if our spirits are starving, then we may crave him and his food. The trouble is, consuming Tobacco unconsciously means that only a little bit of the Power comes in, and, more important, it doesn't reach your Spirit, the depths within you that are crying to be fed. Consuming Tobacco unconsciously is like the unconsciousness of compulsive eating, and it becomes compulsive for the same reasons. Both of these compulsions are manifestations of a starving spirit. (You even see how people who stop smoking often gain weight because they take up overeating instead.)

It also, because it magnifies the power of prayer and intention, magnifies the intention of Tobacco companies to make people addicted and funnel money to them. The commercial Tobacco growers and companies dedicate this intention to the Tobacco they grow -- to feed the spirit of addiction in us. That addiction is intentional and it is because the Tobacco companies put that intention in, both physically (through the hundreds of additive chemicals that can legally constitute 20% of dry weight, not to mention tons of pesticides) and spiritually (through their Intent) dedicate this most sacred of Power Plants to this purpose, of creating addiction. This is a spiritually Powerful plant -- you tell a lettuce leaf to addict people and place them under your command and intention, well, you might not get much results. You take the most Powerful of Power plants and say, "Addict millions of people and place them under our command so they have to feed us money" -- that Power plant will give you Powerful results.

Tobacco also shows how when sacred powers are used carelessly and unconsciously, they can cause harm and sickness. There is only one Power, which can be shaped and used in different ways, up to us.

Blaming Tobacco for how he is used is like blaming electricity for how it is used.

And with some sacred things, most sacred things, the power is fragile and must be protected. Tobacco's Power is not fragile. It remains intact no matter how it is used or misused, no matter what other contaminants are also present. This is why ordinary cigarettes can even be used in ceremony. The Intent put in it by the commercial grower and cigarette companies can be cleared by your Intent. (And there are many ways to use Tobacco besides smoking.)

Tobacco is a plant that involves true secrets in its practice. There are things about his practice that are genuine secrets. What I have spoken of is only the public side of the shamanic use of Tobacco, and that is Powerful enough. I don't smoke cigarettes, except under certain circumstances, but I can never say "no" when someone offers me a cigarette, because they are offering me something so sacred, even if they don't know it.

(All the above IMHE, of course.)

Last edited by sachahambi on Mon Jan 08, 2007 12:22 am; edited 1 time in total"

http://forums.ayahuasca.com/phpbb/viewtopic.php?t=11334

Hey Rabbi

Need to learn yiddish as soon as possible, I have some previous experience with it.......the Pennsylvania Deutsch dialect is almost identical

but just between You and me.............damned I love this book

They're trying to guide me down the right direction, whilst I try to develope their minds to see the beauty of the singularity of heroin addiction.......ha ha ha

Jesse is still interested in meeting with you at some point.

Her husband, Matthew, I want you to meet, he's straight up Pa Deutsch, with jewish ancestry............yes, very interesting.

The secret begins to unfold..........

By the way, the dwarf rabbit population has dramatically increased recently........

Frank,

There are a number of places to study yiddish. We should talk on the phone. i still want to get some of those plant for my garden. i am glad the secret is unfolding, maybe see you next weekend.

Reb Josh

whatta they call rabbit shit?

Rabbit= der Haas....plural = der Hasse

Bunny= es Haasli ...plural= es Hasslin

drek= dirt, filth

scheisse= shit

you can put it together however you like, Bruder.

yep, I nearly fired up the wood stove this morning.I still have all the windows open so its cold in here...but I'd rather pull out more quilts/sweaters than close the windows just yet.Guessing the chimney needs a cleaning first,too.

oh,man.. I mixed your silvery seaside flowery new moon mugwort with an equal amount of my PA farmland full moon mugwort leaf for an absolutely awesome blend. Shared half with me lil Sister Jesseky.

The bag was practically vibrating. Looking forward to using it very soon.Thank you once again , Brudha.

Your contribution to the work is most appreciated. We are happy to have you here in smokey spirit! It makes us all smiley inside and out.

MT Bummy

Wasn't it you who told us you gathered ginseng for Mt Bummy when you were young?

Maybe it was Dennis .... thought you had known him.He was from Oley.

I spoke to an old guy last fall who lives in Oley by the name of Morgan Rheinbold who knew Mt Bummy, probably studied with him but he's not saying for sure. Anyway, I called him once because I found some of his salves for sale at Renningers in Kutztown and they were....interesting, very crude...but richly stinking of plants, nonetheless. We tried to get together a few times last fall before Christmas and then it never happened. He also seemed a little suspicious of me. I must dig out his number and call him again.

He told me the last young 'apprentice' he had smashed her car head on into a bridge....decapitating her.....

ooookay...not sure why he told me that but...I am still enormously intrigued by his salves anyway.

SuebeeKy

Yeah it was me, went gathering goldenseal and ginseng, hung out at his used bookstore on east main when it used to be the poor side of town, musta been 68-71.

We also used to sell him pelts from trapping, muskrat, fox, racoon, him or the guy at the ole junkyard at the three mile house on 737 which ever had the best price........

He had the bookstore in the front, and then had a sheet hung over the entrance to the back where he hung his herbs and had a cot, Bumbaugh...........a genuine one of a kind, Dutchie. had good books too........

yeah he was big into the saturday auctions, renningers was the small fish, the big one was down your way, can't think of the name now, you must know it.....

dabbled in antiques...........

+++

Hunter

Oh God, it had to be Zern's in Gilbertsville, I betcha.....I can almost see him there. yeah..Chust his cuppa tea.It's not the same as it used to be in the 60's and 70's ...but still pretty grungy and raw...but now too many Vietnamese guys selling tube socks and watches, you know....less in the way of Dutchies.

http://www.zerns.com

Green Dragon in Ephrata was on Saturdays, too. Always a good hanging place back then and animal auction, too.We bought and sold alotta chickens and rabbits there. Lotsa fun. (More olfactory memories!)

Or Shupp's Grove /Renningers in Adamstown for the more antiquey crowd on Sundays.

Suebeeky

yeah, Gilbertsville and Adamstown were the big league places, he had other storefronts down there as well, he'd be certain places certain days of the week, Niantic and Barto come to mind for some reason......

He had such a "store" in the Ktown Folk Fest as an exhibit or something.

WE would buy fox urine from trapping catalogues............racoons were the worst to kill, I preferred muskrats

I actually preferred beekeeping, but yeah hunting fishing and trapping were mandatory as was gardening and animal husbandry, carpentry, etc.

Hunter

Bruder, have you forgotten what Mt Bummy looks like? Read his sweatshirt.....hehheh. looks like a character.

Susan

Bumbaugh? Schiesse, he looks too shaven, the belly is correct though, holy smokes where did you get it? Must be at wanna his 'places of business' Don't tell me he's being canonized by the ' Drei Schwestere" ?

Hunter

it was in the book I chust ent you the link for by WW Weaver. The caption read "Lamar 'Mt Bummy' Bumbau in his lair" hahahhaha probably in Lyons, someone said. But no mention of him in the book...just the picture! No canonizing here, just saw it last night.

Susan

The pic was in a cookbook? by William Woys Weaver? jeez that is weird, no cook he........I just got Yoder's

"Discovering American Folklife: Essays on Folk Culture and the Pennsylvania Dutch"

Don Yoder; Paperback; $4.00 has that essay' approaching a definition of folk religion.'

Hunter

PS

you should canonize him.At least his stomach was like a cannonballis there a date for that pic? And notice the plaque above the doorway "When I see the blood, I will pass over you"

Hunter

Figure 25 Bumbaugh

My mom still lives on the farm just outside of Morgantown in a small
burb called Joanna.

Dad died in 1988 and she stayed on, remarrying later on.

They bought a completely rundown stone farmhouse with a nice bankbarn and outbuildings from Bethlehem Steel in 1969 and worked on it nights and weekends until it was habitable.We moved in 18 months later. There were trees growing through the floorboards and dead raccoons in the walk-in fireplace. There was a summer kitchen that the last tenants (in the 50's) kept a dog in for years .Probably a good solid 8-10 inches of sheisse and garbage on the floor. They knocked that ricketdy building down completely ...much to the dismay of a few hundred rats that lived there. Its all documented on film in photo albums, that huge undertaking. That was where I grew up, for the most part.

My dad could build or fix or catch just about anything. I havent gone fishin' since he died. I still really miss him sometimes... my bro, tho, is a very good representative of all of my dad's skills

SS

Hey Sis,

Thats some good stuff there, them ole stone farmhouses are alotta work but they are worth it. Any ghosts?

Had the out building too, eh, ground cellar, chicken coop, milkhouse, corncrib, wood shed, outhouse? Any critters in the bankbarn?

Yeah homesteadin is tough real tough but its the stuff you really remember later fondly.

I see its due south of Reading, is that Lancacter County, Berks? Old country..........

My place up here, circa 1880's, the ole lady who owned it before me had like a hundred cats in it so you can imagine...........birds flying in an outa the broken windows, luckily nothing had been done to the place since the forties, its usually the later renovations that destroy all the good stuff.

Hunter

The farmhouse has a date stone of 1814 and had a dirt cellar (which had to be dug down 2 feet, sifted and wheelbarrowed out so you could stand up straight)There was a smoke house in the attic (you can still smell). A nice size bank barn, with a silo that had to be knocked down recently due to its crumbling nature. wagon shed, yeah, a privy..long gone

The foundation of the summer kitchen still remains with a stone fireplace converted to a grill area with a new floor serving as a patio and hottub area hahha...my mom's doing..

There was a corn crib structure and ramshackle slap-together sheds that were dangerously tilting one way or another...all gone now.Alot of tiny rooms upstairs in the house, some leading into others...that were standardized to 4 BRs and 2 baths.It is not all original by any means. But, it had to be habitable and my mom liked wall to wall carpeting.....There are only a few rooms that have the wide floorboards now and of the 5 fireplaces, she only uses one of them...with propane gas and ceramic logs!

(should mention here that my mother grew up on a real homesteading Dutchie farm in Lebanon Co. and refused as an adult to continue the traditions....she was a modern professional RN with no time/or inclination for the old ways...nope) My dad on the otherhand, couldnt (and wouldnt) be tamed that way. Always a lil source of friction, dontcha know.

A smaller frame horse barn served as the wood working shop and was used to store his hunting/trapping/fishing stuff. He used to tie flies, cure the pelts, oil his guns, string the bow and do all his "guy" stuff out there....I realize now that it was his escape place. He liked to smoke out there, too

Dad wouldve liked large livestock but my mom wanted no parts of it, having lived with sheep and cows growing up. So we got away with chickens, ducks, geese and rabbits and many dogs and cats over the years and occaisonal wild babies my dad would bring home like pheasants,squirrels, bunnies etc. I even had a screech owl for awhile that I loved so much.

Ghosts? well, I always claim that I heard someone whistling (like they were working, pushing-a-broom kinda whistling) and no one else ever heard it...I heard it many many times over the years but never saw a thing.

It always gave me a lil shiver, but I wasnt ever scared really.

blah, blah, blah...Bruder....whatta big barn door you opened!!! hahhaha

Freya, the freakin' shamanka is great!... I looked at every single painting on that website and really like that one the best.

Gut Dunnerwedder, ya? Have good rain last night? There is some happy, satiated plant life today.

Susan

Man that's some old country down there, makes Kutztown seem 'modern'

"There was a smoke house in the attic (you can still smell). "

yeah, and there would be fat stains on the floor beneath where they hung da meat

"Alot of tiny rooms upstairs in the house, some leading into others.."

yeah the bedrooms were kinda small, less to heat, and funny steps and window sills three feet deep due to the stone construction

"A smaller frame horse barn served as the wood working shop and was used to store his hunting/trapping/fishing stuff."

yeah we had the wood shop with all the power equipment, my dad would lock it up and hide the key on a nail, but we would find it and do all kinda dangerous stuff on the power equipment to build airplanes or something.

Later on I built all my hives there, and had a neat potbelly stove roaring in January with alittle whiskey in the coffee.......

"Ghosts? well, I always claim that I heard someone whistling (like they were working, pushing-a-broom kinda whistling) and no one else ever heard it...I heard it many many times over the years but never saw a thing. "

yeah these places are usually totally haunted, people didn't go to die in a hospital, ha ha ha

we had spooks in the attic bouncing balls, footsteps flickering lights and full apparitions in the bedroom at night, but it kinda was a postive thing........a kinda energy, it actually would enter your body if you would allow it to...........

I can usually tell purdy quick if a place is 'inhabited'

This place in Brooklyn for as old as it is has nothing. But my mother in laws apartment in manhattan has alittle ole lady 'living' in the closet, ha ha ha

They live in a place all their lives so its only natural for them to stay there.

Hunter

Hey Bruder,

Just got wind of an ugly tale of witch hunting in Kutztown.

Apparently there was a board meeting at the PA German Cultural Heritage Center last night.

Just as the meeting was coming to an end, the aforementioned disgruntled former employee who calls herself a Christian, lept up and went on a tirade about The Three Sisters Center....an hour long finger pointing, accusatory, inflammatory, slanderous tirade. She is demanding we be barred from the Harvest Fescht and from teaching at the Heritage Center in the future. Fortunately, the Director and his assistant are supportive friends who were able to somewhat defend our work but there were alot of people there who do not know your Sisters and they allowed this woman to spew ugliness for the entire hour.

Jesse will be meeting with the Director today, but he has assured us our welcome place at the Heritage Center this weekend. As for my historic costume, guess I better leave the witch's hat and nose at home this weekend and put on my psychic armor instead. yeah...

now, where did I put that corn cob pipe?

Heil Sister,

Who's the PDF picture on the attachment, he looks like someone Jesse was talking to at the event, had a windbreaker with the Masonic sign on it..........

Yeah that term, "Folk Religion" rang some bells upstairs, I had never heard that before, he (Don Yoder) may have even coined it.........he wrote, an article titled, "Toward a definition of Folk religion" back in the sixties, anyway I have ordered a copy/ Also mining along this 'folk religion' vein of gold, I found out as good a translation of

R O T A S

O P E R A

T E N E T

A R E P O

S A T O R

As I've ever seen as well as that cross of letters:

INRI

takes place in ole West Virginia, PA German settlers and some heavy witchcraft, ring any bells?

Frank Blank wrote:

But did Joseph Smith really oppose lacing sacramental wine with psychedelic material to induced visions, or was he responding to public pressure in the same way he did with the public exposure of polygamy? While Joseph publicly denied polygamy and excommunicated those caught in the practice, he himself had initiated plural relationships as early as 1832 and continued taking additional wives as late as 1842.

It is my thesis that beginning at a young age, Joseph Smith

experimented with psychedelic plants and fungi and that his later repression of the practice had more to do with suppressing public opposition to the Church than with actual antagonism to the use of psychedelic material. Further, many of Joseph Smith revelations and much of his behavior can be attributed to the use of psychedelics. http://www.mormonelixirs.org/

Folk religion

"Discovering American Folklife Essays on Folk Culture & the PA Dutch Message List

I just received this book, $4.00 used on Amazon specifically because after seeing Don Yoder this month in Kutztown at the Pennsylvania German Cultural Heritage Center at Kutztown University, www.kutztown.edu/community/pgchc yes you can minor in PA Deutsch studies.

Anyway it has an essay Yoder wrote in the sixties entitled, "Toward adefinition of Folk religion"

In the scholarly circles, Pow Wow, Braucherei, Hexerei would beconsidered, 'Folk religion' Superstition should be considered as 'Folk religion'

Another chapter another essay entitled "Folk Medicine" is even more to the point. In it he and others divide Folk Medicine into two categories (I hate when scholars do that) Natural Folk Medicine which includes the usage of plants and 'home remedies' True they usually are used in conjunction with a verbal spell, but "Magico-Religious Folk Medicine" faith Healing through prayer called Belezen, Brauchen, powwowing are done with verbal spells going back into antiquity which means Europe. In this chapter he has written what he presented to us at the Harvest Fescht on that Sunday, the verbal charm and ritual for ridding the skin inflammation called crysipelas (wildfire)

"Wildfeiewr, flieh, flieh, flieh!

Der rode Fadem jagt dich hie, hie, hie!"

or

Erysipelas, fly, fly, fly!

The red string chases you away, away, away!

Three times, the red string is then destroyed, if you were there you will remember. It also is a good source for other verbal charms and references for verbal charm collections, many of which are in Deutchland. My personal view is this that the spiritual aspect of the first or Natural Folk medicine employing plants needs expansion, plants need to be considered as teachers and through them 'things' can be seen and thus done. This is where our tradition will be expanded, not just preserved, so sayeth I. The scholars however prefer the verbal route which is understandable. But this is far superior to his very popular "Hex

Signs" with Thomas Graves, which is what I call a 'coffee table book' Finally Stackpole Books is a very interesting publishing house, located in Mechanicsburg, Lancaster county, a hex sign painter acquaintance, Ivan Hoyt who became alarmed when he became aware of my views regarding intention in what Lee R. Gandee calls 'painted prayers.' Anyway they must have an unusual list.

Hunter

To: hunteryoder@earthlink.net

Sent: 10/17/2007 4:05:38 PM

Subject: just a thought....

hey Bruder,

Just wanted to give you a head's up about contacting Don Yoder.....

Before I went back to speak with Dr. Yoder, Jesse told me that he 'had forgotten to give her his contact info' the day before, so asked me to get it when I spoke to him. oh boy, big mistake.

As gracious as he was about all the other things we discussed, he scolded me slightly for being so forward to ask. Jesse was 'mistaken' ...he said he would contact us, if need be, in the future. He is a very private individual and doesn't give his number out easily.

Upon further talk, all the academics at KU and Heritage Center agreed....Don Yoder is an extremist when it comes to his privacy and it is a well known annoyance to those who are gifted with such information, he does not return emails or calls easily. sigh.

Also found out that he is a voracious scavenger of other's information for use in his own books.

We were told not to be surprised if some of the Hollerbier Haven newsletter info winds up in his powwow book with no mention of us at all. He has been doing this to student's research papers for decades, apparently.

I wouldn't be surprised if he joined the Hexenkunst...but would be surprised if he contributed lest he reveal his email address. Bummer.

Susan

strange dream

Hey Schwester,

Had a strange dream last night and I wanted to tell somebody before it fades away, I think somebody is contacting me, anyway you know I've never really big into written or spoken spells until very recently, not a verbal person BUT the dream was like this, a charm was spoken I think it was the Powwow charm for snakebite from that Don Yoder book, he has a hand lettered image of the text done in 1837 or something, after it was spoken it changed into a star like matrix, the lines of the star or spider web was the words of the charm, through the channels between these delineations a kind of magnetic force flowed and the impulse was to place a open hand above it and the force would travel through not only me but others, people from our circle and this was the power of the charm, this was done several times. it was a very powerful force. And thus I 'get it' now........

Holy Smokes, Bruder.....

you got the powwow!! This is definitely dream time and the veils are thin. It is also even more concentrated being full moon ."the Hunter Moon!!" wonderful visuals.very very exciting dream. You must sketch it, perhaps you will remember more. In fact, write it all down ...start your own journal for the ages those that follow. yeah. Be open, perhaps there will be more tonight

Bruder, this reminds me that I never told you months ago about the powwow dream I had about you..... Remember? I was to tell you when you came that first time and completely forgot until now.

The scene was my backyard. You were at the picnic table (where we do alot of our training sessions by the 3 elder bushes) I was to powwow you and asked you to remove your hat. I was shocked to see a black hole in the top of your head exactly where the powwow session begins. I was a little unnerved but encouraged by Matt and Jesse to begin .Within a few minutes my hands were majorly tingling and I opened my eyes to see that the black hole had 'opened' and revealed a vortex column of light and colors that expanded upwards through the trees into the sky. Deep within the vortex were moving symbols and plant life forms that were spiraling up and down through the column into your head and out again. Your face revealed nothing of this amazing vision that I was seeing. I was 'told' that the connection was complete and to do no more. We just stood and stared in wonder at the vortex. dream over...... heilige scheisse, Bruder...

A few days ago, Jesse and I sat together and made some amulets using elderberry ink, drawing runes, adding herbs including mugwort. When we put them between us to "charge" them with powwow prayers, our vision instantly blurred and spun clockwise. We had the identical reaction sitting across the table from each other in silence and compared notes after we were done. It was so strong and amazing.

Next Wednesday ,on Halloween, I will officially 'receive' the powwow from Matthew and be officially out of my training period. So much has happened this year it is hard to believe that I am still in 'training'.

Your Schwester in Powwow

Asafoetida research

Subject: Asafoetida research.........

Bruder, Thought you might be interested in this discovery.

I'm writing about the asafoetida bags worn around the necks of PA
Germans to ward off illness (It has many sulfur compounds like garlic
and onions) but here is a magical use for the resinous 'Devil's Drek'

hehheh.....Betcha those ultra Christian Dutchies don't know this
history....

Ritual: Use is primarily external. Often mixed into incense especially for
rituals of a somber, ceremonial nature. It is used to banish all negative
energy, evil spirits and demons. Used to invoke male gods, particularly
of a phallic nature. There is some mythology suggesting that asafoetida
grew from semen of a god of fertility when it soaked in the Earth. Used
to gain insight and to enhance the magickal work of any ritual. Used to
cense the ritual Circle or the temple. For self-cleansing, prepare your
thurible and stand over it, allowing the smoke to swirl all about your
body. Keep your eyes closed, and your mind focused. Asafetida is a
classic for exorcism and purification rites. Use it to smudge a ritual
space with smoke. It is said there is an affinity between a black diamond
and asafetida. Some believe that they should be stored together. The
energy of this herbe is very focused and intense. It is associated with the
Devil card of the major arcane. Used in meditations in conjunction with
this graphic archetype, it helps one discover how the mundane

attractions in our own lives have placed us in spiritual bondage. Once known, this herbe may also be used through rituals of self-purification or cleansing to help us break free of our own negative desires. It would be an excellent choice for those seeking entrance into the mysteries of the Horned God. It is recommended for those who place Priapus (http://altreligion.about.com/library/graphics/bl_priapus.htm) upon their altars, for those who invoke the gods, particularly in their aspect as phallic, fertility deities.

Monday, October 29, 2007

Squaring Off for Intent

Using numbers and magic squares instead of verbal spells to direct intent is a natural way for me to direct my will.

Most of us are familiar with

A magic square of "rotas" or "sator" is a prominent form of written charm practiced by English and German descendants alike

http://etext.virginia.edu/users/fennell/highland/harper/symbol.html

Some maybe also familiar with 'Lo Shu' the ancient Chinese/Tibetan magic square. The Tantra is loaded with these numerical magic squares more complex than 'Lo Shu' and they are used as 'Mystical Amulets' for healing and well being.

"Yantra Sadhana, Healing Through Mystical Amulets" J.L. Gupta

Similarly Hexology is useful in a similar manner, instead of mentally going through all the possible permutations that always add up to a particular number, the various versions of stars and their components can be mentally evaluated in a congruent manner. Clockwise rotations versus counter clockwise ones, an ability to change these relative terms by changing the point of viewing them. Which way does the earth rotate?

Eight be comes obvious at a glance, as does six and twelve. Counting becomes unnecessary and answers are split second and immediate. These mental exercises in both the stars and the squares result in a sharpening and focusing of the mind.

Focusing the mind for physical results falls also within the realm of athleticism. The ability to achieve a desired performance is about the mind and its ability to impose its will on the body as it is about mere physical fitness. The mind is a muscle. In this format, the mind processes numbers and keeps count either in terms of time or in terms of units of work, distance, heart rate, calories spent and so forth. Also the remembrance of past peak performances and the comparison between those and the current real time activity are obviously mental tasks performed by the athletes mind.

So what exactly do I mean by 'squaring off for intent'?

Inevitably in the course of performing an extraordinary task with an 'intentional' result the user must in someway manage time in such a way that the body and other bodies are tricked into performing a task and 'stealing' time when the task is easier so that this 'stolen' time can be used to 'square off' the intent when the going gets rough. this it in its simplest form. Its a kind of averaging out to maintain a pace for an intentional result.

It becomes much more sophisticated and the mind devises strategies to trick the body into optimizing beyond its mere physical capabilities by creating illusions or recycling other unrelated motivational psychological memories. We've all done this, after dealing with an unpleasant personal interaction, using that residual angst to deal with unrelated problems that need attending to.

The mind must also know when to back off and allow the body to relax and perform in a more realistic manner in the wisdom of knowing that the extraordinary is still within, reach if only one is patient and willing to accept the result one way or the other. All of these mental strategies are usually broken down into numerical units of time over movement through space present past and projected into the future which is where the will lives...............

An ability to direct the occurrence of an event in the future is what we do here. How is it done? Obviously there is an urgent need that demands our conscious attention, more importantly afterward the conscious input is processed by our subconscious mind, this is where the real creative solution is completely visualized in such detail that the execution of intent is almost automatic. One merely is completing the 'task' and there is little question about the outlook for success. Success is inevitably necessary to the intentional self's essential world view. If it is seen clearly it will happen, without a doubt. Some call this belief, I prefer 'knowing'

Ah yes the clarity of this season

Figure 26 Robert L. Schreiwer on the Hexenkopf, Williams Township, Pa, Walpurgis Nacht, 2008, Photo, Hunter M. Yoder

Rob Lusch

From the man who started the Pennsylvania Asatru Meetup group, I am trying to contact him to see if he wants to join up with us. I think his emphasis is on our shared heritage, rather than "Norse" specific. (finally!!!)

Patricia

P.S. see also..

http://heidbindnis.blogspot.com/

Good day,

The Tree of Life hex sign has been around and in use as long as I can remember. I do believe it is a direct descendant from the Yggdrasil of our Germanic ancestors.

There used to be a barn in Lebanon County that had a Tree of Life onit, but it burned or was torn down when I was in my mid-teens. Also, there is such a thing as a "Distelfink Tree" which is essentially a Tree of Life with Distelfinks on the branches instead of barn/hex signs.

Rob L.

Viele Griesse un Helle! Message I hope Patricia does not mind my re-posting much of the content of an earlier e-mail I sent to her here, but it is easier for me to rewrite it than to start all over.

My name is Rob, and I am a proud Deitscher originally from Berks County and now from Bucks. I am the founder of the still-ever-so- small Philly Area Asatru Meetup Group. I have long been an activist in the advancement and promotion of the Pennsylvania German language and culture. Although my primary Deitsch sites have fallen behind because I have been focusing efforts elsewhere, you may want to check out www.deitscherei.org for some old content and the old cartoons and stuff. With the exception of the old blog portion, the entire site is in only Pennsylvania German. The survival and advancement of the language is critical to our continued ethnic identity, and I will do my best to help others learn "die Mudderschprooch."

I have sometimes been referred to as a Deitscher "nationalist," and usually it is in a joking context, but I do have a firm pride in the accomplishments of our ancestors. I believe we are often a forgotten minority, but keep in mind that the Amish in Ohio came out in huge numbers to vote (which they had not done before), and Ohio was the state that decided the 2004 election results.

I am a hammer-wearing, rune-reading Heid, too, though I still have respect for those who adhere to the plain traditions or who live their Christian faith true to the tenets. I believe that among the Pennsylvania Germans, we see loyalty to the spirit of the faith more than in most cultures, but I may be biased there.

"Die Iwwerliefering" ("that which is handed down") is a very small group of scattered Pennsylvania German heathens, some who are more comfortable than others at publicizing their faith due to the locations they live in. Hopefully the Pennsylvania German Heathen Alliance (http://heidbindnis.blogspot.com) will grow over time, even if slowly.

Generally we believe in living heathenism in the present. We don't wear period costume (though if it helps others feel closer to the gods and goddesses, then I wish them well). We believe in bright colors and and joy (as reflected throughout the ages in our barn or "Hex" signs, for want of a better term). I do not believe in disrespecting Christians for no reason other than religion because that would be tantamount to disrespecting the parents who raised me as well as the rest of my post-conversion ancestors who survived hardship in Europe and helped build the United States.

However, if someone earns disrespect, then disrespect is what s/he will get. The "Heide gege Hass" (Heathens against Hatred) statement that appears on the site of Die Iwwerliefering (which translates to "that which is handed down") is somewhat different from the usual "heathens against hatred" statements.

Mir schtehne gege Hass, Razism, Homophobia un enniche Bedraage, dieder Schpott wege re Fruchverletzing verdiene.

Translation: We stand against hatred, racism, homophobia, and otherbehaviors, that earn derision on account of damaging frith.

I am still debating the term "Schpott" and am considering replacing it with "Verachdung" ("contempt"), but the implication is that if a behavior does damage to frith, it deserves derision. At some point I may write it to be clear that mindless hatred damages frith and screws up Wyrd, etc. etc.

Anyhow, sorry for rambling... I have a tendency to do that every so often. Just politely tell me to "sei schtill" and I'll cool down. :)

Rob

" Does anyone know whether the tree of life is a traditional German symbol that would have been used by the PA German, particularly in hex signs?"

Yes we have it the work of Ivan Hoyt especially, he uses Himmelbriefs as inspiration it also shows up on quilts, the one here is from the Philly Museum collection and the goddess 'hex' is mine with Assyrian tree and Canaanite goddess as tree imagery:

"I noticed the pictures of the Helms of Awe or Galdor Staves on the website. I tried to look for some additional information on these symbols but haven't found any. Could someone give a brief synopsis of their importance and association with the PA German?"

Helms Awe and Galdor Staves operate in such a similar manner as thePennsilfaanisch Deitsch Hex signs, the two were put together in a book they get a big laugh about here from the Asatru crowd. "Northern Magic" Edred Thorsson, This author makes the connection between the two and I concur..........

As far as Pennsilfaanisch Deitsch fading away and disappearing, cometo Berks County, Kutztown and we'll show you a good time and you'll be feeling the effects for a long time.

Hunter

Figure 27 Rabbi Saltzman holding Tree of Life Hex by Ivan Hoyt

Learning Pensylfaanisch Deitsch

I agree that the "Pennsylvania German Reader and Grammar" is probably the best for non-native Deitsch speakers to work from, particularly if they are already familiar with grammatical terms. Brookshire Publications of Lancaster, PA, published this book and probably has some copies around (as I may, also).

As for Stine's dictionary, I found it on Amazon and cannot believe how overpriced it is (http://www.amazon.com/Pennsylvania-German-dictionary- German-English-English-Pennsylvania/ Ironically, I probably have a few of them stashed away somewhere, plus I know that some of the Grundsau Lodges have them yet. If i find some copies, I will let you know. The Pennsylvania German Society (www.pgs.org) may have copies, too.

C. Richard Beam has recently put out another volume of his comprehensive dictionary (which uses words in context, which helps avoid the problem of Stine's book, which does not help with homonyms or by identifying which words are used in which areas or which are primary).

I have the utmost respect for both Dr. Beam and Dr. Stine, and all their materials have been created as true labors of love and hard work. In the past, I have hoarded some of these books and other items (like the Pennsylvania German flag) because I never knew whether they'd be printed again.

Also, if you are not receiving Dr. Michael Werner's Pennsylvania German newspaper (actually, it is Penn Dutch, English, and Palatine German), then you may want to start getting it. He and some of his German counterparts are in constant contact with the Pennsylvania German community leaders and do a great job with publications such as the paper and "Hans un Yorick," which is "Max and Moritz" translated into

Pennsylvania German. Check out all the links on

I am not sure how many other Deitsch speakers we have here who are oriented towards the Germanic/Northern Traditions, but I would really like to work on getting Havamal translated into Deitsch.

Unfortunately, I do not know much Old Norse (though I can figure out quite a bit), and I would prefer to translate right from Old Norse into Deitsch rather than using English as a pass-through.

I am hoping The Troth or AFA or other national organizations can guide me to places to learn Old Norse. I could take it at NYU, my grad school alma mater, but I don't want to shell out the money right now that NYU charges for classes. There simply has to be something closer to Philly.

And no, Havamal (Words of the High One) is not an Old Norse form of Hawwermaul (mouth full of oats), though I do wonder whether Old Norse "mal" and Pennsylvania German "Maul" are directly related words.

Rob

I must have some low-key form of A.D.D. because when it comes to reading, I usually end up reading parts of several books at the same time, thus turning my head to mush. I think I just find so many things to be of interest that I can't focus on them for too long. lol

I read a couple chapters of Hopeful Journeys last night, and found the recounting of the strife between Lutherans and Moravians to be something I have not seen much of in print. Some sections of that passage were simply horrifying. I was astonished that Muhlenberg, a highly respected Deitscher Vorganger, would hold Zinzendorf, another highly respected Vorganger, in such contempt.

There are a few lessons to be learned in that section.

1). How could Christian leaders treat each other in such a vile manner and still claim to be adherents of a religion based on love? Of course, this is hardly limited to these two denominations. History is full of religious intolerance and force, but it is particularly disgusting when people oppress or kill in order to spread love. How does that work, exactly?

2). All faiths, including Heathenry, can see what can happen when people let their fear govern their actions. Here we had two German denominations, both of which had experienced repression in various ways in Europe, continuing their spats. And to what end? How did those conflicts serve their people or their communities?

3). One thing I have noticed is that the more similar two faiths are, the more vehemently the adherents react to the small differences. Those differences are heresy, which is worse in many faiths than not believing. We even see this among some of the plain sects that have had weird reasons for splintering off one congregation from another, etc. This is a problem with dogma, and I hope that Asatru/Odinism/Heathenism does not start to follow down that path. I once saw a Hindu bumper sticker that read: "My karma ran over your dogma." I loved it. Since Asatru/Odinism/Heathenism, which I will henceforth call der Urglaawe, has concepts that are very similar to karma (and probably related in origin to karma but with some disitnctions), I found the bumper sticker to be deep in meaning as well as in humor.

Anyway, that's just from a few passages of the book.. I could probably expound on it more, but I don't want to seem like a popinjay. lol

Curious what you and others who read the book think? Similar reactions? Different reactions? Am I reading too much into it? :)

We're trying to expand "Die Iwwerliefering" (group for Pennsylvania German Urglaawers (heathens)), but I am also trying to expand the Asatru/Odinist/Irminschaft community in Southeastern PA. The Philadelphia Area Asatru Meetup Group has its initial meeting coming up on the 26th, but I am not sure what the response will be.

If there are others out there who are interested in such offline meetings, we can probably find suitable locations and get to know one another better, etc.

I live in Bristol, which is in Lower Bucks County not far from Philly. I get to Berks County fairly regularly, and I am mobile enough to be able to hit other areas from Carbon County in the North to Lancaster County in the west.

Thanks,

Rob

November 2007

Henbane Ale

For your holiday table:

Henbane Ale

Ingredients

2.6 pounds barley malt extract

2 pounds honey

1.43 ounces (40 grams) henbane seed dried

5grams dried yeast

6 gallons water

Take the henbane (finely ground) and 1 quart of water and mix together (if you desire to add the Myrica do so at this time) Bring to a boil, remove from heat, and let sit until cool to touch. Then take malt extract and honey and 2 quarts of hot water and mix well (until sugars are dissolved) in a fermentation vessel that has been sterilized. Add the henbane (and Myrica) mixture and stir well-do not strain. Then add 6 gallons of cool water. Check the temperature, making sure it is 68-70 degrees F range and then sprinkle yeast on top. Let ferment until complete, then siphon into primed bottles, and store for two weeks in a cool place.

From SACRED AND HERBAL HEALING BEERS, Chapter 'Psychotropic and Highly Inebriating Beers'

Ordnung vs. Frith (Fruch)

Here's a topic for those who know a bit about the Amish and about Heathenry to consider and opine upon.

The concept of "frith" ("Fruch" or "Fried") is central to the daily life of those who practice der Urglaawe or any variant of old heathenism.

I see many similarities between frith and the numerous versions of Amish Ordnung (or Ordning, depending on which dialect you are speaking at the moment).

I wonder how much of the spirit and function of the Ordnung comes out of pre-Christian culture of the areas that most Mennonites and Amish lived in? These behavioral rules are controlled by the local Gmee, which is similar to a kindred in many ways (vs. a remote centralized church authority). I am wondering whether this arrangement was tapping into the heathen culture that simmered beneath the surface after the conversions, or whether it was simply a rebellion against Roman control, or even a combination of both. I definitely suspect both. Would love to hear others' thoughts.

I think you may have answered your own question, after all 'blood is thicker than wine' I think that the Celts, although distinctly different, share something with us, we certainly mixed blood many times, myself included, in part because they are not so hard on the eyes. This mix is practically a tradition in Pennsylvania or as they say, Pennsylfaanisch Deitsch?

Furthermore, I think I figured out at least in part, how the Heathen blood was not to be denied or controlled by nature, and even though our protestant fore bearers broke free from Rome, they did so at the price of all visual forms of 'idolatry' and got into the music business instead. However, the primitive (a good thing) heathen must have his symbol try (is it a word?) which manifested itself in the Hexology, sun wheels in the most basic sense. But your 'Plain' background will lack this concept......

Hunter Yoder

Ah, but the Plain background only "sort of" lacks the concept. Look at the fancy work even of the Amish quilts, for example. Deitsch and Welsh are indeed a fairly common heritage line, particularly in these parts... more so than Deitsch and Irish, Deitsch and Breton, Deitsch and Scottish, etc.

As for the "controlled by nature" portion, you bring up another interesting topic. We are controlled by nature in the sense of our Urleeg (orlog.... the primal layers) and our presence within the universe, but by the same time, we are given certain tools to manipulate our the world around us through our use of our minds and our energies. We are not in full control of our Wyrd (a concept similar to karma), but we can behave in such a manner as to alter our Wyrd for better or for worse. Our successes and failures therefore can to a great extent be controlled by our behavior and our ethics, which gives us every reason to behave as positively as possible. This is certainly not a big leap to the Christian principles except we do not believe that a omnipotent god is sitting in judgment of us and relegating us to eternal suffering, etc.

PS

Heck, look at all the Welsh town names even in Berks and Lancaster Counties... Cumru Township is really Camry in Welsh... Narvon and Caernarvon Townships... and of course the percentage gets even higher the closer one gets to the Main Line. The Welsh apparently settled a band just to the east of where Dutch Country is usually considered to be now... and apparently all around Germantown

Swiss Heathen site..

Hey Patricia,

You read my file........last time I was investigated, they came up with a direct line between the 'Oley Yoders' and the Joders of Steffisburg, a town near Bern. Nice Rossette there, Lee Gandee wrote, "This six pointed figure is the primitive, first sign of Hex, which states the basic truths of being, namely: that the relationship between God and man, and between God and every created thing is of one law and order." Its the iconic ancient sign of protection against evil.

Hunter

So here is what I found the other night..First, I googled "Belsnickel" and I looked at the Wikipedia article.

http://en.wikipedia.org/wiki/Belsnickel

.it was "okay"...then it mentioned "Krampus". THAT got me interested, so I went there.. http://en.wikipedia.org/wiki/Krampus

Scrolled down the page after reading that, and I saw "Pre-Christian Alpine traditions" article(!!!!) and I went to that.. http://en.wikipedia.org/wiki/Paganism_in_the_Eastern_Alps

THAT article was very good..and led me to more links.

It's the Hagal or "Mutter Rune". It is the basis of Runic and Ur-law. I love that we have remembered it in our culture and our Ancestors' kept it alive for us! As an aside, the Poles and some other Slavs put this on their barns too for fertility, as they "know" this sign. Thats interesting Patricia, especially since 'hex signs' are the visual gateway between our two worlds. tell me though, 'hagall' in that form is seen in the Younger Futhark, the Elder Futhark's 'hagalaz' appears as more of an 'H'? Also use of the 'rosette' on barns hear and even in Poland is probably not for fertility but protection, (of course on the Mennonite or Amish barns there would never be any such heathen sign) Protection from fire was and is the big concern. Two most important things on the exterior of a barn would be lightning rods and hex signs. To promote fertility, we post only in the color green......... and use eight pointed 'earth stars' Four works too as does sixteen, but eight is the best.

Hunter

Figure 28 "Hex Spiral" 2007 Acrylic on canvas

Well, I have to contradict you, Hunter.... I think that both eight and six pointed stars were used in fertility signs.... I was handed hex sign info from the Oley Freindschaft, and in that the six pointed star was the one and only sign of fertility. I also see the benefit of the use of the eight pointed star, but I have a feeling the six pointer was first in Germanic areas. I have also seen it used as a protective symbol, and especially in the Greek and Hebrew alphabets there was a sign with six points and a different letter at each point (the center being seventh). I believe it was called the seal of the archangel Michael, and sealed you against evil in all of the seven directions of time and space (above, below, Norht, east, south, west, and within). I think the eight pointed star also had importance within the Greek systems of magic, astrology, medicine, and alchemy that came later... beginning around 1000 ad, but getting really strong in the 1300's (after the fall of the Byzantine empire). In the Greek system there is always an 8-fold division of time and space. This influence is what acted to standardize alot of the feasts in Europe, making them much more in sync with eachother, and this is why so many of the new age Wiccan feasts are held on the dates that they are. The Greek systems were taken up very quickly by the central and northern Europeans. Anyway, I think it is a piece, though decidedly not the definitive whole of either of these long cherished symbols.

Jesse Tobin

I would have to agree with you that six has more strength and power than eight, but I don't think you will be able to show six in connection with the planet or goddess Venus in her myriads of forms and names going back into Mesopotamia, And if you can make that connection with the planet or goddess Venus, bingo.I don't think six will work with PHI in the way that eight does. By the way PHI is a Greek letter. Anytime you can introduce an irrational number into a 'hex sign' its probably gonna work pretty darn good. I mean the traditional thing would be a four, as 'earth star' the cardinal points and then introduce symbolic elements to have a favorable effect on the earth, like sun and rain, but thats pretty

elementary. Venus is the heavy hitter for the planet earth, I hope there is some heathen Venusian tradition beyond what they received from the Greeks/Romans, and I would be very interested in knowing what it is.--- The planet or star not the goddess that is.

Thanks

Hunter

Eight is fairly common among older Germanic cycles of completion, it would seem. In fact, there appears to be some evidence that at least some of the early Germanic cultures were octal rather than denary. Now whether those systems understood mathematical zero or not is a separate question (there is no "zero" rune, and the blank rune is a modern invention that I discount), but once mathematical 0 came into understanding, the numbers ranged from 0-7 before flipping to a new cycle, and I think we all recognize the significance of the number 7 in our heritage. The octal system certainly makes some forms or rune reading interesting because our brains are not really wired to the concept of base 8 (I was terrible at logarithms in school until I hit hexadecimals in college), and we have to adjust numbers related to some forms or rune reading to match the base 8 rather than base 10.

I would actually love to learn more about non-denary cultures (and there are many of them... the Maya were vigesimal and still have the most accurate calendar in existence!).

Figure 29 "Berks County Eight Hex" 2006

So is there a rune that is assigned the number eight in the same way we seem to be assigning Hagall to six? And or is there a rune that is associated with the planet or star Venus, the morning and evening star? If so we can run associations direct and indirect and see where it goes and fit it right into our 'Hexology" and yes, the Mayans and later the Aztecs and their calendar could accurately predict and show the path of Venus which would delineate a Pentagram on their calendar every 250 years or so.

It appears to be The Ingwaz rune, diamond shaped, or two crosses stacked on top of each other (that is eight radiating members folks), or just the square (the easiest way to draw an eight pointed star is by using a circle in a square). also Yngvi, and theres something about the 'House of Yuengling' sounds like beer.........Big time Fertility Rune!

Hunter

LOL... looks like you got it with the association of Frey's (Ing's) rune with fertility, though his sister, Freya, is often more associated with the Roman goddess Venus (both the planet and the goddess - not that they are necessarily the same entity, though). However, both Frey and Freya govern much more than just fertility. They are leaders of the Vanir house of gods and goddesses. More support for Frey and Freya being related to Venus (at least linguistically) comes from the word "Vanir" itself, which has the reconstructed Proto-Indo-European root of *wen, meaning "to desire" or "to strive for." The same root is shared with "Venus." That being said, it appears that the Vanir revealed themselves to the Teutons before contact was made with the Romans, who would have introduced Venus, so the goddess was not an acquisition from Rome but a goddess who either revealed herself as Freya to the Teutons and Venus to the Romans or who is a completely different entity. I do not know too much about Venus, but from what I remember from grade school (hardly a bastion of Roman learning, though), Freya sounds like a much more multi-faceted goddess.

I just got the new book "Frey: God of the World" (check www.lulu.com... author's name is Ann Groa Sheffield), so I may learn some new information about Frey and possibly Freya, too.

Curious question that I do not know the answer to since I always studied Germanic and Slavic languages... but isn't the "-us" suffix in Latin a masculine ending? How did Venus get a masculine name? Worth reading about Freya... By the way, I have also noted the apparent similarity between Yngvi and Yuengling, though I also figured there may be a twisting of a different Germanic name related to "young," too...

Rob

Actually I think that the reason for the six representing fertility has more to do with the fact that originally the Germanic people had the year divided into 6 60 day tides, whereas later the agricultural wheel of the year became eight. It did not become eight very early on, though, and I think this 6 pointer has more to do with the ancient feast days of the old agricultural/pastoral year... in the old days the equinox dates were apparently not as important to the Germanic peoples as the other six days. So, that's my best guess, other than that I simply am relying on oral tradition out of Oley, though I know that in Virginville area the 8 pointed sign was preferred for fertility.

Jesse

Who of course to the Germans, is known as Frouwa Walpurga and she told me to call her that! Your friendly Bucks County Hexenmeister has returned lol! Damn I've missed everyone :) Although the Icelanders preserved much, the Germans retained plenty of our lore and magic both orally and through Jacob Grimm. And while of course I understand the equivalent names and kennings, my suggestion is that we should try to keep our references to our gods and goddesses in German rather than Norse terms, in keeping with our traditions of Hexerei/Braucherei and Deutsch in general. For example, Frey/Freyr is a Norse term, he is known as Froh/Froh Ing to the Germans. Frigga is Frikka, Odin is Wotan/Wodan, Thor is Donner, etc.

Greg

You can make numbers do anything, but in making the correlation between Hagall and the Rossette/six pointed star, we can take the next step in that direction by making the correlation between Ingwaz and our Four/Eight pointed star. if you look at the facts, Ingwaz is the fertility rune on every level, and it just happens to turnout that the runic shape is either a diamond (a square put on end) or my preference, the 'stacked crosses', which if you were to rotate the upper one 45 degrees and superimpose it on the other, the result would be an eight pointed star. Seems like more than coincidence. The connection may have never been made before. The Rossette in providing protection can thus foster abundance, success, fertility....... As far as the abundance of 'eights' in the Virginville area, I can account for sixteen there by my own hand, but they were repaintings of Milton Hill, who was a great old master Hexologist in that area.

Gods and their symbols (which take on a life of their own apart from the corresponding god) are like navigating the NYC Subway system, For instance, their is a stop on the F train called Broadway Lafayette where you can connect with the Six train which designates that station as Bleecker Street, at this same station you can also connect with the D and B trains which call the stop Grand Street. All of these trains stop there, they go on to different destinations but meet there.

The God Inguz is considered to be the name of an old Germanic earth god, who works hand-in-hand with the earth mother, Nerthus. Their cult was most developed in the North Sea regions of ancient times.

Ingwaz represents the earth mother's male consort, and her attending priest. This cult was so large and important that the people of the North Sea were often called Ingvaeones (those of Ing). The Vanic god Freyr was also known as Yngvi, and he also took part in fertility rites in which he rode a chariot in ritual processions. Freyr has basically taken over the role and name of Ing in the North.

In the Ing-Nerthus cult the female element consumes the male to replenish her powers after using up her own to fertilize the earth and people. Here there are strong similarities to the Cybele-Attis cult. The myth of Freyr giving up his sword to gain Gerdhr or the Ódinnic name Gelding (castrated horse), may be depicted here. The male element symbolizes the self-replenishing cosmic food" of potential energy, which is held through winter by the goddess to be suddenly and violently released again in spring during the orgiastic processional ritual.

Inguz is a store of energy that needs to undergo a period of gestation in order to grow to its full strength. This is a principle that applies to all levels of the multiverse, and it's a very strong Rune of magick, for all power must undergo a protected gestation period before it can manifest in its most powerful and potent form. This Rune also contains on of the great secrets of Northern sex magic.

http://www.hafapea.com/magickpages/runes/inguz.html

Then In Richard North's book, "Heathen Gods in Old English Literature" we see in his chapter entitled "Aspects of Ingui: -geot and Geat" and let me add the names, Enguz, Gapt, Got and so forth, we see the ascension of Ing as Woden declined with the advent of the New god Christ. The Christ had been syncretized through Ing no doubt because of the 'death rebirth myth which the Northern ones could identify with and this happened before the actual Christian conquest through something he refers to as the 'Gothic-Arian sycretism of Enguz through Christ'

This same author describes how he claims, Woden, Uuodan, or Odinn developed as a Germanic cult from the cult of Mercury from Roman Gaul." Through warfare and trade between the Gauls, Romans, and Germanic tribes, Mercury, a god of travel and trade in this world and others, seems to have crossed the Rhine into Northern Germania and spread into the North Sea coastal area, England, and southern

Scandinavia by the end of the fifth century. Wodanaz, or Wodan would have the ethic name for this imported god, from the figure of Mercury, inventor artium, which is Caesar's term for mercury among the early Gauls in 54BC"

Hunter

Apparently we have need to come up with a recognized form of the name Gná, a handmaiden of Frigga and the goddess who is the remover of obstacles, among other things. She has sought me out for something and then I got a call about her from someone else who wants to get to know her better. My inclination is to recognize her as Gna (without the accent mark) or Gnaa (which rolls off my Deitsch uvula better) as there is no lore in Deitsch regarding her.

Interesting to note that I found a web reference to gna- being a root meaning goddess in the Rigaveda:

My caller suggested maybe Gana or Ganaa, but the "gn" is a common cluster in Deitsch (with both letters pronounced, but the g almost sounds like a k.. .almost), so there is no need to add in a fleeting vowel. It is interesting to note, though, that if we were to do that, Gana as a name would look a little bit like Ganesh/Ganesha, who, ironically, is the Hindu remover of obstacles. Sets my mind ablaze.

Rob

Rob, we'll have to talk on the phone sometime soon. I'll probably have much more to say up here as I go back through 3 months of posts and add my own insights, both taught and learned in meditations.

I see Hunter mentioned my association with Lee Gandee, who mentored my own mentor. Other than here with people who can fully understand the hedges I ride and the worlds I inhabit, I am very reserved about discussing how and why I became a Hexenmeister and

very few people who actually know me in person are

aware of this- and that includes people who have been friends for many, many years- as much as it is a constant blessing in many ways, I live in the shadows when it comes to the everyday, mundane world and do my "thing" in private.

It's funny you mention Frija, you must be no doubt aware that scholars have confused the name with both Frikka and Frouwa Walpurga. That definitely would tend in this context to link the name more to Frikka in the eyes of the PA Deutsch. As far as Frikka, I've also seen it spelled "Fricka", but the spelling of Frigg(a) seems to be more Norse oriented. PA Deutsch has evolved quite a bit from standard High German in terms of language, that is for sure, but then after 300 years or so away from the ancestral home that could be expected as much as America and England in terms of speech.

Wod(i)n is very close to the Angle-Saxon "Woden", the Frisians (Holland) seem to use "Wodan", Freya Aswynn identifies him as both Wotan and Wodan. So the Norse Odin seems very lost as does Thor to Donner/Donar regarding the Germans. It really makes one wonder why there are so many similarities in goddess names and so many differences in the names of our gods...as well I've never read German materials regarding Norse figures such as Niord or Skadhi, but there are German figures that seem to be unknown to the Norse as well.

All I can say to end this is that they are responsive to the pronunciations I use when communing with them. But then again, they have many kennings I Norse/Icelandic lore as identified by Kveldulf Gundarsson.

Greg

Hi Greg.. nice to meet you... Bucks County resident here, too. Several other Pennsylvania German speakers and I had a long discussion about how to address Frigga, and it seemed all of us kept the spelling Frigga while using the Pennsylvania German pronunciation, which is

more like Free-ya (not to be confused with Freya, of

course). Wodin is the spelling we have been using for Odin, and there was an archaic "Wodinschdaag" for Wednesday out there. Most of the other names we seem to already use the German forms or transliterated the Norse form (which is not what I would prefer, so I am with you on that).

Rob

And while of course I understand the equivalent names and kennings, my suggestion is that we should try to keep our references to our gods and goddesses in German rather than Norse terms, in keeping with our traditions of Hexerei/Braucherei and Deutsch in general. For example, Frey/Freyr is a Norse term, he is known as Froh/Froh Ing to the Germans. Frigga is Frikka, Odin is Wotan/Wodan, Thor is Donner,> etc.

Greg

Seems to be simultaneously Sanskrit and Norse: Gná is, in Norse mythology, one of the three handmaids of Frigg, together with Fulla and Hlín. She is the one who takes care of Frigg's matters around the world. Probably for this reason she owns a horse called Hófvarpnir, who is able to move through air. She is one of the fourteen goddesses described by Snorri Sturluson.

http://en.wikipedia.org/wiki/Gn%C3%A1

Abstract

The metrical distribution of Rigvedic doublets like dyaus and diyaus is one of the foundations of Edgerton's theory of Proto-Indo-European semivowel alternation. The metrical distribution of the forms covered by Edgerton's theory is here compared with the distribution of words having different phonological structure but identical metrical shape, and it is seen that there is no difference between their distributions in statable metrical environments. In addition, a number of constraints on the incidence of Rigvedic semivowel alternation are pointed out, such as its strict limitation to the vocoid semivowels y and v, and it is argued that these constraints are difficult to account for in terms of the Sievers-Edgerton hypothesis. Rigvedic evidence provided the principal testimony for Edgerton's formulation of his hypothesis of semivowel alternation, but it is shown here, on the basis of the same text, that in its usually accepted form the Sievers-Edgerton hypothesis is neither necessary nor sufficient to account for the observed behavior of postconsonantal semivowels in word-initial position.

http://links.jstor.org/sici?sici=0097-

in Sanskrit: (gná) meaning 'wife, divine female, kind of goddess', or (jani), meaning 'woman, wife, mother', and also 'birth, production', as a verb 'generate, beget, procreate'. [Bibl.10,11] All this points into a common origin of not only of these words, but also of the cult of respect for a "Great Blessed Woman" originally maybe as an ancestor, later as a God. The mythologists call her "Mother Nature" or "Earth Mother". Today the Blessed Virgin is her representation.

http://users.tpg.com.au/etr/rovas/clu/clues.html

Gná: goddess from ICELANDIC HORSE NAMES
http://www.tolt.net/names.html

Her name, moreover, is the same as that found in India. There, the Gnas were a collection of powerful Vedic goddesses whose name translates as "The Goddesses". It is also derived from IE words for woman', including PIE *gwen, Skt gana, Av jani, ON kona, Goth qens, Grk gyne, Arm gin, Welsh benyw, Svl zena, Tocharian s'än, and so on (

Eng queen, kin). Lofn, Lofe, Lofua, Lufn, Vjofn ('Love'> She founded the institution of marriage and presided over its ceremonies. She was also the goddess of premarital affairs, and of marriagereconciliation. In a wider function she maintained harmony amongst mankind.

http://eternalmysteries.com/viewpost_292922.asp

I see my mind is not the only one that was set ablaze! Hunter, my man, you just added more fuel to the fire. This info is amazing! Some of it I knew (the relationship of the Slavic zena to queen), some of it is new information.

Rob

We've spoken much in the past of the Indo-European connections with the likes of the Merseburg charms. Some personal info given from my mentor- Lee Gandee traced quite a few things the Germans used to Indo-European roots and believed the Druids were also influenced by them. Lee also believed the Druids spread the knowledge to "Germania".

I also read the post attributed to "Bandelle", who I have known personally for quite a few years. We dedicated our son at her home 2001 at Sonnewendfeuer and led a German ritual in Lancaster during their "Pagan Pride" gathering attended by notables such as Silver Raven Wolf and Ray Malbrough- we still chuckle when we went to call the guardians and all the Wiccans turned East instead of North where a real Hex should always start and end at! The "papers" mentioned, as well as many very old and obscure books from which he based his theories. were offered by Lee to my mentor, who kicks himself to this day for not accepting them. One thing mentioned there I think may be a bit inaccurate- I was told Lee died in 1989, not 1998.

Also, according to Norse/Icelandic sources, it is believed that Frikka has much more than 3 handmaidens.

Greg

Well of all the Gna variants I like the Welsh, Benyw and of course Zena, what is Svl and abbreviation for? Always fantasized about going a couple rounds with Lucy Lawless. As far as her horse, Hófvarpnir, or 'hoof thrower' a stallion, capable of moving through the air and over water. I like the pairing of female rider on a stallion, from my own days on and being thrown off the back of a horse, my preference was mares. There is always that chemistry you have with the sexes, the kind that attracts and the kind that repels and it is very much the basis of human animal relationships. Of course when I get on the back of horse and take off in a nice canter through Prospect Park up here, I feel like a god. If you want to get that Heathen feeling back in your loins, ride a horse.........and don't just walk or trot neither.

Anyway, now that we have traveled to ancient India via Gna, it reminds me of an image I encountered, that struck me in someway as being Deitsch in a distelfink kind of way. The story is this, my neighbor has this image on her wall for many years, each time I would visit her, I would always visit "It". It got to the point where I was making a nuisance out of myself and I was no longer as interested in visiting her as I was visiting this image. Unfortunately she did not share my belief that something sacred was there.This went on for quite a while as I searched for its origin. Now not only do I have an origin but I know where, Orissa a state in India along the Bay of Bengal, from what source, Bhagavad Gita, part of the epic Mahabharata, which I think is the longest epic poem in the world. I think I prefer nava-gunjara to the great form of Krishna is called virat-rupa (omnipresent or vast

form). It strikes me as more "country" More accessible and works better as a sign/symbol which is what I primarily work with in Hexology. The nava-gunjara is a composite magical animal: "In this telling of the tale, Vishnu himself proceeds to a hill where Arjuna is doing penance in a forest. Here, Vishnu reveals himself to Arjuna in the nava-gunjara form, a vigorous animal standing on three legs, those of the elephant, tiger, and horse. The fourth limb is not an animal leg, but an upraised human arm, the hand of which is holding a lotus flower. Besides these four creatures, Vishnu-nava-gunjara also has the head of a rooster, the neck of a peacock, the hump of a bull, and the waist of a lion. A snake comprises the tail. When Arjuna saw this creature, he immediately recognized it as the virat-rupa of Vishnu-Krishna. He threw aside the bow and arrows he had been carrying, folded his hands, and invoked the Lord's blessing."

Figure 30 "Navagunjara" from Orissa, India

Zena and the nava-gunjara

Interesting. I have a copy of the Mahabharata (interesting read regardless of one's faith! I am sure it is even better in Sanskrit, but it's just a fun story even in English). I will have to go back to that section. I see the lotus flower sticking up from the human hand, but what is hanging down? Almost looks like a mead horn!

Rob

Yeah, I know, that threw me for quite a while, but there is no mention of it other than part of the lotus flower. The Horn is a huge symbol all over the place. But as a Nine animal composite it is unique, and the paint them still today in Orissa, much in the same manner as we do hex signs, they are sold cheaply in the markets, here is another version:

http://www.asianart.com/articles/patachitra/gods/navagunjara.jpgWe hold the peacock in special regard, are you familiar with that?I forget the reason, bird of paradise or something along those lines.

Hunter

Figure 31 "A Deitsch Navagunjara" 2008 Hunter M. Yoder

Hexing to Heal? and Lee Gandee and Weberite heresy and The Mahantongo Vall

Going back to the Gandee latter, this was communicated to me today in a note from my mentor-

"I do have the letter that Bandelle has and I also have his official death notice from the newspaper which says 1989. That lady who published that letter is trying to discredit Lee because she feels he slighted a distant ancestor of hers. I've communicated with her some time ago. As best I can figure, he may have gotten some details of the Weberite heresy incorrect but what she objected to was the allocations of sexual misconduct. I kept searching and found that Lee's statements were correct. Other writers from the period basically said the same thing. The Weberites were getting naked, dancing and screwing. You know, I'd be proud of such an ancestor! Go figure".

Greg

Hey Greg

Yeah I had this up beginning of the month. He lived to a ripe old age. I see that his papers were auctioned off which seems peculiar, did your mentor get in on that?

Hunter

Hey Hunter,

No he didn't, those papers and his rare books were the materials my mentor Jack was offered (Jack's book will be out sometime early in 2008 and he had a article recently published in "Hex" magazine), and that he kicks himself over not taking. As far as his age, obviously the year of his death is inaccurate but yes, he lived a long life and hopefully his "Zaida" has reincarnated- Lee's spirit seemed to be more comfortable in a female body and he predicted in advance of his death that he would do so in his next focus.

I was going to comment on "hexing to heal" sooner or later so I'm glad you asked the question. It is a valid procedure, I am sure others here must know of this, and it is simple- you heal using your right hand with the thumb extended (the thumb is referred to as the "Wodenspaenne" in Germanic Hex) in deference to Wotan/Woden, making an equal armed cross (a healing rune can also be used) in a N- S-E-W manner 3x over the affected area. The goddess Eir usually gets the credit as the great healer and physician of our ancestral culture, but when you contemplate the full meaning of the 2nd Merseburg charm, it is apparent that Wotan is the most skilled healer among the gods, and this is often overlooked because of his fearsome reputation! So, what Lee is saying is that you would use your left hand to hex. The exact motion is not the same as used for healing and not one I would describe here on this board because it can cause great harm if not used for the right reasons-this gesture is the same one Lee used when he caused an entire healthy orchard to wither and die, and it's effects would cause the same eventual damage to animals and humans alike. I only learned it because it was shown to me as part of my training, and was well warned of the danger in using it.

Greg

Thanks Greg!

Thats some good instruction there. As far as that Weberite letter, Lee wrote. The part that caught my attention was:

"Information does not exist by itself. Connected with it is the consciousness of all those who understand it, perceive it, or originate it. So there are not records in terms of objective, forever-available banks of information into which you tune. Instead, the consciousness that held, or holds, or will hold the information attracts it like a net. The information itself wants to move toward consciousness. It is not dead or inert. It is not something you grab for, it is also something that wants to be grabbed, and so it gravitates to those who seek it. Your consciousness attracts the consciousness that is already connected with the material . "

That is so Lee R. Gandee, although I think he got it from that wacky spiritualist book that was a best seller back in the seventies, "Seth Speaks" Lee mentions that book in the letter. I think I still have a copy of it somewhere. So its safe to assume that Lee's interest in the 'Weberites' was because they were Hexes.

Any titles for your mentor's book yet? Whats the link on the Hex magazine article?

Hunter

Deitsch Weather Lore

Deitsch Folkways include 'weatherisms': Extracted and Excerpeted from Pennsylvania Dutch Folklore, Elmer L. Smith, Applied Arts Publishers, Lebanon, Pa, 1960:

If the children are boisterous, rain is coming.

A mackerel sky,

The wind will be high;

Then bring in the grain,

Close by there is rain.

If the ears of corn burst, a mild winter will follow.

If the ears of corn are plump, a cold winter will follow.

A thick husk on corn means a long, cold, hard, winter. If the ears of

corn protrude from the husk, the winter will be short and mild.

If the rooster crows at 10 p .m., it will rain before morning.

If the rooster sits on top of the fence to crow, there will be a rain

storm during the day.

Early morning rain and old women's dances don't last long.

If the hair on a dog becomes heavy during the fall of the year, one may expect a long winter.

When the women hang their legs out of bed while sleeping, it is a sign that the weather is warm enough to plant corn.

If the chickens moult on the forepart of the body first, the early part of winter will be severe. If on the rear, then the end of winter will be severe.

Whatever the weather is on the fifth day of the month, so it will be the rest of the month.

Whatever the weather is like on the last Friday of the month, so it will be the following month.

When the breastbone of a goose is held up to the light, if it shows dark allover it is a sign of a long severe winter. If it is mottled, the darker spots indicate frost and the lighter spots indicate snow. A general transparency of the bone indicates an open winter. (The condition of the front part of the bone foretells the state of that season before Christmas and the other part the weather after Christmas.)

If it rains before seven, the sun will shine before eleven.

If the wind comes from the east when you start a fire, you can expect fair weather.

It will rain in the afternoon if the fields are covered with cobwebs in the morning.

If the spleen of a hog be short and thick, the winter will be short.

When snow is on the ground, if turkeys go to the field there will be athaw.

http://www.horseshoe.cc/pennadutch/culture/customs/weather.htm

I like this one for no particular reason:

"When the women hang their legs out of bed while sleeping, it is a sign that the weather is warm enough to plant corn. "

and this one, because it is so opposite what you would expect for good weather:

"If the wind comes from the east when you start a fire, you can expect fair weather."

Hunter

Some old ways of my grandmother. Will cause bad luck

Shoes on the bed or table

Hat on the bed or table

Right hand or eye itching

cat crossing your path going from left to right

Signs of impending good luck

left hand or eye itching

Cat crossing your path going from right to left

Hey has anybody ever heard this little kids song.

Here come the spider

He's been in my house

What does he want

Cake, Cake, Cake

Ilsa

Facing North in the PA Deitsch Hexerei tradition and Labrador Tea

I have heard explanations on this but I'm still unsatisfied. Intuitively, its easy to accept, my own 'unorthodox' explanation, growing up in Berks County with a view of a certain mountain visible almost everywhere in that locality, the direction we faced was there, or X. How this works outside of that context was always puzzling. Naturally, my intuition was to go with the greatest magnetic force. It was the magnetic pull of the compass not the ideal north of the polar extremity that held the power. I always felt that magnetic north had the magnitude of potency we find in sexual energy our own and those of the animals. This magnetic attraction exist locally and will cause the needle of the compass to deviate, requiring adjustments to be made in order to determine true north. This is true in Berks County with its Appalachian Rock which holds a certain form of magnetic energy, strongest at dawn and sunset. This also is true for me now at a place called 'Breezy Point' on the Rockaways which jut out from Long Island into the Atlantic Ocean. The Ocean currents, especially strong and organized here seem to be the source of this same energy. I would be interested in the more traditional viewpoint, as long as it has some crackle to it..........

Hunter

Where does the Labrador Tea fit in? :)

Rob

What direction from here does it grow?

Hunter

Henbane Ale

Heil euch,

We recently killed a couple bottles of the most amazing Henbane methaglin

(mead), brewed by a friend, while at a Jul rite in Michigan last weekend.

Absolutely amazing. This is the recipe she sent me. I am not sure where she got

it (I'll have to ask) but it may have originated in SACRED AND HEALING HERBAL

BEERS as well. It is sublime!

Although not in the habit of photographing our garden, I will get some photos next season, as I am quite convinced that for some reason, we have the healthiest, largest henbane plants known (some get as tall as 6 feet). We have a really good strain around here, it's feral to the point that it's been classified as a noxious weed in the state. Regarding the datura, it's definately D. Stramonium and grows here as an annual. It's just too cold for it to overwinter. We live in a mountain valley so it's not too "high desert" feeling here but just over the montain range you'll find desert (no cactus) and if you continue north from there you'll meet the edge of the Frank Church wilderness area and that is absolutely the wildest part of the lower 48, replete with wolves, bears and anything else you may (or may not) want to run into. Hundreds of square miles of roadless wilderness there. We spend a lot of time there in the summer months. As far as amanita muscaria goes, it's reportedly found near one lake here in the state about three hours from here but I've never seen it....yet!

There are so many questions I would like to ask, but I understand that this information is hard won and not easily gained. Perhaps in time I

Henbane Metheglin

1 quart honey

3 quarts water, divided

1 pkg yeast (I used champagne yeast)

.5 oz henbane leaves or seeds, finely ground (I used leaves)

Check the directions on the package of yeast to prepare it correctly.

Add henbane (I tied it in a coffee filter so I wouldn't have to strain it) to 2 cups of water. Bring to a boil, simmer for 30 minutes.

Mix honey and remaining water, heat until 165 or so degrees. Simmer for 30 minutes, skimming off scum. Combine honey water and henbane infusion. Pour into prepared plastic bucket. If using a carboy wait until it has cooled. Cool to 70 degrees, or the temperature recommended on yeast package. Add the yeast. Cover and let ferment for 16 to 26 days. I racked this after a couple weeks before bottling. You may add a little sugar to each bottle before bottling if you want it to be bubbly.

Figure 32 Henbane, grown by and photographed by Hunter Yoder

Pennsilfaanisch Deitch Appalachia Schamanische

I have an interesting Yuul tale to tell as we gather round the fire. About a year ago, a friend of mine Frank Blank, through his various South American connections became aware of the fact that the center for High Andean Shamanism in North America was, near Roanoke, Virginia, more specifically in the Blue Ridge Mountains. My friend snapped, couldn't believe it, being of PA Deitsch descent from Northern Berks County, he was very possesive of his Mountains, his Appalachian Mts, even the ones in Virginia. He was determined that he would create through his own life experiences in Berks County a tradition of Shamanic thought, rooted in the the ways of his ancestors, the Pennsilfaanisch Deitch. He contacted childhood friends, old lovers, to see if their experience corroborated his own. Through his old habit of painting eight pointed stars he came upon the word, Braucherei and then Hexerei, it was like the most unbelievable verification of what his intuition had insisted existed. He had a tradition that had been waiting all along for him to discover it. His love of his Mountains has brought him to this place. It is a very strong emotion.

*Of this I am glad of, it sounds to me like you are HOME.

BE WELCOMED HOME, Hunter/Frank!

I sit with you beside this Yule fire Hunter...

Patricia

Re: Pennsilfaanisch Deitch Appalachia Schamanische

Here we are again by the fire, my deepest thanks to you Patricia for

letting me sit here aside of you and the others on the list to enjoy the heat and light, tonite. Here is a recent picture of a certain Mountain in Berks County taken very close by, actually across the road from Jesse's place at the foot of this promontory. Her Mother-in Law, a wonderful women, told me where to go early in the morning to take alittle walk and get a good shot of
it.....

Figure 33 The Pinnacle, Berks County, PA photo, Hunter Yoder

My attachment to these Mountains is not unique, but there isn't a lot of direct supporting literature other than the ole Foxfire publications of the early seventies. certainly within Deutsch mysticism the mountains play many a key role, In fact when I was a teenager, and the filmmaker Leni Riefenstahl, who was only allowed to be shown in clandestine underground screenings, prior to the featured event, "Triumph of the Will" was such a maiden/mountain myth shown in a 'short' cinematic form. We're talking the early seventies which was a very different time, the private screening was at the 'Old Dutch Mill" and it was organized by the local branch of a group out of Chicago, led by the recently deceased charismatic, George Lincoln Rockwell...........I experienced this and more and have very mixed feelings about this great Teutonic tragedy. Hopefully this content is not too strong or offensive to those of the list. Seems to have been the 'karma' of Deutschland to be unified, built up and then down torn down over and over and over again. This had a great deal to do with my hesitancy to once again embracewith those ancient Germanic ways.

Definitely your attachment to those mountains is not unique... I hold a warm love for the same chain of mountains, probably just some different peaks and ridges. lol

There are some stories that I remember from when I was a child... some are recorded, some are not. I guess I am going to have to pull out my Echoes of Scholla book to see whether I can find some of the Neversink tales.

The Eternal Hunter still rides through along the Blue Mountain ridge right where the Lehigh Tunnel passes through it... People still send others out on Elbedritsche (snipe) hunts. Lol Eileschpiggel (known by like 14 different variations of the Eulenspiegel name) still plays his pranks of the Deitsche. Hexenwolf still frightens some people out in the woods near Oley.

The ghosts of Hessian solders still haunt Charming Forge and Hessian Camp.

The Torchbearer spirits, a tale that I have not heard in ages, may still roam some of the back roads of Mt. Penn from time to time. Dutch Mary/Mountain Mary and South Mountain Man are still out there. While looking for lore on Eulenspiegel, I came across this:

http://tinyurl.com/3ckl5w

Rob

You are a Carbon county man? Mau Chunk or Jim Thorpe is really something, really historic, Back when anthracite was black gold, I think there were more millionaires per capita in Carbon county then anywhere else, yeah that Lehigh tunnel and the ole turnpike. Some of those coal mining towns are still frozen in time. I know those falls just behind Mau Chunk pretty well. We'd hike over from Berks Co up to where 309 crosses over, guess that lehigh County.

Hunter

I grew up in Berks County, but both of my parents grew up in Carbon County. The mountains in Carbon County are definitely beautiful despite all the destruction wrought by the coal and zinc companies. My family has tracts of land in numerous places, some of which are still like driving back into the 1950s. Peaceful towns, salt-of-the-Earth Folk, still heavily Pennsylvania German and more than a bit attuned to the old ways in many of the towns (though Carbon County is also pretty much the northern limit of Deitscherei.

Oh yeah

I almost bought a place in a funny ole town, Lansford, between Tamaqua and Mau Chunk, there, coulda gotten the place for practically nothing in the early 2000's on foreclosure.Mostly Eastern european churchs and such. I really like that area into Skuykill County there, Barnesville is nearby for the Beer fest. Yeah the strip mining or all those hills of mining slag don't help realestate prices, much but I kinda like it. Centralia is my favorite with the 100 year old underground mine fire. Visiting Centralia is pretty wild, especially during a snowstorm. The movie "Silent Hill" should have been set there. Lol "Centralia during a Snowstorm" sounds like a painting by, J.M.W. Turner, Any favorite promontories along the ridge, Rob?

Heres another view of the Pinnacle from Owls Head:

Figure 34 Pinnacle from Owls Head, photo Hunter Yoder

Hunter

I have a pic of me somewhere on a rock at the pinnacle of Hawk Mountain, which is one of my favorites. Ever been to the River of Rocks? That would be a good place for a blot or for meditation. Pictures don't do it justice, but for those who are not familiar with it, it is a mile-long swath of land full of giant boulders. It is almost like several layers of the Earth got totally reversed.

http://en.wikipedia.org/wiki/Hawk_Mountain

Then in Bucks County we have Ringing Rocks, which is truly an amazingplace. Another place that would be great to meditate and blot.

Rob

Yeah, Frank's autistic too started back in the seventies when he got hit on the head and wandered around for a couple of days without knowing who he was, finally ended up in Lenhartsville, where he took up residency at the Deutsch Eck Hotel and drew this image on a napkin while he was sipping some Heaven hill with a beer chaser: don't look like no hex sign neither...........

Hunter

Greetings Patricia!

Thank you very much on all accounts for the warm welcome and kind words. Again, it's my pleasure and honor to be here with so many kindred spirits! Regarding the Wolfbund, there are actually several folks there with a healthy interest in Hexerei and Braucherei and one woman in particular who hand paints a tremendous amount of hex signs for her personal work but I believe she's going to be making some available to the public before too long. I'll see about getting them here, as I know they will be highly interested in the conversation held here. There is a GREAT deal of crossover between what we are doing and what the folks here are elbow deep into. We utilize peculiar strands o Traditional philosophical and magical knowledge, and Hexerei is an exceptionally potent discipline. But most of us weren't fortunate enough to have been raised and "educated" within the cultural matrix of the Pennsilfaanisch Deitch!

Thank you again and best Julfest wishes to the list members and their families.

Wodesheil,

Cody

An oldie for Hunter and other Kutztowners

Reading, du aarmi Schtadt

Drucke Brot, un des net satt

Kutztown, du reichi Schtadt

Jellybrot un allfatt satt

- an old insult rhyme from the Kutztown area...

Reading, thou poor city

Dry bread and never satisfied

Kutztown, thou rich city

Jelly bread and always satisfied

A counting rhyme we used to use to choose who was "it" when playing

games:

Een, zwee, drei

Hicker, hocker, hei

Zucker uff 'm Brei

Salz uff' 'm Schpeck

Haahne, geh mol weck

Du schtinkscht noch Hinkeldreck

Wilkum and Background

Heel Cody,

Well gee, thanks there mate. Hopefully this will give Swanhilde (my wife) the much needed context for her emerging craft. Swanhilde seems to have an incredible natural ability to create and paint these powerful symbols. Of course I'll let her tell more about herself and perhaps share some of the images of the Hexes she has produced.

And I look forward to the continued thread here as well.

Prosit!

Walawulfaz

Quoting Hunter Yoder :

Well my experience with odd numbers in this respect is that they usually are the preceding even number plus one, Say the Heathen number nine, it goes eight plus the center Midgaard, A Pentecost to use a Greek term is a week (seven) of weeks (seven) plus one or 7 X 7 plus 1 or fifty. Seven is included in Hexology by the great Lee R. Gandee's "The Great and Seven Lesser Seals": which he describes as "the six steps of Creation, and to the completed Creation" But despite what Greg says, Gandee was Christian and this six days of creation and the seventh day of rest is Biblical, and I assure you that the Amish/Mennonites served the Seven sweet and Seven Sour dishes on a certain Sabbath.

Hunter

While I'm not a numerologist, I am a runologist, and the number 7 figures very esoterically in the scheme of things. Seven is a 'prime' number, meaning it cannot be divided equally, it stands as a 'fixed' point in the multiverse. Seven is the rune :gibo: (Elder system) which means 'gift' on a basic level, it follows the rune of creative power :kenaz:, and precedes the rune of 'ecstasy', or :wunjo/wynn:. Using the method of number reduction within the parameters of the Elder 24 (any number greater than 24 is reduced by adding the components together), 7x7=49 or 13(4+9), the rune :eihwaz: emerges, the rune of life and death. Adding 7+7 gives you 14, the rune of :perdhro:, the rune of the Norns

and wyrd/fate. Finally, if you work the numbers in terms of their runic opposites, an interesting pattern emerges - 1+24=25 (2+5=7), 2+23=25/7, 3+22=25/7, and so on til you reach center or 12+13=25/7. So then, a great deal of mystery and power is wrapped up in the number 7, and in many respects, it is a number of completeness.

Valulfr

Finally a number guy! Its completion exists in Hexology as a six sided figure or star if you like, with a CENTER as in Gandee's Great and lesser Seals: The runes have the Gematria too? no doubt.

New Year's Day Pork and Sauerkraut?

Finally a number guy! Its completion exists in Hexology as a six sided figure or star if you like, with a CENTER as in Gandee's Great and lesser Seals: The runes have the Gematria too? no doubt.

Heil Rob

Well in PA Deitsch kultura, you will run into this all day long and I has been a source of problems here initially. The Christian aspect is almost impossible to remove. Its not really an issue for me, because I wasn't a very good Christian and probably not a very good Heathen, but the Hexen/Shamanisch aspects I fair somewhat better. I compare it to pieces of cloth, fabric a structure lets call it a religious faith, place several together and pour water on top, it passes through all of them, they all become wet from this water. That is how I see this kultur

Hunter

Absolutely agreed. We are all influenced by our histories, ancestry, ancestors' actions and experiences, etc. I don't feel the need to try to wash out Christian influences per se and to pretend the conversion never happened. I honor my Christian and my pre-Christian relatives and ancestors.

However, I do want to get an idea of where some of these traditions come from and what undertones of the culture come from practices not recognized by the "Church" as Christian. Christianity absorbed many Heathen practices, and Heathenry will forever have an imprint of the Christian experience on it. What we do with that imprint in the Heathen context is what's up to us.

I can happily sit for a 7/7 dinner with a group of Christians or a group of Heathens, and I will happily incorporate the Deitsch tradition of the 7/7 into modern Urglaawe practice regardless of its origins; it's part of our identified culture at this point. :)

Rob

Heel,

Well, in the fine tradition of seeking the meaning of symbols I came across this, don't know if any here have seen it before or had it posted here-

I have also come across a site that details the immigration of Mennonites to a district in Russia if anyone is interested -

Valulfr

Heel Valufir

Hopes that right, anyway, nice links, the first one with the headstones is of course completely christian, the second is very interesting, "Catherine II of Russia had invited Germans and other Europeans to settle lands vacated by the Turks in southern Russia. She granted a special charter of privileges to the Mennonites including the right to control their own religious, educational and civic affairs. Among the privileges was the guarantee of complete religious independence and exemption from military service for all time. Catherine also granted them permission to brew beer and distill brandy.

The new colonists suffered poverty, disease and death. The promised government assistance of 500 rubles per family was delayed, wood for construction was slow in arriving, and horses were lost or stolen for lack of fences. Nevertheless, in only two decades, 400 Mennonite families had become established in 15 villages. They were farming 89,100 acres of land. In 1866, Russia revoked the Mennonite exemption from military service and required the Russian language to be taught in all schools."

I have through my native american affiliations found the Mennonitesin the Mexican Chihuahuan desert "The Mexican government desired to settle the barren northern areas of their country with industrious farmers such as the Mennonites. In 1922, at the invitation of President Alvaro Obregón, 20,000 Mennonites left Canada and settled in the state of Chihuahua. Mexico agreed to sell them land at reasonable prices and level no taxes for 100 years if the Mennonites would produce the bulk of cheese needed for northern Mexico. President Obregón granted the Mennonites full control of their schools including maintenance of their language, independence of religion in both home and schools and exemption from military service.

Canadian Mennonites began arriving in 1922, loaded with livestock, farm equipment and household goods, intending to reproduce their industrious farms in Chihuahua as their forefathers had done on the

prairies of Canada. They invested large amounts of capital in farming and transformed desolated stretches of sand and cactus into prosperous farms. They maintained well-equipped machine shops, large farm buildings and motorized transportation, although Mennonites prohibited the ownership of automobiles for common use."

http://epcc.edu/nwlibrary/borderlands/19_mennonites.htm

My interest was in the Tarahumara indigenous tribe who use peyote as an entheogen and now the two are neighbors...........the Mennonites immediately took the Tarahumara to school and introduced them to a new variety of sunflower that the Tarahumara now include as their own "Tarahumara White: This rare variety with solid gold flowers has all-white hulls. Canadian Mennonite in origin, but obtained by the Tarahumara from Chihuahuan Mennonites and cultivated for 40 years by them."

http://www.nativeseeds.org/v2/content.php?catID=1057

Hunter

If I am right, the ones in Mexico I think are the ones that we refer to as the "Old Colony Mennonites" and their garb is pretty unique. Only ever saw a few in person when they came to PA.

Rob

Hello Everybody,

I am a new member here.I have been reading the posts and find them all so very interesting and quite informative. I am from Pa. Dutch background and some of my people were Dunkards who settled in Roaring Springs, Blair County, Pa. They carried with them traditions rooted in the old country. One of them was to have pork and sauerkraut on New Years eve served at Midnight. A suckling pig was slandered and prepared (roasted) and served with sauerkraut and dumpings with mashed potatoes. I married into an old Southern Maryland family and it was their tradition to serve black eyed peas and greens with their pork. So I serve both meals, one on New Years eve and the other on New

Years Day. I now live in an area where Cuban Pork is a big thing made by marinating it in sour orange or Mojo for a day and roasted in a coffin over night and served with black beans and yellow rice. But of course, that is not Pa. Dutch tradition, but just good eat'en !!!

I grew up with my grand parents who were both of Pa. Dutch heritage, born 1894. I learned many things from them, one was the use of Psalms in healing and hexing. Does anyone know of such practices ??? In my home we also celebrated Yule with making a log and setting candles along with Christmas. And as a child visiting our relatives who lived on the ridges, talk of changelings was common, and precautions were made to keep children safe from being stolen. I would be interested in your input or thoughts on these topics.

Many New Year Blessings,

Orva

Where you at now? I'll be right over, ha ha ha Sounds like Miami or East Bergen, NJ Thats a good tradition, in a coffin, maybe I'll try that this year tell us more..........

Hunter,

I live a few miles out of Key West and have loved here for about 10 years moving from Southern Maryland. As I mentioned my mother and her parents were from Pa. A lot of Cuban and Caribbean cooking has found its way into my cooking, especially with pork and chicken dishes. When living in Maryland I learned from my husband's family how to stuff a ham the Southern Maryland way using a corned ham...very local, it can be found only in 4 counties there. It is stuffed with greens and onion and red pepper. The greens used are cabbage (lots of it) mustard greens and kale. Collards were not used much because they are a bit course or tough in texture. They made a lot of low country dishes from the Carolina's and cajun food too. As far as my Pa. Dutch cooking goes, which I learned from my grandmother's knee, was how to make egg noodles and dumplings, pork and meat dishes. Chicken pot pies. All the veggies were home grown and canned in our summer kitchen. Roots were stored in a root cellar and home made ale and root beer was brewed and bottled. Of course, cider. Apple butter was always on the table.

Pasta was un heard of and I didn't eat spaghetti or Chinese food till I was grown !!!

There was much in my Pa. Dutch up bringing that I would like to understand more. I want to pass some of this stuff down to my grand children and want to know more of what it is all about and understand more of what I was taught growing up.

Thank you for the warm welcome.

Orva

Re: New member

Hey Ovra1

Like I told my Schwester, who just sent me an insane seed catalog (all those plants you wanted to grow but your mother wouldn't let you) After reading your post, I immediately went out to purchase a nonstick coffin for the pork and sauerkraut dish for New Years day......maybe you could tell us some more about that? Wow, just out of Key west, I guess thats the Keys, I love Miami and South Beach, Have some Cuban friends here in Brooklyn, real good people and some great food, I'm big on the plantain 'madura' with the yellow rice and beans with roast pernile, maybe a bacalao salad on the side, and some flan with cafe con leche for desert.........yum but if you want to quick track it into some real good Pennsylvania Dutch food, checkout this link:

http://www.dietrichsmeats.com/index.htm

Maybe they'll ship you something- You have good life experiences there from your Grandmother, you are very lucky for that. The Schwesters will take real good care of you. The tradition of sympathetic magic we discuss here is Hexerei, and it is far older and more primitive a form of witchcraft then wicca. The Christian form is Braucherei. Perhaps your Grandmother also passed some of these things to you! You have a unique perspective, and some of us here also recognize the the brotherhood and sisterhood we have with HooDoo, VooDoo, Santeria and Macumba.

Hunter

Hi Hunter,

There are a couple of ways to roast Cuban Pork.. but using a coffin is how we roast a whole piglet.

I marinate the pork shoulder or butt or little whole pig in Mojo Criollo sauce over night with lots of crushed garlic and onion added. Rub it down good with salt and pepper. You could also use sour orange if you can find it. Then into the coffin it goes. The coffin is a wooden box lines with metal and a lid that has metal on top. A hole is dug in the ground and the dressed pig and coffin is put into the hole. Then bar b que bricketts are placed on top and lit. When the coals are going good and turn white, palm froms are put over it to keep the heat in. As the evening goes on more coals are added and it is kept burning low all evening. In the morning the coffin is lifted out, and the lid comes off and the pig is nice and brown and when touched falls off the bone... makes my mouth water thinking about it. I am going over to a friends house tomorrow late afternoon to have some. Rum is the traditional drink served...actually mojitos.

My husband's family roast hogs (the really big guys) using large oil tanks that have been cleaned and seasoned. They put grates in it an then cooks it over a open fire all night. It takes about 4 men and about 14 cases of beer to get it done... but it is all so very good. The weddings and funerals lasted for days !

Nothing like Cuban cheese toast and a con leche light with two sugars to jump start you in the mornings. For a hang over the cure is Bucie... pure liquid caffeine. Just one once and it will take the rust right out of your pipes.,,,, been there done a many time... Key West is a very interesting town. Nothing like Miami or South Beach, which I really like, but Key West and the lower keys where I live (Big Pine Key) is very colorful.

You have good life experiences there from your Grandmother, you are very lucky for that. Thank you, they were very basic and very loving. The tradition of sympathetic magic we discuss here is Hexerei, and it is far older and more primitive a form of witchcraft then wicca. The Christian form is Braucherei. Perhaps your Grandmother also passed some of these things to you!

Yes this is what I am very interesting in learning about. Growing up and what was taught to me at home was NEVER talked about outside of the house. My grand father settled in Washington DC after the depression form Pa. and got a government job working as a machinist in the Navy Yard. Then when I was 2 yrs. old we moved into a rural part of Southern Maryland where my grand parents continued in the Pa. Dutch traditions. Now here is where my mind flows with tons of questions about the Hexerei...terms like this are not familiar to me. Is this the hex signs and such ???

You have a unique perspective, and some of us here also recognize the

the brotherhood and sisterhood we have with HooDoo, VooDoo, Santeria

and Macumba. Yes I can see such in these practices, Hoodoo is familiar to me, and similar in some of the root practices. Santeria is also interesting and I have had many interesting encounters with it and the people who practice it. I mix it with my own belief system at times, especially when hurricane season is here, oh yes... candles to Oya / St. Theresa big time.

Thank you for the links and for again, a warm Welcome ... I have much to learn here and I can see a very generous and friendly place to do it.

Orva

Re: [hexenkunst] Re: New member

Hunter wrote:

The tradition of sympathetic magic we discuss here is Hexerei, and it is far older and more primitive a form of witchcraft then wicca. The Christian form is Braucherei.

Not quite as simple as that, Bruder.

There are many, many, many pre-Christian elements incorporated into the practice of Braucherei as well. (Speaking for us at the Three Sisters here)The use of those elements depends on the practitioner. It is our main effort to reclaim those lost pieces of Braucherei that were thrown off and discarded possibly in the name of Christianity but it is also important to honor those in our Freundschaft that came strictly from the Christian tradition. Like Rob mentioned, they are all our elders and ancestors, and they kept the lineage alive for us through much adversity. We are so fortunate to have access to a huge ecelectic historical blending of practices. It is especially more meaningful and powerful if it strikes a chord within you or the person you are tending to which is much more important for healing than strict dogma and rules...whether it's a heathen or Christian charm or prayer,It all works. Using the same words that many elders before us have uttered is good medicine but so is incorporating information directly from an ancient handwritten charm or from helping spirit guides. Its all very intuitive and creative...and not at all strictly Christian.

Don't want to get hung up on semantics again, but just wanted to make it a bit more clear.

Susan

Figure 35 Salvia Divinoruum, collection of Frank Blank

Mother's Night...

Here's how we were taught to do it in the old country manner- Tonight
at dusk, the season of Weihnachten (the holy nights) begins, lasting
through New Year's Day. The children and I will decorate Patty's chair
with balloons, ribbons, and thank you notes for all she does throughout
the year. While that happens, Patty will begin the official ritual taught to
us by my Austrian advisor, as it has been done for untold centuries in his
family. We will open the windows and doors. Using a mixture of
incense, Patty walks our property 3x starting at the North and invites
both our ancestors as well as those discarnate spirits in need of
merriment and warmth into our home, using an incantation also taught
to us that will draw the spirits like moths to a flame. All spirits are
invited to stay as long as they are peaceful and leave any negativity at
the door. It is a highly profound experience, I have felt the sensation of
being held, smelled cologne and perfume, and the presences of my
father, grandparents, and friends. This year will be hard because my
mother passed over in January.

On Sonnewendfeuer/Winter Solstice, we will make our wishes for 2008.
After they are written in English, I have everyone rewrite them in runic
form to give them special power to reach our gods and goddesses, and
then each of us tucks them into the wreath of evergreen that I construct
from a living tree. This is displayed above our altar and prayed upon
each night during the season. A ritual also takes place.

We have another ritual that we do on the evening of the 24th and another on "Twelfth Night", New Year's Eve. We hide the Weihnachten pickle on the tree after the kids have gone to sleep and they have a blast trying to be the first to find it. On New Year's morning at dawn (my family just loves this part, ahem), I go into each room with our altar bell and ring it in the corners, under the beds, and in the closets, giving the spirits notice that the season has ended and that they are free to leave should they wish to.

I hope that adds some further insights into our people did during the season. The ability to contact the world of spirit is at no time higher than the exception of Samhain (also celebrated by the Germans for those who didn't know). Happy Weihnachten to all, and many blessings!

Oops, I neglected to mention that the wreath containing the runic wishes is burned on New Year's Day to send them on their way to our gods and goddesses. Also, on Sonnewendfeuer night, at midnight you should light the log so that it is burning brightest at dawn. This symbolizes the return of Lady Sunna. The ashes from the log should be saved (if no fireplace, you can do this with the wreath). They can be mixed with vervain, rue, amaranth, and nettles for protection from the ice giants, and can be wrapped in a Himmelsbrief or placed in a muslin bag and carried.

Greg

FYI list information on Pow wow book...

Do you have any opinion on this:

"Hex Craft" Dutch Country Pow-wow Magick by Silver Raven Wolf

I think Greg knows the author, but is it based on reality or not?

Well, I have met the author several times and respect her on some levels, but she is not interested in furthering our ways at the expense of her eclecticism. Otherwise, her training by a legitimate Pow Wow was for real*

Anything by Silver Ravenwolf is...kinda questionable. I don't discount that she does know something, and has presented it to an early audience several years back, to get them aware that the German-American community *had* a *native healing* tradition. For this, I am grateful to her, HOWEVER...when you read the book, it reads like a wiccanized new age version of hex spells, and it uses the "goddess" formats traditionally. In a Heathen Pantheist Native faith, I've always got to question the Wiccans with "Which Goddess Now, is it you're referring TO?"

As I always like to say, if I have one "Aunt" I am referring to, that does not mean YOUR aunt is *my* aunt, just because both of them happen to be "Aunts". Gods have very real personalities, and ways of their own, and I believe this does a disservice to our forebears, and to the reclaiming of our Primal faith (Urglaawe).

It does do a disservice. I have a lot more respect for a Wiccan who follows one pantheon with dedication than one who will worship anyone at any time for whatever suits them.

I know that she has some "Tradition" that is supposed to have some links to the Old Country in her "Black Forest Tradition" in Wicca.

I think one or two persons on this list (who have left since, I did NOT throw them off btw) had been members.

***Her Black Forest tradition is a mix of Pow-Wow and Celt/British trads. Breid FoxSong and the late "Lord" Serphant was her initial mentors, the late Preston Zerbe of York County taught her PowWow. And yes I'll back you up, the Black Foresters that left did so on their own**

If you can get it cheap, on Amazon.com or whereever, a used book store, I'd say it's ok for "comparison's sake" much like the earlier books were in Asatru's formation, just because there was nothing else out there. Now, that there are a lot more Heathen Authors and Scholars, doing research in a more scholarly approach, as in the previous book I'd mentioned, Pr. Kreibel's "Pow wow" book. Llewelyn had a few good books here and there, but they are famous for getting an author in it's "stable of authors" that use 2nd and 3rd hand information, and passes it off as "scholarly work". It is nothing more in most instances, as light reading for the new age crowd. I'd call it a #101 book, if at that. It can also give you erroneous ideas of how things were practised, if one took all this Goddess stuff to heart.

The problem is most traditional cultures did NOT look upon Witches kindly, they didn't want them around. They could throw spells at a village that could make the cattle sickly, cause stillbirths to happen, and invite ill luck in, that would spell the end of the village and any prosperity they could wrest from an already acknowledged existence farming or with animal husbandry.

While I know that what you say is possible to do, in my mind it was a case of a few bad apples ruining the bunch for those wanting to live simple lives close to nature and not wishing anything more than either to help their community or to be left alone. On the other hand, people have sought out witches for cures as well as for hexing, which precisely fits the description of quite a few Hexenmeisters such as Lee Gandee, John Blymire, etc, etc

The New age community does not care to know about this, and
continues to treat a lot of these articles like Silver Ravenwolf's "Teen
Witch" series in a fluffy manner for the crowd that experienced "my
little Pony" as children. (if you catch my drift). Our Urglaawe is NOT
sunbeams and pixie dust. I am telling you to get it if you must for
comparison's sake, but not to use it as a resource, it is more akin to
Ralph Blum's book on Runes, use it for the table or chair leg that needs
a firming boost. That's mostly what it's good for.

**There is a lot of valid stuff in HexCraft that makes it a good primer.
The problem is, she Wiccanizes the material in place of the
Christianizing that was done prior to it, and obviously neither way is
true to it's roots. If you understand the lore and the functions of the
Germanic pantheon, it is not terribly difficult to identify whose ears the
charm or spell was originally intended to reach. I've converted many of
them and they work every bit as well. SRW contends that they will work
with any system as long as you have faith, and while her way is not how
I think it should be or originally was done, her point is well taken in
comparison to how the Christians have madeit work among our
people**

Greg

Howdy Bruder,

Ask Schwester Jesse about her thoughts on Silver Raven wolf. She
probably won't give her honest opinion on the list because of Greg's
connection with her. Or than again....she just might! SRW tried to take
the Christian right outa Powwow and really made alotta people mad. I
have a few of her newsletters I could share with you. It is purely
Pagan....with no regards to Christianity whatsoever. She made up her
own rules, so to speak

Susan

Galdr and Seidr

"There were two types of sorcery, galdr and seiðr. Galdr is supposed to
have been first practised and spread abroad by Odin; it was regarded as
more permissible than seiðr, and probably consisted for the most part in
magic chants and formulas,2 to some extent in combination with the
cutting of runes. Seiðr, on the other hand, owes its origin and diffusion
to Freyja. Women especially were instructed in this lower type of magic,
considered disgraceful to men. Nevertheless seiðr continued in some
measure to be practised by men, as late as the beginning of the
Christian era"

http://www.vaidilute.com/books/munch/munch-03.html

Where does Hexerei fit in here? I see this as a nonchristian discussion Simply what roles do Galdr and Seidr play in our Hexerei. Its my limited understanding that Seidr has a feminine gender connotation as in the Volver and Galdr, male. the former strong in soothsaying roles the latter in spoken or written 'charms' obviously way oversimplified

Does one or the other dominate our tradition?

Hunter

Ok, sorry, I had thought that you had wanted to know how the roles may have developed for our Christianized Ancestors...but ok, on we go.

Simply what roles do Galdr and Seidr play in our Hexerei.

The role is to be a healer within the folk, using various formats that are learned by them through their teacher and their own abilities. That is *my* interpretation, However...I guess you had better ask one of the Hexenmeisters then for further clarification, since *I* am not a practising Hexenmeister. I will wait till one have spoken.

Its my limited understanding that Seidr has a feminine gender connotation as in the Volver and Galdr, male. the former strong in soothsaying roles the latter in spoken or written 'charms' obviously way oversimplified

In the modern era, in Asatru, there have been both sexes going into both forms of magical systems. It is not like it was practised in the old days. The Wolfbund members, for one, may have their own traditions. Both sexes, for instance, can practise Runic Yoga. Some may also practise a form of Martial arts.

Does one or the other dominate our tradition?

They "should" realistically work in tandem, as harmony and the health of a society is always the goal.Is there any reason or purpose that you are seeking beyond the answer to this/these questions?

Patricia

It seems there is some difference of opinion here on list as to how Hexerei is defined. Though, regardless of one's specific definition, my simple answer would be it fits as one of many threads in our rich tapestry of Germanic magical folk traditions.

In Old English "galdor" means "song, incantation", and "sihð" means "thing seen, vision" (Pres. 3rd pers. sing. of Séon, "to see").In our Anglo-Saxon traditions we have many words for different magical practices:

drycræft - witchcraft, magic

galdorcræft - magic using song, incantation, (sung) charms

leechcræft - herbalism, magic and/or healing using herbs

lybcræft - skill in the use of drugs, magic, witchcraft

lyblác - another word for lybcræft

tungolcræft - star-craft, astronomy, astrology

(there are at least 5 other words relating to "astrology"!)

wiglung - soothsaying, augery, witchcraft, sorcery

wortcunning - another word for leechcræft

The Anglo-Saxons had at least 10 words for "sorcery". This would lead me to believe these practices were well known, and important to their folk traditions.I'm sure there are more I'm forgetting, but what I'm getting at is there are many practices, with probably some of them overlapping.

Galdor and sihð may be practices unto themselves, but may also be "techniques" applied to various other practices. While I'm not familiar with Hexerei specifically, I definitely see it as a tradition fitting in along side the many other magical traditions of the Germanic peoples.

I hope this has been helpful in regards to your question. It's very early, or late depending on one's perspective. I'm only on my first coffee; I'm hope I'm at least being coherent!

Rob Hewitt

Wilkum!

German's "Wilkommen" comes to us as "wilkum" or "wilkom" in Deitsch, depending on where you are from... (I usually write it "wikum" but you'll see "wilkom" a lot, too). Both forms appear on hex signs a lot...

I think Zook usually used "wilkom," if memory serves me right, while the others primarily use "wilkum."

The verb "to come" is "kommen" in German and "kumme" in Deitsch, hence the discrepancy in the two forms of the word "welcome" in the dialect.

There is also a rarely used form of "wilkummt" for when speaking to multiple people, but it's not common anywhere outside of Carbon County that I know of... and, being that my family comes from Carbon, that shows up in my usage on rare occasions. Usually we just use "wilkum" all the time with no element of verb declension, though I think one of my sites actually uses "wilkummt" now that I think about it.

Rob

Snow days and research

I would like to introduce myself. I am Swanhilde. Over the past year, Ihave been painting hexes. I have always been drawn to this practice, and lately I have come to understand why. Between geneology research and looking into my self, I have gleaned two specific things. My kin in the line that I feel the strongest draw to was German Refomists that settled in VA and then OH. When looking to my self, I realized that for as long as I can remember, I have been drawn to geometrical patterns. I am also empathic and do readings using the runes as my tool. When I do a reading, there is a process that starts with geometrical images in my head that represent emotions. I do not know how to explain how that works, it just does. What I do know is that when I am creating and painting hexes, I am completely at peace with myself. I will upload the fruits of my labor over the past year so you can see. I was challanged to produce one a month which I did. You can see the progression of technique as the year progressed. I could do this all day every day if life would allow it. I have found my passion and I want to learn more about the practice.

Swanhilde

Yngona Desmond

I was reading through some old mail on the Hexenkunst list when I came across this blurb. Your wrote this January 1st, so I apologize for the lateness of my reply.

[[Vцlusp6 - Seipr as Wyrd Consciousness" Yngona Desmond is a self styled

Vinland's Vцlva.]]

** I am NOT a self-styled "Vinland's Volva". First, I am recognized as a volva and thule by a tribe here in the Southlands; second, "Vinlands Volva" is a name gifted to me by Saami Noiade ('shamans') while living with them for three months. I just wanted to make that clear!

... Yngona

Hallo Yngona

The Plants and animals have been my teachers, Patricia suggested you as a human one. I am looking at your book, I like it.

Hunter

I didn't recognize this as a throw down, but so it is. You can live with whoever you want to for as long as you want to and they can call you whatever they want to. If you are "volva and thule by a tribe here in the Southlands" who is the one in the North?

As far as the southlands, I know this place, the place with the gigantic peach by the side of the hiway. You can have that place but not the

Mountains, they are all mine! I was born and raised in a place called Virginsville, a place where the Saucony and Maiden Creeks join in a place called Berks County Pennsylvania. Here we did not study the grimoires, here we studied the 'hexafoos' with a clear view of the Appalachian Mts. You have your place of power but it is not here!!!

Hunter Yoder

** LOL! No .. nothing that dramatic .. just a clarification. Dont want anyone to think Im makn' up titles. I just use the one folk yell at me.

[[If you are "volva and thule by a tribe here in the Southlands" who is the one in the North?]]

** Dont know of any volva's in the north, but I do a competant seidhman in PA.

[[As far as the southlands, I know this place, the place with the gigantic peach by the side of the hiway. You can have that place but not the Mountains, they are all mine!]]

** Uh-uh! I live 45 mins from the Appalacian Trail ... plus ride the Harley all through those hills!

[[I was born and raised in a place called Virginville, a place where the Saucony and Maiden > Creeks join in a place called Berks County Pennsylvania.]]

** Sounds lovely. I was born in the backseat of a 1958 baby blue Ford, on a US Army OD green blanket.

[[You have your place of power but it is not here!!!]]

** LOL .. you forget .. I am "Vinlands Volva" .. all

of North America is mine! :b

.... Yngona

Hallo again

"You have your place of power but it is not here!!!]]

** LOL .. you forget .. I am "Vinlands Volva" .. all of North America is mine! :b"

Your tribe, the ones who you say bequeathed you all of Vinland, the Saami Noiade may have been indulging too much in the usage of amanitas muscaria or drinking too much reindeer urine.

The Nordic expansion into North America was not altogether successful if I recall correctly.

My tribe on the otherhand, the Pennsilfaanisch Deitsch have a much longer continuous tradition here in as you say, Vinland. So in a sense, I wilkum you as our guest. May your stay in Georgia be productive.

As far as riding up through the Mountains, I prefer a Cannondale, to measure the mountain through my own will alone, and some expensive Italian components, maybe a French wheelset, German tires for power. I do watch the 'Tour de Georgia'

The first time I saw the word, 'kenning' used it was attached to discussion on the Tello Obelisk from the archaeological site of Chavin de Huantar in north-central Peru. Kenning seems to originally be used in reference to ancient Celtic or Norse 'phrases' that have multiple levels of meaning. I see them as metaphorical artifacts. I like them. Kennings can be used on strictly a visual level, and in that manner cut through thousands of years of written and verbal culture in an instant.

Not a graduate student, I like to think of myself as a simple Hexologist who sees these 'hexafoos' as windows into my tribe's deep past.

I see in your book that you have mentioned some interesting plants and trees. I too enjoy the universal language of plant growth and have experienced the 'plant consciousness' Growth, fertility, weather, protection are of interest and the desired intentions in visual prayers. I live with my family in NYC, Brooklyn. It is close enough to PA and far enough too. And there is the Ocean and the beaches very closeby. The Ocean moderates the climate, I like it and I grow Brown Turkish fig trees here. I fertilise them from the droppings of my Netherland Dwarf rabbits which I breed. I also grow cactus and anything else I feel like.

I am enjoying your book and reading it as I do, from back to front and then skipping around in it.

I don't see yet however the Saami Noiade reference..............

I see that you do reference to the Sami word 'sieide' in the introduction. and the linkage of the word Seidr to speja, spyrian, seance, and then to shaman saman, samana, sramanah.

My attraction to Seidr is exactly along those lines. I did not feel completely comfortable with Galdr or the more traditional form of Northern European witchcraft which seems to be driven by verbal or written spells. I have an aptitude for a more intuitive, visceral approach. This 'seething' you speak of is a primitive process.

The connection to the Saami and the Finno-Ugric tribes reminds me that recently it was discovered via the new DNA technology, that this group is most genetically similar to prehistoric Cro Magnon man, which is where this shamanism really begins. I particularly respond to the cliff peckings and cave paintings of geometric shapes, animals, snakes, and antlered humans who are clearly shamans.

Trance state, or altered consciousness is a requirement frequently via entheogenic plants. Strong associations with overall geometric patterns and singing or chanting.

These are elements not usually associated with Northern European Witchcraft, Hexerei and the PA Deitsch, Braucherei but there certainly is enough overlap in these related traditions. Maybe its a matter of emphasis, what are your thoughts?

But back to your book, 'Voluspa-Seidr as Wyrd Consciousness' It seems to be a loose comentary on already existing ancient texts within the 'Codex Regius' But you also mention thee'Elder Edda' the 'Hauksbok' and 'Gylfaginning' which you intersperse with more personal 'pieces'

I read the piece on Yew as Ygg'drasil and for some reason, I couldn't identify it in my head. Frequently I know the plant before I know the name. Then when I found three of them across the street from me functioning as 'hedges' I said 'Yew' of course! Interestingly enough the three house with the Yew were once owned by a German woman, Hildegaard, who liked me and would give me cans of sauerkraut from Germany which instead of being suspended in water, it was in white Rhine wine.

We have a native one here that I respond to after reading your Yew piece, its called Eastern Red Cedar but isn't really a cedar, it is Juniperus Virginiana. Grows very slowly, very upright though, and they have a flame like appearance on a landscape, like a tree spirit embodied and have a curious vibe.

Netherland Dwarfs, heres a pic of my oldest,

Figure 36 Dr Octagon

You need a yard with a good fence. No vet bills, they never have to go. Food is cheap and they are strictly vegetarians but will eat catfood if its around. My cat was terrified of them but not of dogs. That particular breed of rabbit is feisty and will growl, bite, and lunge if cornered, LOL not too much to be concerned about. They can be trained./

San Pedro cactus, also known as Huachuma or Trichocereus Pachanoi I have it and Peruvian Torch or Tricocereus Peruvianus as well as the Bolivian, Trichocereus Bridgsii or Achuma. If in pots, its best to have it in unglazed ceramic. They should almost be able to stay out year round in GA. They can take freezing temps if large enough and come from the Peruvian high desert. I assume you know why the name San Pedro........

Within the tribe I use Hunter Yoder, because the name means something within that context, outside the tribe I am Frank Blank kind of a pen name/persona. You can call me Hunter.

Hunter

[[..the Saami Noiade may have been indulging too much in the usage of amanitas muscaria or drinking too much reindeer urine.]]

** Anything is possible .. but who am I to look a gift in the mouth? ;)

[[So in a sense, I wilkum you as our guest.]]

** Lol .. in that Leif Eriksson discovered Vinland, Id say that makes us both 'natives'!

[[As far as riding up through the Mountains, I prefer a Cannondale,]]

** Ah .. so true. I ride my mountain bike more locally. I am, afterall, 12 miles from Stone Mountain, and, again, 45 mins from the AT.

[[I do watch the 'Tour de Georgia']] ** BRAG is fun .. I havent done it yet .. but maybe for my 50th birthday (that and a tattoo!).

[[The first time I saw the word, 'kenning' used it was attached to discussion on the Tello Obelisk from the archaeological site of Chavin de Huantar in north-central Peru. Kenning seems to originally be used in reference to ancient Celtic or Norse 'phrases' that have multiple levels of meaning.]]

** The word is rooted in 'knowing', so that a kenning was another way to know something.

[[Not a graduate student, I like to think of myself as a simple hexologist who sees these 'hexafoos' as windows into my tribe's deep past.]]

** Well, I was a grad student, then a doctor, so can say: When your in the box, you gotta keep your head there. The air and Art is much clearer outside! ;)

[[I see in your book that you have mentioned some interesting plants and trees.]]

** Sure .. its an integral part of what we do.

[[I live with my family in NYC, Brooklyn.]] **

I didnt know you were in NYC. Do you have a home or apartment? Does either have a yard? A few years back I visited Manhatten and noticed the inner-city gardens .. jungles and wild habitats really. Absolutely wonderful energy. I was impressed enough that where I stayed the night, I asked if my room could be on the 'inside' wall, so my window looked out over the inner-garden.

[[..I like it and I grow Brown Turkish fig trees here.]]

** I have one in my yard as well! It has enough figs for eating, brewing mead, and feeding the birds. Its a lovely tree!

[[I fertilise them from the droppings of my Netherland Dwarf rabbits which I breed.]]

** Wow! How cool is that! Ill have to google them, to see what they look like.

[[I also grow cactus and anything else I feel like.]]

** I recently 'commandeered' a San Pedro cactus from FL. It is growing nicely now in my garage (protected from the cold here in GA).

[[I am enjoying your book and reading it as I do, fromback to front and then skipping around in it.]]

** Ah .. well, if you have any Qs .. feel free to drop me a line.

[[I don't see yet however the Saami Noiade reference.]]

** I mentioned them on my blog. My book is not about their practices, since I am not of their tribe, but about Heathen ones.

Btw .. which name do you prefer .. Hunter or Frank?

.... Yngona

Hallo Yngona,

(Ledum Groenlandicum) Have you tried Labrador tea ? Also as an 'incense'

I believe this is you configuration for Aurgelmir: Its working spatially as an enclosure, equilateral triangles This usage of three equilateral triangles is an iconic sign in the North but recently I came across the nine pointed star from the Baha'i faith, which is some new religion originating in the Middle east. My interest is not in the religion but in the potential this star has for Hexology, mine in particular. Our six pointed star and its subsequent rosette are based on the Yantric star of two equilateral triangles, one male and the other female joined together uniting these two opposing forces in the universe. This is also the origin of the 'Magen David' The nine pointed star is simply three equilateral triangles unified. From the Hexologist's perspective it works nicely, nine goes into 360 degrees forty times. More traditionally, the eight pointed star with its four directions could go nine if the center is counted, the Heathen world in the center of this star would be Midgaard or the world inhabited by humans. As mini cosmologies, hexafoos or hex signs have the capacity to integrate new/old ideas and concepts within a loosely traditional context and thus acquire that knowledge. This last one incorporates the Aegishjalmur into a hexafoos configuration originally done by a Virginsville artist, Milton Hill. Virginsville, Berks County, PA my origin.

Incidently, the San Pedro cactus or Huachuma, is also known as the 'cactus de los cuatros vientos' certainly not very German except that the leading collector and horticulturist of the cactus of Peru and this one in particular is one Karel Knize. Varieties of this cactus are designated by KK numbers. The Germans in particular have been avid collectors of cactus for a very long time.

Hunter

[[I see that you do reference to the Sami word 'sieide' in the introduction. and the linkage of the word Seidr to speja, spyrian, seance, and then to shaman saman, samana, sramanah. My attraction to Seidr is exactly along those lines.]]

** I also include: sidhe (Old Irish), and siddhi (Hindi), but do not have linguist support.

[[I did not feel completely comfortable with Galdr or the more traditional form of Northern European witchcraft which seems to be driven by verbal or written spells.]]

** I agree. For me, the reason behind this is that spells are in a constant state of flux. Now, with that said, there are charms of creation that, when repeated over many years, do build and maintain a tremendous amount of energy.

[[I have an aptitude for a more intuitive, visceral approach. This 'seething' you speak of is a primitive process.]]

** It is, yes.

[[I particularly respond to the cliff peckings and cave paintings of geometric shapes, animals, snakes, and antlered humans who are clearly shamans.]]

** As do I. Here in GA, for example, we have several petroglyph stones. They are tremendous power spots .. as you can imagine.

[[Trance state, or altered consciousness is a requirement frequently via entheogenic plants. Strong associations with overall geometric patterns and singing or chanting.]]

** I agree; in fact, part of my research has led to the study of brain function .. like NLP, for example.

[[These are elements not usually associated with Northern European Witchcraft, Hexerei and the PA Deitsch, Braucherei but there certainly is enough overlap in these related traditions. Maybe its a matter of emphasis, what are your thoughts?]]

** I think it represents one branch of the metamorphosis. I 'see' the earliest tribes as shaman-based. This position morphed into seidhr, which morphed into several branchs, like thule (law), leech (physician), veterinarian, and the like. What many commonly refer to as 'witchcraft' is little more than folk magic; making Hexerei and Braucherei, for example, a particular form of Germanic folk magic.

[[But back to your book, 'Voluspa-Seidr as Wyrd Consciousness' It seems to be a loose comentary on already existing ancient texts within the 'Codex Regius' But you also mention thee'Elder Edda' the 'Hauksbok' and 'Gylfaginning' which you intersperse with more personal 'pieces']]

** All these other works contain 'filler' for Voluspa, so when read together, gives a bigger picture. So, for my book, I filled in the blanks (so to speak) with not just the Lore based information on this text, but the magico-mystic information that naturally accompanies it.

[[I read the piece on Yew as Ygg'drasil /snip/ Then when I found three of them across the street from me functioning as 'hedges' I said 'Yew' of course!]]

** We do not have true European Yew here in the states, unless it has been brought here. We do have, as you note, many similar genius of this tree.

[[..Juniperus Virginiana. Grows very slowly, very upright though, and they have a flame like appearance on a landscape, like a tree spirit embodied and have a curious vibe.]]

** I have noticed that most trees along this similar line do have an interesting energy pattern around them. Their berries also make a wonderful mead; mildly hallucinagenic.

[[San Pedro cactus,]]

** I admire the spirit of this cacti.

.... Yngona

Figure 37 "Virginville Helm" , detail spray paint on scorched wood

contagious magic

I always find the subject of contagious magic to be an interesting one.

Contagions (I'll mention them for you Thall lol) such as blood, skin, hair, urine, etc were often used in Hexerei, for many reasons. It's only been in the past few decades or so that we've seen the very common practice of using blood frowned upon. As a result I first I had an issue with it, mostly due to medical warnings and my early Wiccan training which said the use of blood should be avoided, but as I learned from Jack it is a powerful tool when used correctly and it is not how a traditional witch would view the practice.

We've talked about personalizing Hex signs with the use of contagious magic, and it is the same principle with a runic stave. Most times when you carve a stave of runes, you use a color of some sort as part of the process. Commonly used colors (no surprise here to most of us) are traditional Hex colors of red or black. You can use blood to personalize the stave, or if you have an aversion you can use red ink and another contagion. Depending on the purpose of the rite, you can also choose an appropriate wood and infuse ink with plant extracts to give it extra power in addition to the contagions. It all works as long as your intent (wish) and desire (will) are there. A very curious German reference follows.

A German version of "Odin, Vili, Ve" that I have used with great success in healing and other rites is "Wotan, Wunsch (wish), und Willo (will)". These references to our one eyed wanderer you can find in Grimm's"Teutonic Mythology". In this thinking, Wotan's brothers are his wish and his will, which fits perfectly with both intent and desire. Has anyone else here picked up on this?

I agree with the definitions of "blot" used here thus far. During the time of the Wolf Moon, Donner is honored and I have noticed that Asatru teachings have also mentioned him prominently during this time, I believe the "Thorriblot" is done during January. There is also a very quiet nod to Donner via the traditional herbs used in the favorite German dish of January, pork and sauerkraut, that has not escaped my notice. I believe it all goes back to the ancient idea that Donner fights the "ice giants" (personified during the weather this time of year in the old country) to protect his chosen humans. Now that we move into February, female aspects will come more into play.

Greg

Interesting, and of course Blot is a sacrifice. When I was a child I was taught about the power in the blood, as well as other bodily fluids. (NO, I am not naming them). I also use my own blood in my rites. I have read (think it was on the Irminsul Aettir site), of ritual sacrifice of an animal, in that case a goat, where the blood is used in the rite, and then the animal is used as part of the feast. I know that through the years, I have spent time with different shamans, including time in the Sonoran desert with a Yaqui medicine man. Whenever I 'made' something (e.g. a rattle) part of myself was always put into it, breath, saliva, blood. When I created my runes, it was with my own blood as well. This is cross-cultural.

When I perform a blót there is blood, my blood, sprinkled upon my Ve (altar), on the ground, and in my mead. I will use a sprig of evergreen (usually freshly cut Yew) to further bless the working area. This is dipped into the mead/blood mixture, and then walking around the working area widdershins, it is sprinkled upon the ground to hallow it. I might then carve staves with specific formulas, bloody them as well, and offer these up to Valfather. Though I 'ask' for nothing from the gods, I do honor them with the appropriate Rites on an organic cyclical level - lunar phases and the seasonal 'tides'.

Valulfr

Bruder Greg wrote [[I always find the subject of contagious magic to be an interesting one. Contagions (I'll mention them for you Thall lol) such as blood, skin, hair, urine, etc were often used in Hexerei, for many reasons.]]

** I agree, it is an interesting subject. One of particular note is spitting; a fluid often overlooked based on how it is perceived in modern society. Akin to the use of blood in sacrifice, but not considered nearly as 'bad'.

... Yngona Desmond

The spitting brings to mind still another yet to be named bodily fluid, the two are frequently used interchangeably as in this story

from Popul Vuh: "In the Popol Vuh, a Quiche' Maya epic, the lords of the Quiche' underworld kill Hun Hunahpu and hung his head from the branch of a gourd tree or calabash tree. No tree of this kind had ever borne gourds until Hun Hunahpu's head was hung in it. While Hun Hunahpu's head hung in the tree, the daughter of a lord of the underwold stood before the tree. Blood Woman was her name. She stretched out her right Hand. Hun Hunahpu's head spat into its palm and the spittledisappeared. Soon she came to realize that there was life within her body and in time she gave birth to the set of twins whose names were Hunter and Jaguar Deer."

The entheogenic perspective would be in regards to the amanita muscaria mushroom or Fly Agaric, the principle intoxicating agent is ibotenic acid which passes through the body intact via the urine. Thus the urine was drunk as an intoxicant and also used to attract reindeer who have a huge monkey on their backs when it comes to certain mushrooms, this is how Santa gets them in the air after attracting them with this urine. Its also why he wears a red and white suit and enters and leaves places via the chimney.

Hunter

Interestingly enough, there are only 3 beings that eat the amanita, reindeer, ravens, and man.

Valulfr

The Fly Agaric also grows symbiotic ally beneath certain fir trees which is why top quality grade plus caps are from Washington state this is also the origin of the tradition of putting presents wrapped usually in red wrapping paper beneath a fir tree brought inside for the Yule holiday. The mushroom can be deadly poisonous which is why it is dried which renders it 'safe' for consumption. It is perhaps the oldest entheogen known to man and has been in use by the schamanische since the stone age.

Hunter

Jah, I am quite aware of the use of it, and have used it, both red and yellow variety, for the purpose of 'traveling' through the 9 realms of being. Of course this isn't something I engage in regularly, perhaps once or twice a year. But when I do, I do it as part of my Utiseta, or 'sitting out', complete with drumming, reindeer and wolf pelts on hand, and plenty of galdr to last the night through. Living in extreme northern Michigan, we have our share of these items. I have been known to follow the deer trails and have observed them, along with the ravens, eating it first hand.

Valulfr

Thats a beautiful thing! That mushroom is good for effecting deep levels of concentration. It is important to observe animal behavior in order that you might also think like that animal. This is the key to good 'hunting' Under the guidance of a plant teacher it may also tell you a great deal more. Regarding our last nites conversation on Galdrstaves and my lack of knowledge about them, let me say first that I am less 'intent" driven then most here. I find that conscious intent and subconscious desires frequently are at odds. Intuitive thinking ties them together to greatly benefit the ability to succeed in conscious acts of intent. When it comes to making objects with a potential charge, I prefer something in a larger format, for instance, those picture stones photos that you have placed in the photo section. They are functioning as cosmologies, much in the same way as the Pennsilfaanisch deitsch's 'Hexafoos' I am a huge fan of Aegishjalmr and all of its variants, and now I also see Gandreiðarstafur, these are the ancestors of our Hexafoos and are more sophisticated in many ways.

Hunter

Well, you're right Bruder I am a Hexenmeister and when I make a Hex sign it is rarely for the joy of painting, there is a purpose behind it and a contagion involved. Although in my eventual retirement I surely hope to find much joy in painting them for family and friends. Right now in my life, after family and career, I have very little time to enjoy such simple pleasures.

Greg

I've been around long enough to know that everybody fancies themselves as hex sign painters, truth of the matter is that people will be looking and painting hex signs long after we are all gone. Sometimes its the 'simple pleasures' in life that are the most important. For me the pleasure of breathing clean air deeply, drinking clean water and thinking clean thoughts (Yes believe it or not sometimes I do) are what is important in the experience of living.

Hunter

The spitting brings to mind still another yet to be named bodily fluid, the two are frequently used interchangeably as in this story from Popul Vuh

** It has been many years since I last read this work. Thank you for bringing it up.

Otherwise, the story of Kvasir comes to my mind when considering spit:

Yngona Desmond

"In witch lore this is the term meaning the spit of a witch. Witches caused their evil spells or curses to be effective against others by using their own saliva or spit when producing them. Some witches spit on stones while rubbing them when reciting curses.

There were various uses for spittle. In Lapland, witches could bring many kinds of illness and misfortune on people by spitting three times upon a knife and then rubbing the knife on their victims. Another Lapland witch charm for dooming someone to destruction called for tying three knots in a linen towel in the name of the Devil, spitting on them and naming the victim.

This practice of spitting during the casting of spells still exists, especially in tribal societies. Marquesan sorcerers spit into leaves and bury them while reciting incantations against their enemies. Malay sorcerers place spit, blood, urine, and excrement into clay effigies, which they roast to curse the victim to death. In necromancy, the practitioner sometimes spits when conjuring the spirits of the dead.

Likewise, in other practices of magic, some practitioners believe the saliva of the victim helps to increase the power of the spell. Therefore, various people think it unwise to spit indiscreetly because it is believed that demons capture one's saliva and use it for evil purposes. Among the tribes of East Africa, South Africa and New Zealand, spittle is hidden lest it would fall into hands of sorcerers.

European witch-hunters during the Middle Ages and Renaissance believed witches were incapable of shedding tears, and to fool the inquisitors they would smear spittle on their cheeks.

Spitting, in folk magic, is a universal defense against the evil eye, bad luck, illness, and witchcraft. The custom that dates back to ancient Roman times includes spitting into the right shoe every morning; spitting into the toilet after urination; spitting on the breast or on the ground three times; and spitting while passing any place where danger might exist. Pliny recorded the effectiveness of spittle against various disorders, such as boils, eye infections, epilepsy, and leprosy.

It is thought spittle is especially potent in protecting infants and children against fascination. In Italy, for example, those persons suspected of overlooking children (casting the evil eye on them) a re requested to spit in their faces to nullify the harm done.

The practice of spitting in both hands before fighting to strengthen the blows dates back to Roman times."

Pillaged on-line -

From - Guiley, Rosemary Ellen.

The Encyclopedia of Witches and Witchcraft.

New York: Facts On File, 1989

And let's not forget the ever popular 'bird spit' used to bind the Fenris wolf -

"At last they invented the tricky Gleipne made of cat noise, a woman's beard, mountain roots, the breath of a fish, and bird's spittle and that fixed it. But they had to ask Tyr to put his arm in the gap when they made the knot." Edda

Valulfr

backdoor shamanism

I just wet my pants laughing at this, dear Bruder. You are fucking hysterical.

((sigh))

really funny...gonna go back and read more.better not change my drawers til I'm done!!.

Schwester

Kiara said: "you've drawn a blank, frank. such fear limits you from a harmonious dance with the divine unfolding. do not be so arrogant to assume that aya has no play in her exposure to the 'children' of the planet. there is a bigger picture, a sweeter flow; than can be seen from such a narrow window as the one you are seemingly looking thru."

_____

Frank says: "You didn't like the part about spreading shamanism through anal sex with a 'real shaman' either? I do admit it is a rather , as you say, 'a narrow window' to pass through" ha ha ha You gotta be kidding me with this harmonious dance crap, snap out of it! Heck this is starting to sound like the TV cable channel WE around here. If you think you can judge me, think again. You may be mistaking yourself as a spokesperson for Ayahuasacan shamanism, doesn't seem like such an egoless role you've set yourself up as.......... You might stay with the Peruvian tourism angle, the touritas go big time for all the harmonious BS. Over at Edot , there's a joke circulating that you can get Gucci 'el purgo' buckets to go with matching designer luggage" By the way ole Frankenstein here lives in Brooklyn, NY, thats NY as in New York City, pleased to meet ya.

Hey Schwester

yeah I kinda gave them the ole cattle proder treatment They actually go on to taking my idea of making a 'ayahuasca shaman' computer game seriously.

I'm like a ticking time bomb on these forums................

Bruder

Hunter

Yeah THE BACKDOOR HEXOLOGIST is just gonna be Hexefus images, plants and shamanism, maybe dirty jokes...

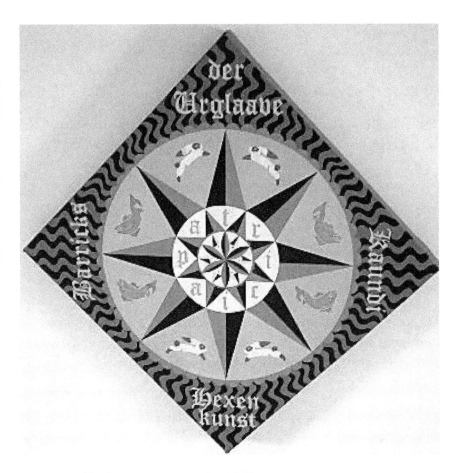

Figure 38 gifted Hex, Hunter Yoder 2008

A Sad Story

I wonder if you can tell me anything about this hex sign I came across on ebay

Patricia

Hey Schwester

Its not a 'hex sign' It has an indigenous feeling as in 'turtle walker' the seller If you like I could paint you one for free.........

Maybe the Berks County one, an eight pointed star, black, yellow, white and red center or a rossette inside an eight what ever you like. You could look at it and be in Berks County, staring at the Pinnacle at sunset This is why the center is always red. It would be our little secret.

Bruder

I would Love whatever you painted for me Hunter!

Here's another situation. I was talking to Rob on the phone (he calls me a few times a week!) Sometimes a few times over the course of a day if we haven't finished our conversation. I guess he travels in his job, and he can do this..

But he suggested talking to you, so here I am. I don't want this to be a burden on anyone.

Now, he was talking to Orva on the list, and seeing where things tie up in geneology for them. He knows, as all of you do, that I am adopted, and the links to Pennsylvania tie in with me through my birth father. (whom I know "of" slightly, but don't know.)

He says I should see if you may have ever heard of him...his name is Alan (or Allen, I don't know which spelling is correct, as I've only heard the name) Fisher (could be Fischer too.)

I was born Aug. 29, 1959, and he was in Chicago, obviously 9 months before that, so it makes it roughly Thanksgiving time I was conceived.

He played in an orchestra, he was a musician. I think he played trumpet for them, or some wind instruments. I think hearing that he also could play the drums. It was one of those travelling orchestras back then, he played in a hotel downtown Chicago, where people may have dressed up to go hear some music and dance, not unlike how kids go to bars today. In fact, my adopted folks (who are deceased now) met at a dance hall.)

So, he travelled around, to Kansas City, and Virginia Beach, etc. In fact, I recall my birth mother, (whom I HAVE met, she lives in Eau Claire, Wisconsin) telling me she phoned him in Kansas City to tell him of the fact and the last she heard from him as he was in Virginia Beach. He never came back for us. So, I haven't been interested in HIM per se, but in the family heritage. That is the way of the world, and some men (not you or the men on the list) are not honorable men. Or they may be just scared.

I had an uncle (adopted family) marry an aunt, she was his second wife, as his first wife had died. He had an affair in the mid-time between meeting my aunt, and the death of his wife, which produced a daughter, and the mother never told him. His daughter had contacted him when he was in his late 60's or early 70's, and she was about 45. They were very close after that, and he was so happy to have met her, so sometimes these stories can work out..sadly, she died of breast cancer not too long after my Uncle had passed back in the late 80's.

So, maybe I hold out a little hope. This is more of what I know of the family. That he came from a good family, a wealthy family, that were in construction. (that is where Rob had the problem, as he said that he knew of many Fishers, or Fischers, that had families in construction.) I do not think the family was "religious" anymore, at least, if they were from Mennonite/Amish. It seemed that they had a debutante picked out for him, and he didn't want to strap the yoke of marriage on, and he had a love of music, and was accomplished enough to play for a band, so he "postponed" things for a bit, met my b-mom, and then things happened. He was 26 or so, just as she was, when I was born. I do not know if my larger family knows of me, my b-mother's family was aware of it, but didn't 'say' anything.

That is what I know of him, and that is all she was able to tell me, as they had dated, and not of course, lived together, especially during that era. She had waited tables, and served at the Stouffer's restaurant, which was once famous, it is now closed, at least in Chicago.

I told Rob, the other day that I am so happy that you folks are finding links way back to the old days when our common ancestors came and settled Pennsylvania. It is good to hear of this. I said "I don't expect to ever find out about mine", and he said that someday I will find out. I am more interested in finding out my family's heritage, so I can find out my links to Germany, our Heimat. It is a bit unusual to be in a folkfaith which proclaims such a link to heritage, and then, one doesn't even know of the one that one has. I felt kind of disconnected to mine for several years, so I focused on the Slavic side, which of course, I did know of, and I was raised in by my adoptive parents. But then something funny happened.

My mother died (adoptive) in '94, and I was heartbroken, as she and I were quite close. My father, whom I was close to as well, kind of went nuts, and basically cut ties off with me, married another women, kind of went with her family (she was a widow) and her grandchildren. (I have no children, first husband didn't want any, and he left me for a woman that had 4 go figure.) He disinherited me, formally, and I lost any claim to my inheritence when he passed in '97.

After that, it seemed that things started changing for me, some for the better. Last Year, when I worked at the Chriskindlemarket, I actually was around a lot of folks that "looked like me", were German, and were very accepting of who I was. It also seemed that something "woke up" and that may have been my Ancestors, who remembered, had a grandchild over on "this side" and it may be important to get to know her. Right after that, I seemed to take over the Hexenkunst list, and here we are.

It is a remarkalble thing that we have all gotten to know each other. I have told Rob, that it is not unlikely that we may have been together, in other eras, working with each other. In Heathenry, it is how we work things out together, through the years.

So, Rob told me to ask if you have any knowledge of someone that could fit that bill, but again, I don't know if Fisher is a very common name, I know it is one of the first names in Pennsylvania, I was reading somewheres online in some geneology tract.

So, that name could be a dime a dozen. I don't unfortunately, have a town where he was from, or anything other than he was a musician, and that he was 26 or so when I was born. And that the family was in construction, and were well-off. He may have married that girl, or another, and have kids and grandkids by now, in fact, I'd expect him to.

I am not interested in upsetting the family, but just interested in the history of the family.

Of course, I don't expect anyone other than myself to possibly contact this person. This is just a basic inquiry. But this could be the chance that introduces me to my personal heritage, and the birthright that you folks take for granted.

If you don't know anything, that is ok too. It was just a query, or a chance. I know that you are a very fine father, and the thought of one that is cut from their family may stir a "dad's heart."

Take care Brudder. Of course, If you want to make one for me, with the Red center, I am grateful and humble for it. I would love to be in Berk's County at the Pinnacle!

I want to take Susan up on her offer, last weekend in July, she told me, of having the 2 of them, Jesse and Susan, give an informal "class" of sorts, and have me over there. I hope, if possible, and family vacations down to S. America don't get the better of you that weekend, that you *could* make it! I would love to meet the person that is the Shaman of the Reawakened Urglaawers...

Thanks for reading this long, and possibly tiresome story.

As you said, if your birth father referred to himself as being 'Dutch' that could only mean one thing with that name and one point of origin. Oley. Dutch as in PA Dutch is what we were called and called ourselves until very recently. But why Oley? Is that the county that called themselves "Dutch" the most? I am unknowing of these things, so I am dependant upon you and Rob's best knowledge on these matters.

That's the "haunted county" that you are thinking of? That would make sense! I have that book by Dennis Boyer, I am going to have to reread on Oley County.

Patricia

Shun

Not a very popular subject, but, Shun is actuallly a "Plain" custom, maybe you could elucidate for us...... I put up some views of up on the ridge you in particular might appreciate.

Hunter

Hunter, there is an old saying that some of the cunning folk or prophets are not accepted in their own town or community. Here is where you are needed. You're home now, none to shun anyone, you or yours. I am, as always, standing beside you at the fire...

Patricia

Shunning is a very difficult subject to address. Even in everyday life it is a word that is unique to our deep rooted customs and beliefs. When ever anyone says they have been shunned or they are going to shun someone it is well understood. The custom is a very harsh one and reading about your experience and the account that Rob set forth brings very painful memories to all of us that have been the object. I do not like the practice and the pain it causes, but I am sure it is a way that our ancestors wanted to protect us from outside influence and it was a primal way of protection.In spite of the heavy consequences shunning inflected, it did help preserve a very unique way of life without outside influences.

I was raised by my grandparents with an absentee Mother. My aunts and uncles hated me because I was favored and chosen by my Pap, and would remind me every time they had a chance that I was less then they were. BUT I was well loved my Pap and Mom and am a better person for their efforts.

Hunter when you found love in the woman you married and had beautiful children (blond hair and blue eyed or perhaps may have had dark hair and rich beautiful skin and eyes) so much the better.

My youngest daughter married a man by the name of Mathew Levine. He is Jewish and I have beautiful grandchildren...AND we celebrate ALL the holidays to boot!!! I adore his parents who are wonderful folks and share Grandparent stories.

After giving birth as a young single person to my oldest daughter who was born with Spina Bifida,,, well that also set my mother back a few hundred years, but regardless...I feel blessed, and as my Grandmother used to say " we're from good Pa. Dutch stock".

Orva

Yesterday was a momentous day for me, for today, I was introduced to my birthfather's family by way of book and research knowledge. It is a most important step, because now I have confirmation of my heritage, which for most folks, is taken for granted. Not of course, for Adoptees.

I want to thank, from the bottom of my heart, my little "black crow" sister, Orva, who is a crack genealogist, and hunter of family lines, and souls. I am amazed that I was able to get as much information as we did, so soon, but with genealogical information online now, many things go much faster.

I still have to go to Berks Co., for information on the actual family history, for I see it has been written there, in the library's section on family history of Berks County. My family has been in this country since the father-son team of Johan Christian Fisher, (senior) and Johan Michael Fisher, (son) came from their part of Germany in 1724. (Orva didn't get that far yet, we were just working in America right now.) My family has been for the most part, in Berks and Lehigh Counties, working as what was told to my birthmother, builders that had Construction companies that built this section of America. Always landowners, always building, both sides came from this. Carpenters, workers of wood, always holding land. My family tree seems to be stout and solid Germanic. ALL Pennsylvania Deitsch. For that I am so very happy and proud. My birth father, Allen Henry Fisher, has been gone now since 1993, so there is no chance of reunion, until my passing. His elder brother has passed on too, and I doubt if I will present myself to my cousins, as I have already been through this once with the birthmothers family, and sometimes it doesn't go well. It is hard to encounter a new face, a new person when one is set in their feelings about their family, and the secret life they may have had, and the repercussions from it later on (my existence). It is not necessary that we need to wear it on our sleeve, if it is worn proudly, secretly, in our heart. I can live with that.. Some may ask me why I did this..

When I lost my adopted father, I had the dubious privilege of being formally disinherited, due to my father having remarried after the death of my adopted mother. It happens, as Hunter has mentioned. So, I was, in a way, without any FORMAL Familial Wyrd as the ties had been cut, legally. It is unique in a situation that people take up such an ancestral-loving faith that had been treated this way. I had always been one of those adoptees interested in the truth, whatever it was, and now I have found it. Orva was interested in telling some of the details, since she is worked on it, if you folks are at all interested...she has my permission to tell the tale. I think it is worth telling the history of my kinfolk, "The Fishers of Berks Co."

ORVA, my black crow sister, I OWE you a debt that I do not know if it can be repaid in this life, but I thank you from the bottom of my heart. I am sure, sister, we have traveled many lives together to get here. Do not doubt it.

THANK you ROB my brother, because of the strength of your statement "you WILL find them", I had the courage to ask at this time.

THANK you HUNTER, because your stories, and optimism cheered me on, and because you knew before I had confirmation that I belonged here.It is good that our relatives worked together, I can only hope. They were Lutheran too.

THANK YOU list, in your patience for reading my tale.

Patricia

Geilskimmel, Hexegraut, und Wachholder

Found some ole friend's names in the 'dialect' Das "geilskimmel" is the subject of my next promised 'Hexafoos or Hexezeeche' for 'meine schweschder'. The 'eins' who has the ability of 'Blanzeschwetze' 'Hexegraut' or Hypericum perforatum which is usually harvested in my month of birth but on 'yuni' 24, I don't know much, but I like the name. Und 'wachholder' as Yngona Desmond says. "I admire its spirit and a meade made from its berries is somewhat hallucinogenic"

**I sell St. Johns Wort. Named after the church/Saint Holy-day (holiday) it bears, on Sonnenwende/Midsommer, which was Holy before Byzantium ever got it's paws on it! lol.

I never used to sell a lot of it, because most folk didn't know what to do with it besides enjoy the yellow flowers, which are fine enough. Last year, my personal store..outside of our company stores, was in a neighborhood that had the influx of German folk that had escaped the Lincoln Ave./in-city "German-town" and located to this suburb. They were amazed I had the herb to sell, and bought a lot of it up. The other folks that had bought it were from India, or the Middle East and had lived in Germany, and thus, were familiar with this herb.

This, and calendula, I love, and think that they are "sunshine-y" herbs. Mix in some pansies, and the winter blues are g-o-n-e.

Germany has done some good work on this herb, and have had it for sale there and here for quite a long time. Good for the winter blues, or 'cabin fever' as was the old time expression for it.

I have been inundated with placing the last of my orders for the stores, for the main things I want, my bushes and shrubs, so, I am dreaming of things that are growing today. Spring will be here, before you know it, so it is time to relish the last month of what Winter gives one..silence, and reflection.

Figure 39 Geilskimmel Hex", 2008,Hunter M. Yoder

"

Still thinking about Ukrainain Cosmos/Trypillian Civilization in particular an image of:" A double helix was carved over the goddess's breasts. A diamond-shaped sign, crossed twice to make four sections, was drawn on her belly or loins. A wheat grain was pressed into each section of the sign before baking. The breast helix symbolizes the heaven: it is a lightning, after which the rain-semen falls on the ground. The diamond-shaped sign with grains represents a plowed and seeded field. This is another fertile place on the goddess's body."

http://www.trypillia.com/articles/eng/he3.shtml

"Authors are always trying to play that "Isis" game and say that the Europeans had no culture and had to learn it from somewhere else. I say WE HAD it from what some of us call the "DREAMTIME" as a folk as we remembered it from our proto-indo-euro days around the Ukrainian Black Sea area after the ice shelves started retreating and left some incredibly fertile soil. I think that this is a genetic memory and goes to the heart of any serious farming culture."

Heel,

I couldn't agree more with what you said above. This is much like the 'fylfot', or swastika, no exact point of origin, though it's found all over the world. I too believe this emanates for the collective unconscious of mankind in general.

Valulfr

there is also the story of the discovery of flax and Frau Holle (Holda, Hulda). A peasant shepard follows a chamois up the mountain where he finds a door in the side of the glacier. Inside he finds the goddess in the jeweled cave. Overwhelmed by the sight of the goddess and her attendants amid the wealth, he feel to his knees. She told him that he could choose from anything that he could carry away. He looked around and found that he could not stop going back to the little nosegay of blue flowers that she held and asked for that.. She gave him the flowers and some seeds and told him that he would live as long as the flowers did not droop or fade. His wife gave him hell for not choosing the jewels. He paid her no heed and planted the seeds as instructed and found that he had several acres worth of seed. The plants grew and bloomed all the while he wondered what use they would be. When they had gone to seed Holle came to him again and taught him and his wife how to harvest, spin and weave the linen. They found that people were more than willing to pay for their goods and they became rich beyond their dreams. The man lived to see his grandchildren and great-grandchildren grow up. One day he noticed that the nosegay was beginning to droop. He knew what this meant and again went in search of the door in the glacier (which he had unsuccessfully tried on many other occasions). He found it with ease and was never seen again.

I have flax in my garden, and would love to have fields full of it. It is amazingly beautiful, and has so many uses.

It is finally here

I just got 'Strange Experience' through inter-library loan. I am so excited. Will let you all know what I think when I am done. There are some really great hex signs in it. I saw one in there that I painted. I did not know that this was it's origin. Thank you all for reccomending it to me. (esp. you Hunter) Well it's off to reading for me!

Swanhilde

"Strange Experience" is our "A Separate Reality" and both written the same year, 1971. The book is out of print but is bound to be reprinted, its not easy to get, only as used. He puts all the pieces together.............enjoy!

Hunter

The Nymphomaniac & Sexually Perverted's Cookbook, 1931

Looks like some pretty good reading, interesting use of plants, I won't say which Schweschder it was I have so many now, LOL Gives me an idear for another hexafoos though..........

" An interesting guide to the world of sexual stimulants that ranges widely through datura, peyotl, nepenthes, strychnos (nux vomica) and even yohimbe, and of course the opiates: "As to opium, a small dose may act as a provocative upon certain natures; to me it is a begetter of dreams, blissful, un-erotical; a contentment so plenary that to break in upon the trance with idle embracements were folly and almost impiety."

NO RESERVE!!!!!! SO TAKE IT AWAY!!! REMEMBER ELVIS "It is Now orNeveeeeeeeer,!! Tomorrow Would be Too Late.""

Its up to $83.96

If you really care about the Schweschders, please buy this book.........(LOL)

Frank

**wasn't ME, but they forgot Damiana..that is pretty good. There is a damiana liquor that I had in a Mexican restaurant that the owner let me try, and whew, I only had one small glass but it went down nice and smooth, and it left a lady with a nice w-a-r-m feeling. He told me that in Mexico, it is given to a young lady on her wedding night to invite marital bliss between the new couple,but in today's world, they're marching down the wedding aisle with their toddler children watching mom and dad finally get hitched...sigh...better late than never, I suppose. anyways it is in a nice bottle with a large woman I used to call her "La Gordita"...nice and lush she is. Bring some home for your wife, she and you will love it Hunter. Nice taste too.

Patricia

Hey we're all 'professional' here I just couldn't resist, (she's gonna kill me) That part about, "It wasn't me" sounds like the story of my life with the three ladies I live with........The mama bear says, "Well it wasn't me", and then the sister bear says, "Well it wasn't me, and then the baby bear says"Well it wasn't me either: fifty degrees F in Brooklyn I just purchased, 9 trees, 5, Juniper and 4 Witch Hazel I think the sap is running up the trees again

Hunter

uh, wasn't me, either......but $95????? Holy Smokes I've made damiana cordial a couple of times but not in a bottle like that! Have a recipe here somewhere... I don't know though. Just give me a few cold 'local' lagers or stoudts and I'm way good to go. Don't need to be importin' anything for me..

Susan

this is just gonna lead to a lot of more plants............ Yohimbe being the one that pricks my interest, Is it African? or Caribbean then theres

Horny Goat Weed:

oh brother, Brother...LOL

you should really read up on these plants somewhere other than Ebay, where they want you to buy their products! Horny Goat Weed is purported to be one of the biggest quack 'aphrodisiacs' on the market and a Wild Lettuce infusion bath once made me so incredibly limp and relaxed that I fell into a deep sleep in the bathtub until the water was ice cold. Can't imagine that being conducive to any romantic interlude!

Susan

Oh well

Living with a family of rabbits is stimulus enough Mostly now its trying to prevent the romantic interludes from occurring I already did my fair share, now its up to the rest of ya's make Deitsch babies! yeah! $95 wow, I was gonna bid $100 but it was too late.......I'm raking it in with record Sinicuichi sales, LOL

Hunter

Honoring/Blot to Wodan

"The Deitsch are a practical people; we take what works and attune it to our cultural context). In fact, once free from the thumb of the church, some of these practices very likely flourished where they may not have otherwise."

"But let me be clear on one thing... I have seen some disturbing references on other lists to the Pennsylvania Germans somehow being ³inferior,²either culturally or linguistically."

My position is that we needn't replace one set of restrictions (christianity) with another set, (Asatru) which is why the concept of Urglaawe is exciting.

"I am sure that more than a few of us here have either experienced it ourselves or heard about it from our parents or grandparents. Much of the anti-Deitsch bigotry surrounded the general fear of Germans beginning before WWI and continuing beyond WWII."

This accounts for the generation that skipped acquiring the 'dialect;' In my own case which probably is a common one, the Grand parents spoke, but for those reasons cited the parents did not, although exposed to it throughout my childhood, I am acquiring a 'taste' for it. And the pronunciation is there already LOL

Maybe you could explain the origins of the usage of Urglaawe. Is it an original term you are involved with in its conception? Why should I as a Pennsilfaanisch Deitsch want to know more?

Ferwas der Urglaawe? Why the Urglaawe?

Hunter's question is extremely important, and I am going to take my time in answering it. My opinions are subject to change as I learn and grow not only from our own community but from others as well.

I suspect that we are on the edge of a cultural reawakening here in the Deitscherei. Unfortunately, many of those who kept the cultural, non-sectarian fires burning for the last 60 years are passing on, and, for numerous reasons, many in my generation have lost conscious ties to the past. One such reason was the legislative actions in 1911 that targeted the use of Deitsch in schools. There is currently a study (Alice Spayd; I can put anyone interested in answering her survey in touch with her) going on regarding the repression/suppression of Deitsch in schoolyards and in classrooms. I am sure that more than a few of us here have either experienced it ourselves or heard about it from our parents or grandparents. Much of the anti-Deitsch bigotry surrounded the general fear of Germans beginning before WWI and continuing beyond WWII.

People have been predicting the demise of the Pennsylvania Germans as a distinct ethnic and linguistic group for literally centuries, yet my understanding is that there are now more speakers of Deitsch than there were in 1980 (thanks mostly to Amish and Menno birthrates but also due to efforts in the non-sectarian communities to provide language resources for those who want to learn it). Meanwhile, the folk art has continuously thrived here in Pennsylvania, even containing symbols that pre-date Christianitys overlay our our ancestors communities in Europe. Other practices, such as Braucherei and Hexerei, have continued here in the Americas (with some influence from other sources... The Deitsch are a practical people; we take what works and attune it to our cultural context). In fact, once free from the thumb of the church, some of these practices very likely flourished where they may not have otherwise.

William Parsons called the Pennsylvania Germans a persistent minority. This applies to numerous aspects of our being. The organic aspects of our culture as handed down by our forebears continues. Even with the Christian overlay, our ancestors brought with them, in various facets of life, aspects of the pre-Christian culture are persistent. The concept of organicis whence the Urglaawe comes. Identifying organic cultural facets is difficult unto itself because of the extensive adoption of various practices among tribes. I submit, though, that voluntary adoptions can be considered organic. Such discussions are one reason we are here: to identify that which is organic to our Volk vs. the result of forced adoption or conversion. As Patricia cites below, the same questions are being asked by other tribes worldwide. Even great minds (such as Dostoevsky) pursued some of these questions throughout their careers.

So what does all this mean?

318

To me it means that the voices of our ancestors are calling on us to restore the organic order to the Volk as much as is possible and practical. This is not a matter of hatred, feelings of superiority, etc., because such notions are counterproductive to the positive growth and the increase in consciousness that is part of the development of humankind. Although our tribe did not exist as an entity during the pre-Christian era, our ancestors were members of various tribes, so their experiences live on in the genetic memory as well as in the cultural developments of our Volk. This makes us as much of a valid Germanic tribe as any other, and our isolation from the blights on Europe from 1681 until the present time may have preserved elements from several tribes that otherwise might be lost. My belief is that we can work to find remnants of the organic, primal belief and life system. As we search our lore (everything from our folk stories to Hexology to Braucherei), we should record what we learn and offer our tribes experiences to the wider community.

But let me be clear on one thing... I have seen some disturbing references on other lists to the Pennsylvania Germans somehow being inferior,either culturally or linguistically. I reject such notions. Our ancestors left Europe before there was a German state and before there was a standardized German language. It is not that one language was correct and the others Any dialect might have been chosen as the standard. We do not need the approval of other tribes to pursue our distinct heritage and Wandel (mode of life). We can certainly learn from everyone else from different Teutonic tribes, but the voices of our ancestors have as much right to be heard as do the voices of the ancestors of tribes that remained bound to the continent.

Thus, the Urglaawe is the pursuit of the primal, organic faith as handed down through our unique tribes ancestral lines (including influences from the Christian overlay... We must not dismiss our Christian ancestors, either... We owe them frith, and without them, we would not exist at all... But I do not believe the Christian religion is organic to our Volk, which is why Europe was plunged into the Dark Ages when the Church controlled it). There is much work to be done, and, as Patricia says, there are no rules per se. It seems each of us has unique skills and experiences that will play an important part in reconstructing our faith and in developing it forward... this is not a static way of life!

I hope this explains where my head is at with the basic reason for the movement. Please feel free to ask for more clarification, particularly if this comes off sounding like I hold any disdain for any other group, religious or ethnic, because I don't feel that way at all. :)

I am not sure if that clears things up at all or if it muddies up the waters!

Rob

I agree with almost everything you said and you are most wise for saying it. A lot of things we know today were written down by scribes and clergy of other faiths. I agree that we should not ignore or overlook the contributions made by those of other faiths, who purposely or not helped to give us at least a vestige and a building block to start with. But, it must also be pointed out that the X-tians also took the faith of our ancestors or we still might have it intact. What they did not outright destroy was altered, and we need to be cognizant of this. My view, thankfully and gratefully shared by others here (and thank you most especially to "Uncle" Thor and "Aunt" Audrey for being among the first to recognize this), is that we can use what they left us. We can turn it around and change it in the same way it was changed, only back to our ancestral faiths. Not all among us who practice our magical arts will agree, I know that Jack appreciates the direction I've gone in but it's not endemic to his own practice. He has been very supportive as my mentor, and even suggested to me that this direction would be one that Lee would have approved of. Somehow, I feel very strongly that Lee knows...

I also welcome our Norse cousins to our club. Partly because in addition to being German, I am also part Swede among other things- mutts rule lol! But now it is time for us to shine, and shine we will. We will not reject the witches among us as "Wiccans" like the snobbish Irminists and others have done, or "Satan" worshippers as those of the monotheistic religions have labeled us for centuries. Rather, we will seat them in their rightful and honored place at our community table, and welcome their contributions to our faith. The faith of our traditional witches like myself in our gods and goddesses, is as strong and abiding as anyone who follows it.

This is my view, for whatever it's worth. I always read my email and I appreciate the contributions of everyone here. I stand in service for anyone who needs my personal assistance, whether you need healing or a little bit of advice towards a problem. Ths is the way it once was and should be again. Let's keep it going!

Blessings and frith,

Greg

Salt

Contagious magic in Hexerei is also a way of setting a psychic spell or as I call them; a magical intrusions.". I worked with a wealthy, well-educated couple in 2005 from TN who had been under a curse from the wife's former husband and his family. Their plight was dreadful or they would not have approached me for help.

One thing we eventually discovered is that the ex-husband "set-the-spell" by burying a charged item in front of their back door in front of the steps into the house. As the couple entered their home after work, they stepped on the contagious charm and carried the negative engery into their home, infecting the entire atmosphere and creating a channel for further intrusions. When I asked them to dig around their porch, they found it and destroyed it by encassing it in a jar of salt.

Over the years, I've also made "love charms" for two wives who desired their husbands to be more vigorous in the bedroom. In this case, I fashioned a wax poppett and added a sample of the husband's hair to persoanlize. Then the wife persoanlized it with her personal lubrication (in private) and then returned the poppett to me, I sewed it into a red sleeve and fashioned a small erect penis from a High John Conker Root aand ounted it onto the poppet before closing the sleeve.

The wife then inserted the poppett into the mattress directly beneath where the husband slept. In both cases, the results were exactly what the wife desired, in abundance! The contagious magic was activated when the husband lay down over the charm. One woman eventually had to take it out as she was tired out by his new vigor. This example shows the use of both sympathetic and contagious magic.

BTW, this contagious magical practice is also used in and by "rootdoctors" in the African-American communities.

As for spit, it is a way of personalizing a charm. I have used spit and blood for the ones I make. As long as care is taken with hygene, there is no danger to yourself or others

Best wishes, Jack Montgomery

Wow Jack Can't believe nobody posted on this, Mention the word Hexenmeister and speak of the devil, LOL

That charged object, I guess you can't tell us what it was, but can you elaborate on 'charged objects' alittle. I also would greatly appreciate some discussion on 'salt' I've spoken to Greg about it and I have a rabbi as a close friend who indeed is a 'Saltzman' but I'm still foggy on the issue. Does it function as an intent enhancer, but there is some mystical aspect, I'm missing. Is it the crystaline aspect or the sea? I am a big fan of HooDoo and VooDoo, especially being as mere Hexologist, I feel a kinship to their images and have enjoyed yor post enormously and I thank you.

Hunter

And now you can speak of two devils lol! We talked about how salt carries it's own "mana" and how salt is very much amenable to, let's say, suggestion. It has never failed to do exactly what I wished of it and is so simple to work with. My 9yr old daughter learned this last year from us while helping shovel, now she lol has to learn that it's uses are not in keeping her brother away! I'm sure Jack will elaborate if what I've said hasn't been sufficient.

Greg

Dear Hunter,

Brother Greg is a wise and seasoned Powwow. What he says you can take to the bank. As for the TN couple, I do not know what the object they found looked like for they only told me that they had found it and destroyed its power through containment as I instructed. I suspect it was a small, charged parcel of herbs, nails and written spells stitched into a small packet of cloth. Some folks put them into a bottle. It works the same regardless. I actually flushed one down the toliet one night but that is another story.

In my book, I have a transcript of an interview with a Appalachian Granny-woman in Southern Virginia. She told me of a "witch ball" which she described as a ball of hair, pins and other materials that entered her kitchen one afternoon and proceeded toward her of its own volition to posion her home. Knowing how to stop it and to contain it, she prevented this from happening by stunning it, then scooping it into a jar of salt and burying it under a oak tree.

Salt, is a universal disruptor of psychic energy. It has been used so since ancient times. Water is also a effective disruptor and is used to prevent aa psychic attack from going any further. If you ever feel assaulted psychically run, don't walk to a shower and get under it. Take an Epson salts bath, it is very effective in removing negative energy from your person. The magical properties of salt aand water relate to the movement of energy. Have you ever noticed how psychically fresh it seems after a good downpour? That is also why some Carribean women deliver their babies in the surf at night. The water and salt protect them both at a vulnrable time. Probably hygenic as wwell.

I actually practice both Hoodoo and Powwow. I do know of St Augustines in Chicago and they seem to be reputable. Such places are in every major major city. You just have to know the right person.

Hope this helps, with love, respect and blessings to you all.

Jack

Now that the subject **of Hoodoo and Root work** has come

up....here are a few thoughts. This sounds to me like the object must have been crystalline or asubstance like a crystal or stone. They can be programmed and used to focus an intent. I have used crystals to do various kinds of work as well as the work you have described, and then when I was done "cleared" them by putting them into salt or salt water. I find bottles buried with personal effects in them to be more effective. Usually they are found under porches or steps. To rid yourself of a curse, or crossings ,many times spiritual baths are used with the aid of saying the proper psalm. The the most popular one as you know is Psalm 51

"Purify me with hyssop, and I will be clean. Wash me, and I will be whiter than snow." Bathe at sunrise for 9 mornings using hyssop and letting yourself air dry. I have used hot foot powders to get someone to move on. The mostrecent will be leaving on Feb. 14. She became a real problem to me and my fellow staff members I work with (not a team player and caused a lot of drama) so a little hot foot power and now she is moving on to greener pastures. A win/ win situation for everyone. Honey pots can sweeten someone to you, either in love situations or in court cases to sweeten a judge or jury to be sympatric to your cause. It can also be used to sweeten teaches to give you good grades, of course you have to study, and in divorce cases to help sweeten things up to get a settlement in your favor, it is a great aid and helps focus your intent.

Name papers or petition papers are used frequently in Hoodo practices and I can remember by grandfather "my Pap" using a very similar method to throw a hex on someone who abused me as a child. He put her name onto a paper and said a "chant" and then into fire of the old cook stove it went and then he spit in the coal bucket for good measure. Dressing candles and poppet's is also used in Hoodoo. I had to use one to lift a curse off of me a few years back. I was in St. Martaan's when a old Island woman wanted me to buy some of her things, I said no and she then put a foot track trick on me. I know it right away because shortly there after I took a bad fall and banged myself up pretty good. I waited till I got back in the States then had to do some heavy duty Uncrossing and Hex breaking measures. Amoung other things, I fixed a poppet and then set the whole mess by a cross roads. The curse was lifted and I dressed a candle and said a prayer to St. Lazuras on her behalf, to send her a blessing as well. Healing was the speciality in my home gowning up and it was what was taught by my Pap. He had different methods to heal and find things. I am a Root worker and have practiced for a number of years. Ihave a small following here on the Island where I live. Folks hear about me from word of mouth and usually catch me in the grocery store or the post office or in the doctor's office or any time I am out and about to ask me for my help. Hoodoo however, is a folk African American tradition. I can see many of the Pa. Dutch practices that were carried down into the south by way of migration and picked up by the slave population early on. Because I study migration patterns, I find a bit of cultural heritage and folk lore and traditions travel along the way as people move about from place to place. But if you wanted to back track it, a lot of folk medicine and practices can go back into Pa and then travel back across the water to the motherland where our ancestors held it as a part of their daily lives integrated in their beliefs. This belief system was so embedded in our ancestors that it has trickled down to us today in bits and pieces. Hoodoo appeals to me for this reason, I learned it to try and untangle my Pa. Dutch Roots. I also studied the Wiccan Beliefs and the various neo-pagan religions to uncover the Heathen part of my childhood. Nothing is quite like the Pa. Dutch traditions that I knew but it has broadened my perceptions. ....As Jerry Garcia said" I'm going to Hell in a bucket, but at least I'm enjoying the ride" !!

Blessings ..

Orva

Ooooo! excellent reply Orva!

As Brother Greg was saying recently we often do not talk that much of intent as a process in magic but it is very real and powerful! I had not considered it but I think you are right about the crystalline aspect of salt. Brother Hunter asked me if it disrupted both good and bad projected energy and I have always found that to be the case. The idea of programing it is really interesting.

When travelling in spirit, if someome lays a line of salt in your path it is like stepping on a hot coal and you need to find a way around it to go where you intend going. Have you had such an experience?

I have used black salt like hot foot powder as a way of ridding my self of the presence of a living person. I laid it accross the doorway of their office and in two months that person was gone. Have you heard of this?

I too use Hoodoo and know that the traditions are interlinked historically.

Best wishes, Jack

Hello Jack, interesting discussion going here... and it has given me much thought.

Pretty much salt will do anything you tell it to do. It has no ethics it adheres to and it can be programmed to do what you want. Crystals are pretty much the same way. The question of Ethics comes from he "doer" not the "receiver." Salt in it's natural state can absorb negative energy (guess that is how you would describe it in today's terms) Back in the days of yore, salt was used to dehydrate things to the point where they can be preserved, like in curing, thus ridding it from decay. It can corrode metal so it again break down one's weapons of defense and communication, like phone wires and computer wires when exposed to too high of salt content in the air.(like when living in the Florida Keys ...lol) So salt is very powerful to work with as an agent to rid or purify things depending on your intent. Salt can be programmed because it is a crystal and vibrate releasing energy I have had success in programing quartz crystals to do healing's, as I mentioned earlier by clearing them first then placing my intent into them. I have programmed them to draw off pain after surgery on myself and others. I had some nasty hand surgery last year and was able to heal it up to where I have full range of motion and without pain. The only way I can describe this is like this, using a crystal watch as an analogy. When you place a crystal into the watch along with a little battery the combination of the crystal vibrating and the battering running the mechanism allow the mainframe to tell time.The quartz crystal tells it what to do by transmitting the message... Now lets say you want to program a crystal. You will put your intent into it and you acting like the battery will set it into motion what you desire to happen. The crystal runs off of your body bio rhythms... Say...wheww, now that is a mouth full and way over my own head ! Anyway that sort of kind of how it works for me. . Remember The old crystal radio sets, receives the message and transmits it. I did a programing a week or so ago and it is really talking up a storm for me.

Pap used to ring the house with salt to keep snakes away. Mom used to scrub the steps with a broom and salt water... and Epson salt was put into the hole with a match before planting tomatoes....

When travelling in spirit, if someome lays a line of salt in your path it is like stepping on a hot coal and you need to find a way around it to go where you intend going. Have you had such an experience?

I have only astro traveled a few times and it was in great need to go to someone very sick and dying or when in a cone of power during a ritual and I went out the top. Salt was used to draw a circle and I was within the circle. I just went straight up and over the top. When going to someone in need, I put salt around my bed and used it as a safety net... I have not come across salt in my path before, only used as guidelines. Perhaps if you carry a little vinegar with you it will counter act it for you and break it down . My Pap used salt and vinegar in his workings and so do I when I want to move something out of the way or go around it. "Piss and Vinegar " was actually the formula. That would pretty much break anything...Hex or Jinx or Crossing.... a little of that stuff in a ball jar with a chicken egg and a rusty 2 penny carpenters nail in along with it and you had best head for the hills !!! lol. My Pap used to dream walk..and I can do it too, but the difference is we dream off somewhere and talk to the dead and they send messages back with us. Now I am not sure if this is a German folk Pa. Dutch thing or if this is because he was born with the veil on his face and has passed it down to me. I am still trying to figure that part out.

I have used black salt like hot foot powder as a way of ridding my self of the presence of a living person. I laid it across the doorway of their office and in two months that person was gone. Have you heard of this?

>>> Hot footing is a really great FAST way to rid someone from you. I like to use the red peppers and mixed with black pepper. I have made my own black salt and used it some, at my door or around my fence for protection. ... but for me it is easier to use the red pepper and made up a little hot foot oil to do candle work or dress a hot foot mojo hand. The latest hot footing I did sort of back fired on me. The girl I wanted to leave did...her last day is the 14th... but my little young girlfriend stepped in some of the residue and now she wants to find another job and move away... she called me last evening with the news. I told her she got exposed to some of the powder that I didn't get all off the carpet and told her to wash herself in Black Tar Soap and then take her shoes (berk sandals) and put them down in some octagon soap and

Florida Water to get it off.

I never had that happen before, she didn't know I was hot footing Cathy, but when I told her what I had done she was understanding on the remedy she need to do. She is from Germany and has her green card. I am helping her with her Citizen's test. I will sure hate to see her go.. she is a real sweetheart and a good worker.

I too use Hoodoo and know that the traditions are interlinked historically.

So Jack, guess I got a little long winded here. I like working with HooDoo. But would really like to learn more about the stuff I grew up with. Some of it is coming back to me in bits and pieces.

I would be very interested in hearing about more of your experiences.

Best Wishes Orva...

Pennsilfaanisch deitsch sex magick

Most powerful force in the subjective universe? maybe. certainly our rossette is based on the unification of the opposing male and female forces in the subjective universe. A force that is most useful in channeling its energy. Love charms aside, transmission of our ways is from male to female or female to male. Down on the farm sex power is very useful with the creatures, they are always way on top of this subject. Raising rabbits as I do (always raising something)my pulse is on the way sex glues these creatures together. If in possession of a female, there is no worry of the males ever escaping.

Sex power magick, very useful tool. Anyway, sex exists everywhere, animals know this.

Two thoughts:

I could never own a neutered animal, it like the equivalent of a human having a lobotomy

Good hexafoos are never limited to any particular shape most commonl , 'the circle' now all the expert hexenmeisters and brauchers here will disagree, BUT to limit a hexafoos to a circle will doom it to infertility, it is important that they are able radiate forth and not confined as if wearing a prophylactic device.

This is metaphysical sexuality.

Hunter

Braucherei's Fallen Angel/ Mt Bummy

Gonna be pretty hard to top Orva's post, but I'll give it a try......... Back in 1968, way before most of you were born my mother apprenticed me out to a certain 'Bumbaugh' He had a used bookstore in Kutzeschtettel on East main street not too far from the Saucony Creek bridge. Yeah, the rong part of town back in those days. My Mother was known as the 'Purple Lady' back then, well because she was alway dressed only in purple down to the eye shadow. Anyway she stopped into his place looking for antiques, another one of his sidelines. I guess he made a pass at her, which happened alot with the 'Purple Lady', ha ha ha but it was 'Nix so gut' and instead he got stuck with a fourteen year old kid to help him out around the store and gather herbs on field trips. Bumbaugh had several of these storefront used bookstores throughout Barricks kaundi including one in Niantic which I think was his old stomping grounds. he was also a fixture at the Saturday markets such as Renningers in Kutxtown and down there in Adamstown. This was common back then, all the "Dutchy operators" were into antiques, herbs, hex signs and whatever there was an interest in. He was also a fixture at the Kutztown Folk festival where they put together a replica of one of his bookstores for the tourists. He also dealt in 'pelts' Yeah he'd buy muskrat, raccoon, fox, and deer pelts. Sometimes we'd sell to him or there was another buyer out at the junkyard at the 'three mile house' He also bought and sold ginseng which was a big cash herb as it still is. He also was into goldenseal and was always recovering from some health issue or another, probably more like recovering from a hangover...... He alway bragged how he was popular with the college girls that inhabited Kutzeschtettel, a college town but I never saw any. Susan hooked me up with a pic of him which was taken years later, guess he moved his operation to Lyons station, not too far away, its included in a book by Dr Don Yoder...... Its in the file section under 'Mt Bummy' its a PDF file, its definitely worth a look. So anyway, while most of you were merely a twinkle in your Daddy's eye, I was hanging with Mt. Bummy, Braucherei's fallen angel. If anybody has more info on him I'd really enjoying hearing it, I doubt if anything would be a 'shock' ha ha ha

Hunter

He looks like a real character for sure. Outside of collecting herbs for his hangover (which sounds to me like a pretty worth while effort !) what were some of the other things he taught you. From the looks of his establishment it looks like it was a real fun house, right down to his curved walking stick and the goodies in the ball jars. And the "Purple Lady" ... very cool indeed.....sounds to me like there could be a making for a book here. Please tell more !!!

Orva

Heck yeah Orva

The Purple lady drove a lavender LTD stationwagon , one of those 12 passenger ones with a big V8, AC and a brand new 8track stereo system, heck we'd get out on the super hiways stick on some tapes and put the pedal down......problem was she'd get so carried away with the music, AC and the speed that we'd always miss the exit, hell why stop now........... Yeah she even had purple lipstick, purple patent leather purse and a purple poodle that got too old so she took'em to get put to sleep........happens We'd call it the purple solution

Humter

Oh My God Hunter... what a Dream Queen your Mom... She is the Purple Priestess of all time... I can just see it now...cruising in the lovely Purple ride with her very Purple elbow length gloves, behind the wheel...rhinestone studded out and rolling in style... listening to tunes from ... lets say " Smoky Robertson" or perhaps a bit of " Rubber Soul" ??? Yeppers!!! Don't I know it. A Girl after my own heart...

You are a Blessed Child...and I am not kidding ...you really are.. Mom's like your's are a Rare Treasure.

A Toast to her and her son...young Hunter. Lordy Lordy... you must have been (and still are) some child !

Signed: Her Pinkness ...My signature color...

Aka Madame LeFeye...

Orva

Thanks so much Orva! yeah, thing I like the most about her, she was such a ruthless killer, we'd go huntin fer deer, and she get the lever action winchester, kinda like the one the "rifleman" had. Anyway round 8Am she'd open up and shoot some poor creature all up, then motion to us and point down in the brush where it lay, yeah we'd have to drag it up for her, poor critter, LOL i still get nervous when I'm around a woman with a firearm.

Oh yeah Mt Bummy.......well he didn't teach me too many Bible verses I can tell you. Showed me the power plants of Barricks Kaundi though at age 14 in 1968. Yeah wild Appalachian ginseng, golden seal, secret places. Between him and the Claypoole brothers with their crazy Leprachuan dad, Johnny who was the reigning king of hexology at the time, I wouldn't be hanging out at places like this..........ha ha ha

Hunter

Mei Gaarde iss glee: sie iss schee Am beschde es Monet in (??) mei gaarde es der Summer awwer es beschde nicht deheem. Die Familye enjoys (??) nicht es Haus waarem.

Erika Yoder.

"in my garden" = "in meim Gaarde" The family enjoys = "Die Familye gleicht" adder "die Familye luschdert"

Heel die Mudderschprooch!

Rob

Hexenkopf

I was up in Bethlehem yesterday, and I came across a booklet in the Moravian bookstore. At least one of our list members will know this book as his family is connected both to Hexenkopf (am finding their family surname throughout it) and the author, Ned D. Heindel.

The book's called "Hexenkopf: History, Healing & Hexerei." I can't speak to all the accuracy contained within as I've not started reading it yet, but many of us here are aware of Hexenkopf to one degree or another, particularly as a site of supernatural activity as reported by Pennsylvania Germans since arrival and, apparently, within local Lenape lore before us.

The Hexenkompf Rock is also associated with the term, LEGEND TRIPPING: "The legend trip itself is usually made by foot, by groups of at least three adolescents. On the way to the site, the legend is usually retold, and additional legends are told that tell of the frightening consequences of past legend trips to the site. Sometimes, sexual experimentation is part of the legend trip; like horror movies or frightening amusement rides, the legend trip environment encourages people to get closer. Alcohol or drug use also may take place."

Figure 40 Hexenkopf, 2008 photo, Hunter M. Yoder

337

Hi Hunter and Rob,

I grew up a few miles from Hexenkopf Rock,on Morgan Hill as it's know to the locals, the rock itself is south of I-78 and to the west of 611. Best way to go is take the Easton Exit on I-78. Once on the Ramp, don't go toward Easton, go the other way on Morgan Hill Road, up onto the Ridge(Two blue water tanks will be in front of you, as you head up Morgan Hill

Follow Morgan Hill Road for several miles. (Note: quite curvy) You will come to the top of Morgan Hill and you will pass Waltman Loop on your right. (I will give you landmarks on the right) The next intersection on your right is Morvale Road. The following intersection on the right is Jeanette Street. You will pass a Blue Church (on the right) The old Municipal Building (Intersection of Morgan Hill and Diehl Road) There is a stop sign at this intersection. The next small intersection is Stage Coach Road, which can easily be missed. The next landmark is the Williams Township Elementary School and two Churches. This will take you to the Morgan Hill Road and Texas Road intersection. Just past the two churches, Morgan Hill at this point will start going downhill and gets curvy. Continue down Morgan Hill Road. The next intersection on the right is Cider Press Road, the next intersection is where you'll turn. Continue on Morgan Hill and on the right is Hexenkopf Road and on the left is Spring Valley Road. Make the Right on Hexenkopf Road and continue up the hill.

Note: if you miss this road, Morgan Hill will take you to Raubsville/Hellertown Road. The Rock isn't marked but will be on your left as you get to the top of the hill. Should be two stone farm houses on the right. If there isn't any leaves on the trees, you'll see the rock sitting back in the woods. It can be reached from Hellertown by taking the Hellertown and Raubsville Road. Hexenkopf does intersect Hellertown/Raubsville Road, but it's easier to find from the Morgan Hill Road entrance.

Kevin Frankenfield

P.S. I don't have pictures of the rock, but if you want to see one I can get you in contact with Ned Hiendel. Since it was basically in my back yard, I never bothered to take pictures.

Hi Hunter,

I do have stories to tell but not of interest to this group, it has been know as a parting place for local younger generation. Which I will have to say I was guilty of too. But my brother lived in one Ned's properties in the late seventies and early eighties and he talked of a white fox that lived among the rocks. It was during these times that I took my friends to see the rock. I never been there on Halloween to find out if the witches do gather. There is another place in the Township called Elephant Rock, which is outside of Raubsville.

Kevin

Very interesting places, and I too would like to visit some of them in the future, and perform the rites necessary to bring about potential 'contact' with the unseen.

For my part, here in Northern Michigan, I have sought out the places off the beaten path with a good deal of success. Around here, we have many hills that were carved out during the glacial period. Many of these places are either sacred, or taboo, to the local Odowwa tribe. Years ago I made friends with the tribal 'medicine man' who told me of such places, and being the magician I am, I ventured to these places. Most often, there is a very large boulder at the very tops of these hills, no beer cans, graffiti, or any other sign that a human had been there. These are places of great power, and are linked to what is called 'bear medicine', obviously these are places where the land-wights gather.

They are usually surrounded by either birch or beech trees (some so big, it would take 4 people to get your arms around them - old growth). When camping there, I would offer up tobacco, or juniper, along with either mead or ale. Many of these hills also have springs that flow out of the sides of them, this water I will bath with and also offer up to the wights on the stone. I will spend the day taking 'signs', like the flight of eagles or hawks, the number of calls they make, and general breeze direction. Other local places of power are the cedar swamps, very spooky places when the swamp gases are being emitted. It is there I have performed some of my most potent work, usually the Ravens will fly through and acknowledge my presence. Spending the night in the swamps are usually sleepless as I seem to be on my toes much more than on the hills. Just thought I would share what goes on up this way.

Valulfr

Hey Bruder

real nice post there are early Ernest Hemingway short stories take place up your way. I hope it hasn't been too discovered. Yes the swamps and lowland near the water is where life lives. and the old ones also lived, here it was the Lenni Lenape. Their names still linger in the names of our rivers and streams. Usually the question is to have a fire or not. In my youth the fire was a necessity but now, I go without. Any sort of artificial light is also avoided. Night is the time to dilate the pupils of the eyes. And there is plenty of light for sure. I like the phosphorescent fungi growing on rotten logs. Full moons are too bright. The darkness is not so dark.

Hunter

Ja, the old Hemingway stead is about 20min. north of me, a place called Horton Bay. I Painted several houses up that way in the past couple of years.

I understand about the fire, never in peat bog swamps, those things can burn underground for years. I too prefer the darkness. In fact, one night while 'sitting out' (ON Untiseta), I had deer almost in arms reach of me, it was very exhilarating.

Valulfr

Don't forget me on this one Rob, if permission is granted I HAVE to be included. Sorry I couldn't make the blot due to other commitments, the next one I will try to appear.

I have seen pictures of the formation and have recently obtained some Bucks County maps that show it's location on Hexenkopf Road not far from Riegelsville and the Bucks County border. It isn't much to look at from what I remember. When I first saw the picture I did place my hand on the image and did pick up some very interesting energies similar to those I have felt before from Frouwa Walpurga. Also, there is a small creek/stream maybe a mile or two west of the rock called (maybe coincidental, maybe not) "Frya's Run". It would almost seem the early settlers knew or recognized something. I got the distinct impression that the spring from where this water runs may be just as special as the rock itself, especially if it runs in an eastward direction. If gathered before sunrise it can be highly useful.

I also heard it is designated private property and there may be a public utility in question also involved. I probably would have gone by now since I've been in Bucks for 2 years, but I am not one to trespass unless I have clear and urgent reason so I have never made the trip. I would most definitely enjoy this, and, I would be happy to lead a Walpurgisnacht ritual there if permission could be obtained and enough people are interested.

Greg

Permission has been granted for an initial visit, and when I meet with the owner, I may see whether he'd be open to us using the site. I don't want to overdo it right off the bat. If he's amenable to it, we'll see what we can develop.

Will definitely include you, Greg!

Rob

Figure 41 Mark Eppihimer and wife Sarah on the Hexenkopf, May 1, 2008, pic by Hunter M. Yoder

Gods and Goddesses

The Urglaawe is the [3]primal faith[2] as it comes to us within the Pennsylvania German culture, language, wights of the land, symbols, traditions, and, yes, the Gods and the Goddesses, some of whom never disappeared fully despite hundreds of years of discouragement or outright contempt.

Rob

Vaygar Yngvi Elmersson wrote:

Sooooooooooo, is this just another form of Heathenry?

"Jordsvin" wrote:

Rob, please tell us more about the Gods and Goddesses who "never fully disappeared" in Pennsylvania German culture

I would not say "another form of heathenry", more like how heathenry was kept alive in the folk despite the stronghold of christianity which sought to abolish all connection to the traditions that were the heart of the folk. While in the more urban areas it was easy to enforce, and these things were reduced to quaint folk art and such, the practices were very much alive in the more remote countryside where many of these folk immigrated from, bringing with them their remnants of the old ways. It is not another form of heathenry, it is one of the most direct connections that we have to the original heathenry. To those who have kept it alive, I raise a horn to you and your ancestors!

Swanhilde

Not to butt in on the conversation, but for what I know, it is always the folk culture that carries the Gods and Goddesses. The whole festival and before that, the folk tale surrounding Belsnickel was a descendant of the Perchentlauf (ie."Perchta" to the Allemanic/Southern Germans or Mother Holda to the Northern Germans). Alfather is depicted in the wild hunt, etc. I think I may have some images from old advertising of products now long gone, that advertised our Gods around the late 1800's, early 1900s.

this is just for starters, let me see what I can come up with....

Patricia

Re: Gods and Goddesses

Any cursory examination of our Hexology will quickly reveal the presence of one of the god Frey's more ancient manifestations, Yngvi or Ing. Ingwaz is the old German Earth God of male fertility, we call Enguz. He appears as the Runic Diamond. This diamond manifests itself in the Deitsch eight pointed star which is almost always in the color of Enguz, yellow. It is the sign of the sun, fertility, the husband, I would also add the farmer to this list. He is the sexual energy of May, symbolizing the proverbial "birds and bees." In fact all of our Hexology is Heathen. there are some xtian symbols of course, but even their presence goes against the predominantly Protestant doctrine of the exclusion of the visual 'aids' Our Rossette, a six pointed florette design is straight from Heathen Europe as is Deitsch Kultur.

Hunter

I'd not say "pseudo" tribe. We are no different from every other tribe that formed throughout history – individuals from different tribes may split off for one reason or another to form a new tribe. Such is the case with the Pennsylvania Germans, though the bulk of the population comes from the Rheinland-Pfalz or the German portions of Switzerland. Mixed in are many other tribes if they emigrated at the same time, including Hessians who fought on the losing side of the Revolutionary War, etc.

Rob

The new tribe for the new world. From my 'new' heathen perspective, it becomes increasingly clear that the Deitsch tradition is the 'King Solomon's Mine' of North American Heathenry. Imitation is the most sincere form of flattery. Heathen publications for example. Our Kultur is a goldmine, a 350 year old goldmine None is richer in North America. This is becoming increasingly clear. ARE minds me of the first time I applied for a mortgage at the the First National Bank of Fleetwood and filled in the application questionaire regarding what ethnic or racial group I belonged, I filled in PA German instead of checking the white box. They laughingly objected saying that I couldn't say that, I asked why and they said we're all Pa German here.

Hunter

Similar anecdote!

I remember trying to fill out the 2000 census. In the question about what languages were spoken in the home, there were not enough boxes for Pennsylvania German, so I ended up drawing more boxes in.

I agree with your assessment, Hunter, that our Kultur is a treasure-trove of information and maybe some lost traditions, etc. I am starting to see the need to hit the libraries in Reading, Pennsburg (Schwenki), Allentown, Lancaster, etc. to look into some of the older books. Heck, even the archives of the Readinger Adler (what eventually became the Reading Eagle) may carry some tales.

My 6th grade teacher, as I may have mentioned before, was a Berks County historian and very knowledgeable about Deitsch life all throughout the county. When I was in 6th grade, I did not appreciate his sheer brilliance as much as I do now. I have one or two books by him, but I should seek out others. His name was George M. Meiser, IX. Just googling his name turned up a lot of stuff.

Rob

One last detail on that Fleetwood National Bank story, the president of the bank's surname is FREY, a common Deitsch name. I meant to see if you could tell us some more about the Sonoran Desert experiences. I have as I think you know a connection with the Tohono O'odham tribe and have written numerous times about our Mennonite Bruders in the Chihuahua Desert who have taught the Tarahumara tribe a thing or two.

Hunter

The Old Colony Mennonites... Interesting brand. You've not heard anything till you've heard a cross between Deitsch and Mexican Spanish!

Rob

Here are the seeds, Tarhumara white sunflower: Wonder what Mexican Deitsch food tastes like.............sounds wonderful.

Hunter

This just sounds like the Mennonites I grew up with as neighbors, only they are in the Chihuahua Desert, "Canadian Mennonites began arriving in 1922, loaded with livestock, farm equipment and household goods, intending to reproduce their industrious farms in Chihuahua as their forefathers had done on the prairies of Canada. They invested large amounts of capital in farming and transformed desolated stretches of sand and cactus into prosperous farms. They maintained well-equipped machine shops, large farm buildings and motorized transportation, although Mennonites prohibited the ownership of automobiles for common use."

http://epcc.edu/nwlibrary/borderlands/19_mennonites.htm

Hunter

That is the area where my family is from. Nothing beat Mennonite cheese. Yummy!!! It is my understanding that they have made a lot of changes. They are inter-marrying now. It's a very interesting dynamic. I don't have any pictures. What I remember the most is their dress. My uncle had a little store in Rubio, Chih., MX, which when I was little didn't even have a stop sign anywhere. My uncle would send Mennonites to my grandmother's house. They would bring her cheese and would sit and talk with her about what was going on in Rubio and any messages from my family.

My grandmother never trusted anyone at her door except for the Mennonites. If they showed up my grandmother would let them in and even ask if they would like to spend the night. They were always plain clothed, ruddy, very German looking. Which I think is another reason my grandmother liked talking to them.

They would work with my uncles in their orchards and my uncles would help them with their farm equipment.

What I remember the most was that they were very community oriented but not just the Mennonite community but the sounding town/Mexican community. I have heard from some of my family that the girls are now wearing jeans and minimal make up. That's a big step from them.

Micalela

Gods and Goddesses in Deitsch lore

In reference to the Gods and Goddesses, those who were directly mentioned were Holle, Woden, the "Walkeries", the "Aser", the Three Sisters, Sophia "creator of the Dutch", White Haired Woman, and "Walhalla".?

Jordsvin: More, please!

There were a whole host of spirits we were handed information about, I have to look back and check that.? There were also the four birds of powwow.? There are alot of lovely sacred stories handed down orally too, but those can't be written.?

Blessings

Jesse

Jordsvin: why can't they be written? The only reason we have most of what we do of Icelandic lore is because Snorri Sturluson and others decided to write it down.

I don't usually jump into a thread so quickly after joining a new (to me) list, but I really feel the need to second Jordsvin's comment regarding written lore. Yes, I agree that having written lore is helpful and it's a good thing. In fact, I think we should write down as much as we can and record as many different versions as we can. The goal is not to create a tome of unquestionable authority, as other scriptures have become (and I'm not convinced that was the initial goal in other religions that have scriptures/lore; later practitioners decided to uphold the written word as an idol, if you'll pardon that analogy -- but this is really a tangential comment).

As long as we maintain the intention that making a record of the lore is simply to enhance an oral tradition and ensure that the stories are not lost. Always the emphasis must be on "this is *a* rendering of the story of [insert title/name/place/etc. here]; it is not *the* final and last word on the story." In any written version, there must be room for interpretation and embellishment. In this way, later generations (whether next year, decade, century, or millennium) can use the written versions as jumping off points in telling the stories on their own.

At least, that's my two stones worth. I could be completely off base. It certainly would not be the first time.

Brian

They can't be written because they are living beings- to write them is to commit them to stagnancy and death- the inability to evolve with our words and feelings as they have for ceturies. Most of the information I teach can be written and talked about with anyone who is interested (or else I wouldn't be able to offer a course to the general public). The prayers, ceremonies, and sacred stories are another element, however. They have been passed to me in oral tradition with the stipulation by the elders who taught me that they stay that way, and so I honor that request. I only teach those things to apprentices to our "Raad" or circle of Brauchers. This way I am able to be sure of the person before I give them this charged and powerful information. One of the reasons the elders asked me to keep them this way is because they still remember the horrors experienced in their community by those hexerei practitioners who were not using their knowledge for the good of others- but were using it either to strengthen themselves, for egoic purposes, or else to actually cause harm to another. Most of the elders I learned from, and especially the women generally did not use prayers that had been written (although some used bible passages), most of the prayers I have been taught are directly out of oral tradition. I own a copy of the long lost friend, but I don't remember ever using it for a specific cure. I do not mean to imply that written prayers are useless, I am sure they most certainly are not, but these prayers have been maintained in living culture for hundreds of years, and I intend to keep my promise to the elders who passed them to me.

The other reason I was asked not to write these things down was because the elders who taught me did not want this information to be exploited. Most of us here don't remember the pain of the Deitsch people in the early 20th century. After the Hex trails we were branded as backward, superstitious, and "dumb" dutch. That pain is still carried on by the great grandchildren of the people who saw it happen in their day. The loss of the language, the stigma on the healing , spiritual, and agricultural beliefs. We were reduced to funnel cakes, hex signs, and dumb dutch jokes. We are only now climbing out of it. Great care has been taken to pass these things on intact, and to those who will use them in the light of healing, wholeness, and harmony. So I've got to carry it on that way, as I have sworn to do.

As to other things, What more do you want to know about? There is alot to tell.

Blessings

Jesse

interesting opinion.....

So, just to clarify:

There is no elitist element to the teaching of Braucherei stories, prayers, and ceremony. I am not working to deny this information to the people who should, and will recieve it back into their hearts and minds. Instead, I have a notion (according to how these traditions have been taught to me and the others in my wheel) of how I wish to teach these things. I wish to have a personal relationship with any student. I wouldn't teach an unskilled person with no ethics to be a brain surgeon. I'm not saying that anyone on this list is an unskilled person with no ethics, I'm just saying I like to know who I am teaching, and choose what I am teaching them and when. That seems to me to be a characteristic of a good teacher, and I am striving with all my being to be a good teacher. There are plenty of people out there (I have seen some of them) who would put this information to use against others, for the harm of others. And, as a teacher, I do have a certain amount of resposibility for my apprentices for the rest of their lives. I personally do think that people should have to work a bit to develop skills, and gain knowledge as their skill level increases. As I have been taught it, the purpose of our lives here on earth is to grow our spirits and encourage others to do the same, so I like to encourage people to do that work, grow themselves, develop their skills. It is the time honored tradition of learning I am speaking of here, not an elitist claim on exclusive information.

There is pleanty that I've been given that can be written down, and that I do and will continue to.

Sorry for the rant, this is an issue that comes up often and with great passion behind either side. I do understand the tendecy to record this knowledge, but I also have to keep in a harmonious place with those blessed dead who have passed it down to me.

Blessings

Jesse

sorry....not really buying it.....lots of media to record and share things other than paper...

P Hall

And one other element that probably plays a role... Much of what I remember from my great-grandmother and from my own Brauchers was the use of tones and pitch in the speech... How words were intoned and stress, etc., plus associated hand gestures. Thing like that would be hard to capture on paper, I would think. I'll let Jesse, Jack, and Greg speak to that from their first-hand experience.

Rob

And right here, Jesse has provided an exception to my overly generalized stance regarding the archiving of lore. My previous comments primarily apply in the *absence* of a functioning, oral tradition. That is not to say that the archiving of lore cannot work *with* an oral tradition, and in many cases it probably should.

But what Jesse has described is not one of those cases. She is oathed to her instructors (and her instructors' instructors, und so weiter) to *not* let the teachings fall into the wrong hands (er, heads). One way to control this flow of information -- and, let's face it, we're talking about controlling a system (and there is nothing inherently wrong with that, folks) -- is to carefully select the recipients of said system, bind them by the same oaths, and then train them orally (and carefully!).

I, for one, have no issues with such a system. Jesse's oath trumps any reason I might have for wanting to "save" the information on paper, on film, or encoded on marbles. In fact, though I do not know Jesse, I cannot but be impressed with her dedication in this regard. And I applaud her for her efforts.

Brian

New members..

Someone asked me what the color options were available for broomsticks here...................and well, to quote Henry Ford, "You can have anycolour you want, ...as long as its black"

Hunter